▲▼ *Famous Builder*

Famous Builder

▲▼ *Paul Lisicky*

Graywolf Press
SAINT PAUL, MINNESOTA

Publication of this volume is made possible in part by a grant provided by the Minnesota State Arts Board, through an appropriation by the Minnesota State Legislature, a grant from the Wells Fargo Foundation Minnesota, and a grant from the National Endowment for the Arts. Significant support has also been provided by the Bush Foundation; Marshall Field's Project Imagine with support from the Target Foundation; the McKnight Foundation; and by other generous contributions from foundations, corporations, and individuals. To these organizations and individuals we offer our heartfelt thanks.

Special Funding for this title has been provided by the Jerome Foundation.

Most of the memoirs in this collection have appeared in earlier versions in the following periodicals, anthologies and web sites: "Afternoon with Canals" in *Nerve*, reprinted in *Genre*; "Captain St. Lucifer" on *The Joni Mitchell Homepage* (Jonimitchell.com); an excerpt of "Captain St. Lucifer" entitled "Tools" in the anthology *The Man I Might Become: Gay Men Write About Their Fathers* (edited by Bruce Shenitz, Marlowe & Company); "Famous Builder 1" in *Ploughshares*; "Famous Builder 1, 2, 3" as a single piece in the anthology *Open House: Writers on Home* (edited by Mark Doty, Graywolf Press); "Junta" (under the title "Button, Bucket, Blade") in *River Styx*; "Luck Be a Lady" in *Quarterly West*; "Mystic Islands" in *Gulf Coast*; "Naming You" in *The Journal*; "New World" in *Sonora Review*; "On Broadway" in *Provincetown Arts*; "Pygmalion Salon" in *Gulf Coast*; "Refuge of the Roads" in *Santa Monica Review*; "Same Situation" in *Provincetown Arts*; "Wisdom Has Built Herself a House" in *Boulevard*.

Published by Graywolf Press
2402 University Avenue, Suite 203
Saint Paul, Minnesota 55114
All rights reserved.

www.graywolfpress.org

Published in the United States of America

ISBN 1-55597-369-8

2 4 6 8 9 7 5 3 1

First Graywolf Printing, 2002

Library of Congress Control Number: 2002103513

Cover design: Scott Sorenson

Cover photo: Robert and Paul Lisicky © Anton Lisicky

Map of New World © Paul Lisicky

Contents

This one is for my parents.

... in my fame, my shame undone.

Hart Crane, "Reply"

▲▼ *Famous Builder*

JUNTA

I.

"Lisicky."

What?

I try to project my name toward the ridged roof of my mouth. I try to keep my jaw loose, my eyes animated, secure. I think: Smith, Stevens, Bishop.

"Li-sick-y," I say again. "Paul Lisicky."

How do you spell that?

I note the hushed quality of the bank teller's voice, the tender, quizzical lift of her penciled-in brow. She leans in closer to me, palms flattened against the counter as if I've just told her my condition is terminal.

II.

In 1970, at the Bret Harte School in Cherry Hill, New Jersey, a substitute teacher with flame-bright hair and an exhausted, gullible demeanor walked into her assigned fifth-grade classroom and dropped a violet, bullet-shaped purse on the desk. It took but two minutes for us to size her up. She took out a creased sheet from its blue satin lining, called out "Samuel Agresta," and after a pause, Barry Lem raised his hand. Then "Allegra Asher," who was answered instantly by Marguerite Keating and "Brian Boguslaw" by Wendell Waties. In no time at all, others joined in, as steely and determined as plain-clothes soldiers walking through the markets of a corrupt village.

I was Kevin Navins. I huddled over my desk, surprised by the ease with which my hand moved across the paper, my brain supplying me with ready answers to the multiplication tables. I hadn't so much taken on the characteristics of the real Kevin, who cooled his agitated face against the windowpane, longing to be anywhere but in this world of paste jars, milk tickets, and old oranges souring the depths of desks, but rather of someone tranquil and collected, content to live in his skin. When I glanced up at the blond Ewart Greet, who was Paul Lisicky for the morning, I was surprised to see his gray-green eyes fixed to the assignment. He didn't worry that he'd just recovered from another strep throat and missed the last two weeks of school. Nor did he fret about the lunchtime game in which he'd inevitably be struck in the face with a heavy white ball. His forehead pinked with vitality, good cheer.

But it didn't stop there. Two hours later, after we'd come in from the snowy blacktop, and Mrs. Balotin had been summoned by the principal's office to correct the inacuracies on her roll sheet, she called out our names again. Soon Kevin Navins was Carol Campiglia, Mona Chase was Damean Osisek, David Monshaw Marguerite Keating, until everyone had so many identities, no one knew who anyone was for sure. Mrs. Balotin massaged the freckled bridge of her nose between her forefinger and thumb. She glared and let out a raspy laugh. "You kids." She wagged her head back and forth, ripped the roll sheet in half, and tossed it into the waste basket.

That day I walked home from the bus stop with a brisk step, the bottoms of my sneakers skating across black ice. Later, I'd come down with another sore throat, but at that moment, I could have been anything: the spaniel tearing through the hollies, the water sparkling in his deep blue bowl.

NEW WORLD

My father won't sit still. He walks to the sliding glass door, stares out at the lagoon. He paces the bare tile floors of our summerhouse with a solemn, abstracted expression. His footsteps shake the rafters, shake us to the root. He stands in the kitchen, pulls out a sheet of paper, and writes a To Do list in his firm cursive:

—New tailpipe for station wagon
—New roof shingles
—Sprinkler system
—Spotlights
—Wire burglar alarm
—Pump out crawl space
—Jack up porch slab
—Jalousie windows for porch
—Pour concrete sidewalk
—Pour concrete driveway
—Pour concrete patio
—Creosote bulkhead
—Build outdoor shower enclosure
—Curbs?

The raft, however, rises to the top of the list. The orange foam beneath it has lost its buoyancy after two years in saltwater. "We should have bought the good stuff," he says, shaking his head. "They saw us coming." It doesn't seem to faze him that it's ninety-two degrees, the Friday before Fourth-of-July weekend. We trudge outside behind him. Two houses down the Sendrow girls lie facedown on their towels, the backs of their legs basted with Bain de Soleil. Next door Mr. Forte and his friend Fisher, just back from the Inlet, clean flounder, wrap soft filets in aluminum foil. Perspiration creeps through my hair. I touch my scalp just to make sure it's not . . . beetles? My father kneels below us on the raft, fastening the rope to a pitted ring in the corner. Bobby and I stand on top of the bulkhead. Soon enough he jumps up beside us and the three of us pull and strain with all our might. The veins in my neck thicken. I'm not even sure my exertions affect anything: I'm thirteen years old, my arms thick as drinking straws. Although Bobby is stronger, he's not doing much better. Still, just as the rope skins the flesh of my palms, just as I'm ready to let go, to say aloud that we're a doomed, foolish family giving ourselves over to chores we can't possibly complete—why can't we ever *hire* somebody?—we manage to get the wooden behemoth up onto the grass, turning it over on its back. The three of us suck in our breaths. Its underside is encrusted with the physical symbols of shame: greasy mussels, prehistoric white barnacles, and rich green seaweed. The foam has faded to a bleached pink. Exposed to sunlight, it smells like an emptied can of fish chowder.

"Holy Mackerel," says Mr. Forte, who walks over to get a look.

I lie on the grass, breathing, breathing, listening to my beating heart. My eyes follow the tiny plane towing an advertising banner overhead: FOR SUNBURN PAIN TRY SOLARCAINE. Its engine putters, then fades. My father and Bobby sit off to the side, their brows sweaty, their faces the russet of our brick patio. (What does *my* face look like? Surely, they've been responsible for most of the hefting.) Only after my heart has stilled, only after I've made a reasonable demonstration of my willingness to help, do I rise to my feet and brush off the loose grass blades sticking to the backs of my legs.

"I have to pee," I declare.

Inside, I walk past my mother, close the bathroom door, and sit on the cool tile floor. How good it feels to be by myself, to be silent, to be still again. A tingling comes back into the tips of my fingers. I'm no longer part of the larger body of my father and my family, but I'm my own body again. There is a splinter buried in the heel of my hand, which I squeeze till I wince. Things are happening inside my head. One minute I work on a new song, which I'm planning to send to the producers of *The Partridge Family,* the next I think about the street names in Cambridge Park, a development under construction near our house in Cherry Hill. Everyone who knows me knows that I want to be a builder, a famous builder, like Bill Levitt, when I'm older. I want those who drive through my communities to be socked in the head with the sheer beauty of all they see.

I huddle in the coolish bathroom and murmur, moving my lips as if I'm reciting the rosary: *Pageant Lane, Pennypacker Drive, Poppy Turn, Pershing Lane.*

Footsteps heavy on the living-room floor. I rumble the toilet-paper roll, throw the unused sheets in the trash, then flush.

"Where's Paul?" my father asks gravely.

His tone says it all: I'm not serious or helpful, I have a deep, self-absorbed streak. There's a heat in my stomach, a small contraction. My mother stirs a boiling pot on the other side of the wall and makes macaroni salad for lunch.

"He's in the bathroom."

I slip out into the back hall, where I grab a broom and pretend to sweep the floor around the water heater. (His usual expression every time he catches us at rest: "What are you doing, sitting around with your teeth in your mouth?" Or worse: "CLEAN UP THIS PLACE!")

Beach sand flies up against the laundry tub, pinging.

"I need your help," says my father. He's taken off his shirt. He looks down at his nicked, bleeding hands.

"But I thought we were done."

"Done?" he says, with a soft incredulousness. "*Done?*"

I follow him out to the dock, attempting to mask my disappointment, but my face has fallen for sure. Certainly I want to help. Certainly I want to be a good boy, a generous, benevolent, dutiful son, but I want to be my*self*, too. I don't understand why we don't get to fix up our house and make things of beauty like our neighbors: the Foxes' wooden Japanese bridge, the Moores' garden of herbs and wildflowers. Even worse, why is it that we never finish anything? Although we'll work on the raft every Saturday for the rest of the summer (replacing the top boards with fresh lumber, shining the rusty bolts), it will sit on the lawn for two years until the boards silver, until the grass dies in a gray-brown rectangle beneath it.

▲▼

Just as soon as our car has climbed the mountain, we go down, down into the heart of Allentown, home to all my cousins, home to more Lisickys per capita than any other place outside Slovakia. From our vantage point it twinkles with thousands of lights through a scrim of flurries, a landscape with the quality of a Brothers Grimm fairy tale. I already hear the local accent (which my father has mysteriously lost), the vowels infused with a catch in the throat, a lilt, the slightest hint of a yodel, sentences invariably rising on the last word. There's a ridged cylindrical gas tank, at least fifteen stories tall, topped with something like a flattened beret. Aunt Mary and Uncle John live behind it. To the left of that is the only skyscraper in northeastern Pennsylvania, the Pennsylvania Power and Light tower, known locally as the PP&L, a squat version of the Empire State Building, its crowned top bathed in crimson light. The redness of those lights reminds me of an interior human organ exposed to the elements, and sure enough, I feel a contained heat inside my chest in response. To the west, out of the range of our vision, there's Dorney Park, home of the oldest running wooden roller coaster in America, where I'll come down with the first symptoms of chicken pox three years in the future. But the row houses really snare my attention. We pass blocks and blocks and blocks of them (joyless, joyless), none of which seem to be individuated. Although the temperature is in the thirties, it feels like the coldest place in the world. All of it seems impossibly old, musty, dense with the smells of upholstery and cooking: holubky; apple butter; tuna, onions, and vinegar. The place says one thing alone to me: *You will always be you here.*

Get out.

We stop at a red light, watching a window across the street. At the Harugari, the Hungarian club, people with beer bottles in one hand wipe off their florid faces with handkerchiefs. Hands are clapped, and a middle-aged couple in the center of the floor whirls to—I can only imagine it—a manic accordion. They dance so fast that I swear their shoes are in the air more than they're actually touching the floor. "Now that's dancing," says my father. "Not like the crap you kids like." And he takes his hands off the wheel, chugs his forearms like a go-go dancer with a brain injury.

My stomach groans with the same sensation that keeps me from eating my bowl of cereal on certain school days. If he really loves this place as much as he says he does, if he really feels the sting of its absence, then why have we been raised as if we haven't a history, in a township named for its shopping mall filled with ficus, coconut palm, and cages of leering tropical monkeys showing us the pink of their gums?

My father is a storm. His presence charges the air with abstract particles: guilt, duty, fear of failure, fear of death. If he were a painting, he'd be a Jackson Pollack, all splash and squiggle, no open spaces, no room to breathe. If he were a piece of music, he'd be a Shostakovich symphony, brash, shot through with bursts of tympany and horn. I could keep going on like this. I could keep trying to count the instances in which he simply sat down to rest his weary bones, in which he didn't read the stock-market page while shining his shoes then run down the hall to sweep off the porch, then go back to his shoes again.

The house of his childhood. 333 North Second Street, a narrow brick row house with two second-floor windows and a wide front porch, no lawn, no plants, no intimation of adornment. A sign hangs on the wooden porch rail (MODERN SHOE REPAIR), the name of my late grandfather's business, which is later taken over by my uncle Steve, then his son, Stevie. On the block all the houses are similarly sparse, with no defining characteristics other than cleanliness. The front steps sparkle in the weak sunlight that's offered. So clean, my aunt Mary says, that "you could eat right off them."

I close my eyes and hear loud, lilting voices. They shift back and forth between Slovak and English, even the occasional Hungarian and Yiddish, all rivaling for attention. Seven children live in these rooms: Anna, Mary, Steve, Joe, Catherine, Francie, and Tony, my father, the middle child. Their quarters are so cramped that several share the same bed. A modern bathroom with pink fixtures glows in the darkness. Aunt Catherine and Uncle Joe (who later move out to a newer row house close to the fairgrounds) do everything possible to make it cheery (doilies on the backs of the sofas, new curtains), but it feels as if the walls are about to compress all the life out of you.

I have to see it from the street again. I imagine my grandparents gazing out the two upper windows, my elusive grandparents about whom I know next to nothing. Alexander, my grandfather, stands in the left window, a man of medium height, utilitarian wire-frame glasses over his broad face, above thin Eastern European lips, a glass of red wine in his hand, the same wine he makes from the grapes of the backyard arbor. (He stores huge vats of it in the cellar.) Is his smile tinged with sadness because he doesn't know how he ended up in this gritty, industrial city, so far from the vineyards of his birthplace? He takes another sip of wine (why did this batch turn out so sour?), putting off work for another few minutes. It's so hot in his workshop that he sweats profusely, and in order to keep at this pace, he eats salt by the fistful to replace what he's lost. He hears his wife, Mary, who's straightening up the contents of the drawers, folding clothes in the next room. He doesn't even remember their quarrel anymore, but he's aimed his trademark screw-you gesture at her—he sticks out his tongue, placing his thumbs in his ears and fluttering his fingers—in full sight of the children. Tonight they'll sleep in separate beds, separate rooms, though the truth is that they haven't spent a full night together for longer than he can remember. (At some point, it will be a joke among his children that they managed to produce so many offspring. "Immaculate conceptions," says my father.) Alexander dies at least six years before I'm born and is rarely brought up at family gatherings.

My grandmother stands at the other window. She wears a light blue dress patterned with nasturtiums; she's doughy and pale in the arms. A babushka is tied beneath her chin. With her thick gray brows—she wears no lipstick or makeup or jewelry—she looks like an earthier, heavier Georgia O'Keeffe. Like Alexander, there is a tinge of sadness in her expression, but her sadness seems to run deeper, with complex chords in it. Is it that she's been fighting with her husband, who's been drinking, spending too much time playing poker with his friends? Is it that he's been indifferent to the children, and abdicated his responsibility to Steve, the oldest male child, who's begun to administer the spankings? Or is it that she, too, feels homesick and doesn't want to learn this new grammar with its irregular verbs, its blends of consonants almost impossible to pronounce? (Years later, my parents will think she's cursing until they realize that the asshole she keeps referring to is, in fact, our next-door neighbor, *Ethel* Friedman, whom she's taken a shine to.) The weather feels foreign and sticky on her skin. The air doesn't smell as it should. Where, where is the Danube? What are they doing so far from the Danube?

In the fall of 1998, at a Chinese restaurant in Fort Lauderdale, I ask my father a few questions about the grandmother who's been nothing but an outline to me. To my surprise, I learn that she actually left my grandfather for a time. Back in Baltimore, their first home in this country, she wasn't happy with the crowd Alexander was in (reportedly, there was even a shooting at their wedding reception), so she packed up Anna and Mary to stay with her sister, Tetka, in Allentown.

He stood guarding the door. "And what about me?"

"You can come live with us only when you're good and ready," she told him.

The lo mien on the buffet table across the room practically glows beneath the copper hood. For the briefest moment, I feel a presence—a warmth, pulse—then gone.

"Who do you think you are?"

My father weeps over his trig homework.

"I said, who do think you are?" Steve walks past the humble desk on the second floor, then sits on the bed, hunching forward. He crosses his arms. "You think you're better than we are?"

"No," says my father.

"You think you're smart or something?"

My father hangs his head.

"Tony?"

"It's just—"

"You should be out helping the family."

"But *Steve*."

"You're a car mechanic, okay? You're just a Slovak. You're no better than the rest of us."

My father cries again. His eyes blur on all the red slashes and X's on the page. He can't give up now. Not after so much work, not after all those homesick, harrowing times in the War (Texas, Belgium, Germany) when he lived off pennies a week and sent his earnings back home. Wasn't that in payment for this? It had to be for something. He wipes his eyes on his fist. No, no. The work will tax him; it will come close to killing his spirit, but one day they'll see how kind of heart he is, what he's capable of giving.

No more scraps. Finally, he'll be given the prime cuts at the table, just like his older brothers.

"It's two in the morning," whispers Steve. "It's time for sleep, kiddo."

My father blows his nose. He shakes his head. He sharpens his pencil and goes back to work as his brother looks on in fury and awe.

In two years he'll earn his degree in electrical engineering and graduate, to the shock of family and friends, not far from the top of his class.

▲▼

Unlike Slovak women, Anne Homan is tall with long, slender legs and thick dark hair. The daughter of a veterinarian and a schoolteacher, she's half-English, half-German, both sides of her family having lived in this country since the 1830s. Not only does she draw and paint—her pastels and watercolors grace the walls of her mother's living room—but she loves opera, Verdi and Puccini, and sings in the occasional recital. Her mother plays the piano; her older brother, Alfred, is a professional Broadway actor, now appearing in Cole Porter's *Kiss Me Kate*. My father can't help but be charmed and impressed by all these indications of culture. Although he's only known her for a few weeks (they've met on Long Beach Island at an outing of the Collingswood Catholic Club), he's eager to bring her home to his mother.

"She loves me," he says, not two minutes after he's introduced her to the family.

My mother smiles beside him, blinking, bewildered. She thinks, what a funny thing to say.

"She's not so big," says bald, red-faced Uncle John with his trademark joviality.

What has he told them about her? my mother wonders. An earlier boyfriend once called her "shapely, well-endowed," but "big?" "Excuse me for a minute," she says, and disappears down the hall to the bathroom.

"What do you think of her, Mom?" my father says.

His mother nods once, twice. She thinks, where are the broad apple cheeks, the thighs? Such a tiny nose.

"She loves me," he says again, more softly this time.

He clenches his brow. He's in awe of the fact that anyone so lovely could love him. After all, isn't he just a "dumb Slovak," as he himself would put it, from 333 North Second Street?

"Nice girl," says my grandmother.

"You like her, Mom?"

"Fancy," she says, nodding.

My father's smile is shaded with sadness. He thinks, I wish Pop were still alive.

They face each other, waiting for my mother to come back from the bathroom, unnerved by the sudden uneasiness between them—where did this dizziness inside his head come from? My dad's face glows; it's heated from within. But how he wishes everyone had more enthusiasm! Can they already tell that the children they'll bear won't ever learn Slovak, nor appreciate the sweet, granular texture of kolache in their mouths?

Allentown:	Cherry Hill:
Cellar	*Basement*
Supper	*Dinner*
Buggy	*Shopping Cart*
Hopper	*Toilet*
To tootsel	*To snack*
They want rain on Friday.	*It's supposed to rain on Friday.*

They sit side by side on the chocolate brown sofa of their one-bedroom apartment in Haddon Hills. He gazes up at the white metal kitchen cabinets, half of which are filled with tools and engineering books. He knows she'd like that space for dishes and groceries, and he knows the place is a little cramped. He places his hands on my mother's warm belly, feels a nudge, a slight kicking, then remembers the project due at work this Thursday. He smiles, though the bottom half of his face feels tight. He must do a good job, he thinks. He must present it with more authority and panache than any of his co-workers or they'll see who he really is—a fraud. He's a car mechanic, for God's sake. What does he know about engineering, anyway? He'll lose his job; he can*not* lose his job, not now, not with all these bills, especially with a baby on the way.

He gets up off the sofa and stares at the calendar on the refrigerator. "Maybe we should go to Allentown next week?"

My mother blinks. "It's such a long ride."

"*Hon—*"

"Weren't we just there?"

Yes, they were, but the visit felt careful and strained, though he couldn't bear to admit it to himself till now. Why did it seem he had nothing in common with his family anymore? When he tried to tell Steve about the jealousies he's encountered from coworkers (they cannot bear his energy and speed), Steve stared at the football game, fumbled for his cigarette lighter or the beer bottle on the end table. They must make up for it this next time. They must have a warmer, more satisfying stay.

Don't they know how much he loves them? If they only knew how much he loves them.

Maybe it will help if he gives Mom some money.

My mother pages through the new *House & Garden*. "Let's take a look at houses."

My father nods, rubbing his lower lip with his index finger.

They walk out to the parrot red Buick in the parking

lot. (How did he end up in South Jersey? he thinks. Where are the mountains in the distance, all those beautiful languages—Slovak, Hungarian, Yiddish, Polish— on the streets?) In Delaware Township, on the east side of Haddonfield, they drive through the stone gates of Woodcrest Country Club Estates, "The Entrance to Elegance," as it's described in the newspaper ads. They tour the ranchers and split-levels—each decorated in a specific style—French Provincial, Danish Modern, Early American—each named for expensive cars: Fleetwood, Eldorado, Continental, Imperial. (Other developments in the area share a proclivity toward the flash and the glare. Haddontowne's models, for example, are named for Miami Beach hotels.) After talking to the salesman, they check out the houses from the curb. Actually, they're not even sure they like the place. What about those metal windows? And why do the houses look so severe from the side, like, well, bread boxes? But it *is* the up-and-coming neighborhood, says my mother. We don't have to stay here forever. She's right, thinks my father. And wouldn't the family be proud? So much to see and do nearby: the Latin Casino nightclub; the Garden State Park racetrack; the Cherry Hill Mall; the Cherry Hill Inn, and all those other restaurants: Cinelli's, Sans Souci, Irv Morrow's Hideaway, and the Hawaiian Cottage, which is built in the shape of a squat gold pineapple with a jaunty green topknot. Already celebrities are moving onto the township's curving, freshly paved streets. Walking into Shop 'n' Bag you might run into Al Martino, Connie Stevens, WFIL TV-show personality Sally Starr, and some of the major figures in organized crime.

I swim and somersault inside my mother. In but two

days they'll put a down payment on a Continental, which will be ready just in time for my birth.

▲▼

My grandmother is hazy, enormous as a planet. I walk into Aunt Catherine's living room to find her sitting on the red sofa before the TV, a look of emptiness on her face. She watches *Championship Wrestling*, the single program that seems to harness her attention. I'm four years old. A good boy, I kiss her on the cheek. Freshly bathed, she smells of lotion and yeast. "Hello, Grammy," I say. "Nass boy," she answers, eyes fixed to the screen. "Nass boy." It's the only thing she's ever said to me. I know she doesn't know much in the way of English, but I wish she'd try. I wish she'd call me by my name, see me as a separate being from my brothers and cousins. (Are we just puppies to her? A litter of yapping, wide-eyed puppies?) And why doesn't anyone tell us anything about her? What is her favorite food? What was it like taking a ship across the Atlantic? And does she miss the streetcars and markets, the soot and the gray skies of Bratislava?

My father stands next to her. "Mom," he says. "This is my son."

"Son?"

"His name is Paul."

I don't understand why he talks to her as if I'm a stranger. We've had this exact exchange at least twenty times in my brief life.

She looks out at me, then up at my father with a dim, apprehensive expression in her eyes. Her lips move. She mumbles something to him in Slovak.

"No, no," he says with a rueful laugh. "I'm TO-ny. Not Francie."

Aunt Catherine walks into the room, wiping her hands on a dish towel patterned with hex signs. She already looks like a younger version of her mother; in twenty years she'll have the same "Indian nose," as she calls it. She senses something about the tightness of Grammy's mouth and blinks. She lifts her up by the elbow (heavy, how heavy she's become), guiding her toward the orange potty chair tucked in the corner of the living room. Grammy's walk seems to embody a suffering larger than herself, the suffering of every ancestor who'd gone to bed hungry—the parched lips, the growling stomach—before being snuffed out. Is she getting sicker? Or dying? One thing is for sure: she must not end up at the "poor house," as she calls the nursing home. She dreads it much more than death itself, so next week she will be shunted off to Francie and Goldie's, then a few weeks later to Mary and John's. There is no denying that everyone's nerves are raw. As soon as she's comfortable in one house, learning the trajectory of its hallways, the patterns of its sofas and armchairs, she's off somewhere else, where she must start all over again, a permanent exile in the houses of her children.

Once she's back from the potty, my father sits close to his mother on the couch and whispers in her ear. He seems to express far more affection for her than do my aunts and uncles. Is his affection part display? Is he trying to prove his devotion to the rest of the family? Although her eyes are still fixed to the wrestlers' zany trunks (blues, violets, crimsons), her thoughts are elsewhere now, in happier worlds. She's either back in Slovakia, dusting the rooms of the rich people for whom she once worked, or she's already in the next world, nimble and alive, in a flowered dress and blue babushka, sweeping someone's front steps.

Boxwoods, white birches, and cedar diadaras are planted in the backyard. Ethan Allen furniture is ordered from Haddon Wayside. It's Easter, and outside, there's a smell of hyacinth and lilac on the air. It's the day of our relatives' first visit to our new house, a custom-built brick rancher on an acre lot on Circle Lane in the Boundbrook section of Cherry Hill. (How quickly we've outgrown the place in Woodcrest. And those windows: my parents spent a fortune covering them with plastic in the winter.) I'm old enough to know how important this house is to them. It's a symbol, a bold announcement. *I am to be taken seriously; I am worthy of something more than a mere development house; I have done something in the world.* And I've had all the proof I need by witnessing an exchange between my mother and an old friend of hers in the Haddonfield Acme. When she finds out that our house is in Cherry Hill, "in the new Kresson Road area," her face opens; her bottom lip prickles and swells. "Fabulous," whispers her friend.

Aunt Mary gets out of the car first. She looks out at the expansive front lawn, the squat Colonial lampposts at the head of the driveway. She touches the back of her head, swallows. Then Goldie, Francie, Elsie, and John get out, followed by Catherine and Joe, who pull up in their red Rambler.

Once we're all in the foyer, I point to the baseboard next to the front door. "You should take off your shoes."

"No, no," my father laughs uneasily. "These kids. . ."

"But *you* make us take off our shoes."

My father smiles at his siblings through gritted teeth. *"Paul."*

The tour commences. Everyone seems quietly respectful as they follow my father from room to room—the hearth room, the sunroom, the laundry room. Their shoes wisp the gold wall-to-wall carpet. Everything is perfect; every vase, book, and picture frame in proper position. Little do they know that we don't always live this way. It must be the first time in months that my father's papers and magazines don't cover the kitchen table.

"I like the Queen Anne furniture," notes Aunt Catherine. "Nice chair."

"Pretty windows," says Mary. "Are they hard to keep clean?"

"Look at the size of this cellar!" says Uncle John, who cups his hands around his mouth. "You could sell tickets and open a movie theater down here, Tony."

Everybody laughs. I follow the grown-ups around like a spaniel with shining eyes. Afterward, I stand outside on the back patio and breathe in the brisk, lilacy air. I love seeing what we have through my aunts' and uncles' eyes; I love these physical demonstrations of our luck and our worth. The tiny leaves of the poplars glitter in the clean April light.

Once everyone has seen the house, we all crowd in our station wagon to go on a tour of our township. We walk beneath the wet, tropical trees inside the Cherry Hill Mall; we drive across the Barclay Farm development's mock covered bridge; we drive past Muhammad Ali's stucco rancher with its iron gates. We walk through scores and scores of sample houses with the latest features: wet bars, central vacuums, built-in log boxes, conversation pits. And there's something called a bidet, which brings out the suggestive and shy in everyone. "What's that for?" says Aunt Mary. "You know," says Aunt Catherine. Aunt Mary stares at the low-slung, porcelain boat. I'm not sure I know myself. I imagine it has something to do with blood, with pregnancies. Or something darker. Then: "*Oh,*" says Aunt Mary.

The Beau Rivage, The Fontainebleau, The Ambassador, The Mark 70. So much newness! So much vitality, beauty, excitement for life! No more cramped tenements and fire escapes, no more dank lightless wells. History? Who needs it. Out with the old. We're making ourselves anew. "Oooh," we say, and look up at the huge Latin Casino sign against the twilit sky. On the glittering marquee with the gold flashing bulbs: DIRECT FROM THE LAS VEGAS STRIP: STEVE AND EYDIE.

We head out to a restaurant on Route 38 with flaring torches in its gardens and shields on its fieldstone walls. It's in a round sunken pit and is known for its steaks and huge salads: an entire head of iceberg lettuce served in a teak bowl.

"Filet mignon," my father says to the waiter in his official voice. "For everyone."

"Now, Tony," says Catherine.

"I insist," he says, holding up his hand. "This is on me."

Halfway through the meal a coiffed woman in a mink stole walks down the steps. Her husband, a slight, dark fellow with nebbishy glasses, touches the small of her back. She practices an expression of sophisticated indifference as they're led to their table, but she wants us to look at her, to *see* her, more than anything else in the world. It's what she lives for, this moment, this display. I turn to Aunt Mary. The woman has certainly captured *her* attention. "Rich people," she says, her voice tinged with modesty and pain. It seems to hurt to look at them. Is she already thinking of the towering gas tank across Foundry Street, how it throws her humble house into shade?

▲▼

If only Aunt Mary knew what really happens inside the houses of Cherry Hill.

I'm eating dinner at my friend Lisa's house when all the lights go off. Immediately, we know it's not a blackout; we can see the chandelier blazing through the window of the house next door. There's a cone of light on the grass. With an astonishing poise, Mrs. Marx breezes into the dark kitchen, where she opens a drawer for a box full of matches. She returns to light the candlesticks on the table while her husband sits across from us, his head in his hands. Mrs. Marx smiles, but the match trembles between her fingertips until she burns herself. "Ah!" she cries, as it falls to the silver tray beneath. The next day Lisa tells me that they haven't paid the electric bill. The card shop Mr. Marx has operated in Clementon for the past ten years cannot compete with all the chain stores that have opened at the nearby Echelon Mall.

And, of course, there's the ongoing ritual, much less dire, in our own house.

My father stands at the kitchen table with a somber expression and hunts through the bags of groceries my mother and I have just brought home from Penn Fruit. "How much did you pay for this?" he says, holding up a bag of chocolate stars. "And what about this? Why do we need more ice cream? We already have some." She runs water in the sink. She doesn't answer. Hasn't she done enough to scrimp and save? Hasn't she filled the shelves of our pantry with store brands—Bala Club, Gaylord, Top Frost, Two Guys—instead of the pricier name labels? The afternoon sun shines on the yellow kitchen walls, heats up the skin of my forehead, blinding my left eye. Boundaries break down. I cannot tell myself apart from my mother, and surely, my father's anger extends to me as well; haven't *I* asked my mother for the candy? He looks down at the bag of chocolate in his hands, then shakes his head. Surely, we're frivolous, extravagant. We don't understand the meaning of good, hard work. For all we know, this single bag of candy could be the one purchase that ruins us, that brings the whole tower of match sticks tumbling down to the ground in a heap.

He tears open the edge of the plastic and hands me a star, waiting for me to accept it.

Then, with troubled relish, he eats one himself.

▲▼

When my youngest brother Michael tells our mother she's the "most beautiful woman in the world" (something which she remembers fondly to this day), I silently agree with him. She's recently bought her first pair of bell-bottoms, and I'm quietly hopeful: Is this only the beginning? Will she start dressing like the mothers of some of our friends, like Mrs. Kasten, who walked down the Communion aisle last week in a low-cut black mohair top, demonstrating her cleavage à la Elizabeth Taylor, setting off a minor stir among the husbands in the church? My mother wears her new bell-bottoms everywhere, at choir practice, at the supermarket, and when I tell Aunt Catherine about it on the phone (she and Uncle Joe are coming to our shore house for the last week in August), she says, "Come *on*."

"We're serious," I say. "We have a very modern mother."

"Get *out*."

But two weeks later I receive a postcard from Aunt Catherine: *I'm looking forward to visiting your 38-year old, hip swinging, bell bottoms mommy.*

I love my Aunt Catherine; unlike some of my other aunts, she's like a second mother to me. But I wonder if she's making fun. I know that my father's side of the family thinks we're weird. None of us are terribly interested in football or team sports, and I know that it's part of family legend that we were given dolls to play with as children along with the tool kits and the G.I. Joes.

My mother, two brothers, and I are crouching—or hiding, to be more precise—inside the pink bedroom of Dolores Dasher's summerhouse, which just happens to be directly behind the weedy lot across from our own summerhouse. Earlier in the day we received a phone call from Uncle Steve's son, my cousin Stevie, who's been staying with his wife and his son in Wildwood; he wants to know whether they can drop by at around two this afternoon. My mother knows what this means. They want to extend their vacation for another night or two. They'll just sit there, we know it, and wait for her to suggest it, and they know she'll suggest it because my father would be upset with her if she didn't. How many relatives have been dropping by lately? My mom feels like she's always on call; more often than not, she finds herself in the role of cook, while the aunts and uncles sit around the umbrella table, where they feed the gulls and watch the boats sailing by on the lagoon.

This time the thought of it is too much for my mother to bear. It gives her a twinge in the neck—and my brothers and I feel it in the backs of our own necks, in sympathy. At the very last minute her friend Dolores Dasher offers to hide us in the hopes they'll think there's been some miscommunication.

We look up at Dolores Dasher from the floor. Like our mother, she, too, has taken to wearing striped bell-bottoms, even though she's a good twenty pounds heavier. She wrings her hands with a vexed look in her eyes and shakes her honey blond curls off her face. Plans are hatching inside her head.

"Do you want me to go over there?" Dolores paces. "I'll go over there. I'll tell them something came up. Your car broke down. You had to take it to the mechanic. It was an emergency. How's that?"

We give her the go-ahead. We sit there in silence. I get down on all fours, butt high in the air, press the corner of my cheek into the carpet, and laugh quietly. Although we're all on edge, we're having a strange kind of fun. How many mothers would do such a thing? How I love her sense of adventure.

"Get your face off the floor, dear," she whispers. "Germs."

My brother Bobby peers over the window ledge. The top of his moppy head must certainly be visible from Point Drive.

"They'll see you," I declare.

After a few minutes, however, I feel bold enough to take a look myself. Dolores Dasher stands at the fence, gesturing, while Stevie and Janice lean against their car, lifting their faces to the sun. Little Stephen tears through the gardens and smashes the portulacas and petunias like a Rotweiler on speed.

"Little Stephen's destroying the flowers!" I cry.

"Oh, this is ridiculous," says my mother suddenly.

"Don't," I say.

"I mean they're not going to go away. This isn't nice. What's the matter with us? Come on, you kids. Up, *up*."

And just as we stand up, Dolores walks back into her house, flipping through a sheaf of envelopes in her hand. "Well, that was a flop."

"What do you mean?" I say.

"Well, I told them about the car, but"—she rolls her eyes—"they were on to me. The car was parked right in front of them."

"Oh *no!*" we all say.

"They wouldn't take the hint. I'm sorry, Anne. Those two," she says, shaking her head. "So damn blasé."

And so we go back to greet them, cheerily, as Little Stephen starts jumping up and down on the webbed lounge until he breaks through the fabric and shrieks.

Aunt Mary's living room is already cast in darkness, even though it's not yet three-thirty in the afternoon. Arctic clouds rush and tumble across the sky outside the north-facing window, passing over the gas tank. A gust of wind rattles the panes. The TV imbues the room with a thin, bluish light. I sit in the armchair across from Grammy, who's lying on the couch with closed eyes, moistening her lips after a shot of insulin. I hold onto the armrests and tell myself not to be frightened.

Murmured voices in the hall. I sit on the edge of my

seat and strain to hear above the cries and jeers of the football game.

"It's getting to be too much, Tony," whispers Aunt Mary.

I know they're talking about Grammy. Her care is becoming more and more of an issue; it's a full-time job, especially since she fell last week. The brothers and sisters argue about who has her when. I feel something in the air when we're all together, a pulse of frustration, regret.

"We might have to take her to a home."

"No!" he cries. Don't they know how she feels about the poor house?

"What do you mean?"

"She's my *mother*," he says. "We can't just throw her away."

A pause, a pull, a catch in the throat. "She's my mother, too," murmurs Aunt Mary. "Don't you think we love her?"

Aunt Mary has stepped into the doorway, where a bar of light from the kitchen illuminates the top half of her face. It's full of suffering, a drawn-ness in the cheeks, the same suffering I've seen in Grammy's face for years. "Then you take her, Tony," she says finally.

A wave rises then falls inside my stomach. Leaves rasp against the frosty grass outside.

My brothers and I are buttoned up in our coats, our hoods tied beneath our chins. I hold the paper bag of ham sandwiches and M&M cookies she's made for the long drive home. When my father leans over to hug her, he presses a check into the pocket of her dress.

"No, no," says Aunt Mary with exasperation.

"Now listen," says my father firmly.

"It's too much, too much," she says, fingers fluttering against the front of her dress. After a minute she tosses the check at my father. "Too much."

"Now Mary," he says.

We stand in the foyer, heads lowered. I fumble inside my bag for a Hershey's Kiss and pinch a flag of foil between my fingers. The check is tossed back and forth until it's creased. Finally, Aunt Mary plunges it into her pocket. Her face is sweaty. She's breathing hard, but she's already relieved that this part of the ritual is over.

At some point in the next couple of hours, my father must bring up the possibility of taking care of Grammy to my mother (does it happen when I'm curled up in the backseat of the car, sleeping, lying beneath my coat?). She stares at the windshield; the words are dumb in her throat. Of course they took in her own mother during the last months of her life, but this feels harder, more challenging. Hasn't she given up enough of herself these last few years, poured every last ounce of her attention into us? There's hardly anything left of her. She looks at the dried maple leaves blowing along the sidewalk, and for an instant she's a maple leaf herself, scraping against the pavement, lit by the headlights of the passing cars.

Our house is electric the next several days. Every time I touch something—a doorknob, a light switch—I get a shock. I jump every time I hear something. Doors and cabinets are slammed emphatically. Even my mashed potatoes don't have much taste; I leave them on my plate until they're cold. My dad finishes them off, spoons them into his mouth, blank-eyed, with abandon.

I stand in the backyard one day when the house finally explodes. Voices thunder. "Not true." "Responsibility!" "Your mother? *My* mother." I curl up against the trunk of the crab apple, the wet ground seeping through the seat of my pants. I cannot stand fighting. *Any*thing would be better than fighting. (Where do I begin or end? I *know* they're talking about Grammy, but I can't help feeling that I'm at the center of things. I bear it all like a buoy in a squall.) I keep looking over at the windows, worrying a long blade of grass in my hands.

Then peace. The house settles into an unlikely peace for the next several days. My parents are kinder, calmer; what has transpired between them? They start talking about where Grammy should sleep, how to keep her comfortable on the long car ride back to Cherry Hill. There's talk of moving her into one of our bedrooms, Bobby and I doubling up. I picture her lying on my single bed in the dark, the back of her dress pulled up to expose the crack of her naked rear end as she waits for another shot of insulin. I picture her in this land of shopping malls and racetracks and nightclubs, frightened, far from what's familiar. My stomach hurts; my meals go unfinished for days. I must stop behaving like this. Selfish, selfish, I will myself to be a better boy. Then, just as my father decides to phone the aunts and uncles, to tell them, yes, we'll take her for a while, he learns that Grammy has taken a mysterious turn for the better. No need to move her now. One day she actually carries on an extended conversation about the summer when she was sixteen, when she rolled cigars in a factory outside Bratislava. On another day she actually gets up off the couch. She walks across the room herself, stands at Aunt Catherine's picture window, and watches with amazement all the cars and buses threading down the street.

The weeds are tangled around the base of the shore-house fence. They're amazingly thick, like dried reeds. I pull them through the wire links and cut them off with the shears. A rusty smell rises from my fingers. Steve, Myra, Francie, and Goldie are due to arrive at any minute, and sure enough the mint green Valiant moves up the street at an excessively slow pace, jerking to a stop every few feet—someone's pointing inside—before starting up again. I draw my elbows closer to my rib cage and pretend to be absorbed in my task. My head's overheated like the blades of a lawn mower. A greenhead lands on the damp flesh of my neck, and I reach back to slap it, but—*pinch*—it's too late.

My parents have prepared for the visit all week. My father has made sure he's around; he's even gone so far as to do the grocery shopping himself, a task which seems about as comfortable to him as painting his nails in public. (Why does he look so dour pushing the cart through Starn's Shop Rite? Is it the outlandish numbers on all the price tags?) For Steve, he's bought Dietz & Watson, Entenmann's, Vlasic—all the brands his brother expects whenever he comes to visit. One by one he loads the items onto the conveyor belt, trying his best to seem cheerful. "Don't take this so seriously," I'm tempted to say. Fortunately, I know when to keep my mouth shut. It doesn't take much to trigger an explosion these days.

Not in the house for five minutes, Steve sprawls in one of the blue-gold armchairs, yawns, and asks to be brought a beer. The dynamics in the house have shifted. My father doesn't sound as sure of himself; my mother lifts the lid off a pot, trying to make more macaroni salad—the first batch hasn't met with Steve's satisfaction. "Are you okay, Steve?" "Would you like another beer, Steve?" "How about a nice ham sandwich, Steve?" Steve sips from his beer, asks for another before he's finished, watching our every last move—how we walk, talk. Every gesture seems to be recorded and assigned a barely passing grade. Occasionally, his eyes actually widen as if he's appalled by something. A nerve pinches the base of my neck. How are we to live through this? He's grinding us down like a pestle.

Finally, I decide, no, enough; I'm not giving in.

I pull out the poster board of New World (a name I've shamelessly stolen from the Rossmoor Corporation), the prototypical city I've been designing since the beginning of the summer. I've situated my project in southwest Florida on an immense tract of flooded sawgrass out-side of Naples, where we've recently been on a family trip. I'm so proud of New World, of my skills as a city planner, that I've lost any traces of self-consciousness. Am I showing off a bit? Steve leans forward in his chair, squints slightly. I start drawing the tiny cul-de-sacs in pencil. I reach for my art markers, ink in the parks, waterways, shopping-center sites with their respective color codes. Then once I've finished, I start the naming process: *Daily Lane, Danube Lane, Dasher Drive, Daven-port Drive ...*

"What are you doing on the floor?" says Steve.

I drag the map closer to his chair, then hand it to him. In a voice more deferential than I'd intended (how does he have this effect on people?), I describe my city. His breath is scented warmly with beer; the rims of his nails are stained yellow with nicotine. Nevertheless, there's the lure of authority in his eyes, in the steely white hair combed back off his forehead. For the first time in my life I can see that he must have been handsome and full of life once. And that it couldn't possibly be easy to be in charge all the time.

"This isn't going to work," he says finally. He points to a section of the map, a little cluster of homes I've called Jupiter Shores.

"What do you mean?"

"These canals," he says, shaking his head. "Water flows *down*hill."

I don't have it in me to remind him that my city is just west of the Everglades, where there is no downhill, where the water level is only a few inches beneath the surface even during droughts. I'm merely shocked that he'd find fault with my project, that he wouldn't find a single thing to praise in it.

My mother, hearing the nature of this exchange, walks into the living room, wiping her hands on a dish towel patterned with bronze coffeepots. "Paul's been designing cities for years. The *Philadelphia Bulletin*'s even done a story on him."

"Paul should listen," says Myra, who walks into the room from the porch. "Steve *knows*."

How can people be so sure of themselves? He goes on to talk about the nature of physics and water, about sewers, seepage, drainage. For all I know, he's made it up. He hands back my map to me, an aloof, satisfied look in his eyes. His face slackens, bluing the skin of his cheeks. I think again: how can people be so sure of themselves?

Is it even possible to reconstruct what happens next?

I can only piece it together from the bits and pieces I've heard through the wall. ("Why didn't you defend us?" cries my mom later, before taking off in the car.) Drinking, drinking through the night, Steve lays into my mother and father, in a sustained explosion of sorts.

Smoke banks against the windows, stalling in the room like soot from a power plant. For some reason he's made sure Goldie and Francie sit by his side; they pull in the edges of their lips between their teeth. Their eyes dart from Steve to my parents—whom should they side with? As Myra sits on Steve's right side, blank and imperial.

The brands you buy are junk. He holds up his whiskey and jars it; the liquid sloshes over the rim. *You expect me to drink this garbage?*

You didn't even give them the right toys. I had to give them tools to let them know they were boys.

Paul. That Paul was never so smart.

How much did you pay for this place? Who needs two houses? I'll give you seven thousand for it.

All the while my parents sit there shaking inside, stunned. His tirade goes on through the night. After all, they can't get up to leave. They live here, don't they?

On one of those thick, humid summer nights when we're in Cherry Hill instead of the shore, my father tosses his camel-colored briefcase on the kitchen table, buries his head in his hands, and sobs. He sobs so hard that my brothers and I are shy about it, impatient, even resentful—fathers aren't supposed to cry. I stand at the back of his white starched shirt (it's too tight in the shoulders), wondering how I should comfort him. Sweat stains dampen his underarms. My mother walks into the kitchen, blinks, says, "Hon?"

"Ettengoff," he says to her.

We know that name like the backs of our hands. We've heard the stories about the layoff list for weeks— my father's coworkers arriving at the job one day only to pack up their things. Heads are hung in shame, fists shaken in silence, desk legs kicked. Their bosses—Etten-goff, Sorkin, Sass, Degnan, Sellars—aren't even people anymore. Their names curdle in our mouths like un-refrigerated milk.

He throws his RCA ID badge on the table.

His snapshot glimmers in its plastic sheath: the brush cut, the glasses, the stern, commanding expression above the bow tie.

We decide that we must get to the shore house as fast as we can. We drive through the scorched woods of the Pine Barrens, past the failing and abandoned busi-nesses—Betty and Rags Diner, Finerty's Quonset Hut, Johnny Boy Farms. The worst is anticipated. There's talk of renting out the shore house, renting out the Cherry Hill house. There's talk of selling, scaling down, moving into smaller quarters. Will I go to a different school? And what about our furniture, our piano—will they go, too? A numbness takes over my right side. The pines on ei-ther side of the highway are charred. I think of the grit-tiest South Jersey towns—Deepwater, Penns Grove, Thoroughfare, National Park—oily neighborhoods of aluminum Cape Cods, like houses on a train set, in the swamps along the Delaware, within sight of refineries. Cat crackers flare. I see the five of us sleeping together on yellowed linoleum as my father steps over me in the middle of the night, reaching for a glass of Alka-Seltzer.

We drive to the Ocean City boardwalk the following afternoon. Spin art, Skee-Ball, popcorn in boxes of tinted blue glass—we walk by it all, downcast, as cries of plea-sure drift upward from the beach. The sand's quilted with yellow blankets. Baby oil sizzles on someone's hot, freckled shoulders. Frisbees sail. It seems almost unthinkable that anyone could be having fun at this moment. Everything glimmers with the possibility of its loss: certainly, this will be the last summer I'll stroll down this boardwalk. And the sea, the breeze, the open blue sky: I can't bear the thought of them taken away from me. At Wonderland, the red cylinders of the sky divers swoop and soar, scrambling the stomachs of the kids caged inside.

My father trails behind us, face ashen and tight.

That night we eat creamed chipped beef on toast as if to prepare ourselves for the lean times to come.

It doesn't take long for our grave news to travel back to the family in Allentown. (How must they react? With surprise? Or is it laced with something else? *This is what happens when you want too much, when you travel so far from home, from your soul.*) Aunt Catherine and Uncle Joe arrive in the boxy red Rambler. Their cheerful, calm demeanors shock us. "Help take these to the kitchen," says Aunt Catherine, as she nods to the groceries in the car. The bags are filled with all the name brands—Oreos, Fritos, Viva, Hi-C—we'd never think of buying for ourselves.

They take us to the Dairy Queen, they take us to miniature golf. They take us to the beaches along the Delaware Bay, where we collect clear, sea-polished pieces of quartz. I stare at the moss-covered hull of a sunken concrete ship (an old tourist attraction) and want to know everything about it, how it landed there, how they ever got the monstrosity to float. Anything to forget what's going on at home. We go to the movies. We lower crab traps into a dim, brackish creek. Aunt Catherine and Uncle Joe do everything possible to distract and buoy us, but in spite of their kindness and goodwill, I have the sense that they don't quite know what we've lost, what's really been at stake here. "It's all going to be fine," says Aunt Catherine.

"But Catherine—" says my mother.

"Really now," she answers with the slightest impatience.

(Does she already sense that my dad will be rehired within the week, with a raise and a bonus, no less?)

But you don't get it, I want to say. *My father cannot, cannot ever live in a row house again. It would kill him.*

Instead, I rip into a bag of Lay's Potato Chips, gorging on their salty and greasy taste as if they're the last meal I'll eat.

▲▼

Steve and Myra's living room is newly papered with silver. A green ceramic pine, no taller than two pencils put together, blinks on top of the TV console. I'm down on the silver-blue rug, leaning back on my elbows. Ten A.M.: another game show. The whole lot of us are in this room—aunts, cousins, uncles, parents, siblings—tense, fidgeting, waiting for the phone to ring. Outside a passing truck rumbles the front porch of the house.

When it finally happens, Mary and Catherine almost push each other on the way to the kitchen. Their clothes are crumpled, their curls lank, flattened to their scalps. They've been up all night, as have most of Grammy's children—some surrounding her hospital bed, some walking up and down the waxed halls with cups of cheap coffee. It shocks them that it's happened so fast, for on Christmas Eve she'd seemed so well; she'd closed her eyes in pleasure as the hot soup was spooned into her mouth, and then the next day....

The voices are low and hushed from the kitchen.

I tense my limbs tight, tighter.

Outside, a branch cracks beneath the weight of the ice.

My father walks back to the room, finally, looks at my brothers and me for a moment as if he's never known us, as if any passing resemblance between us is uncanny, a surprise. He sits on the sofa and folds his hands in his lap. "My mother died."

The plainness of his voice, the unutterable simplicity of it. (Words fall apart: the sky darkens; a clapper strikes a bell.) From across the room my mother catches my face and smiles at me with a fond sadness. Then the weeping starts, a chorus of it from Grammy's children. It sounds foreign in their throats, almost animal, haunting and deep, as if as adults they've forgotten how to cry.

My cousins turn away. Embarrassed, impatient, they punch one another on their arms.

The hours of the next days move slowly, sluggishly. Intermittent snows, freezing drizzle. Uncle Joe takes the kids to a James Bond movie—*Diamonds Are Forever*—to keep us out of the way.

We dress. (Why am I having this trouble? My pants swim above my ankles. The buttons slip through my fingers.) The inside of the funeral home glows with a rosy, burnished light. Tufted French Provincial sofas border the walls. Nothing about it has anything to do with the life that Grammy led: her troubles and compromises, her stubbornness and will. "No," she'd say, shaking her head. "Not here. Too fancy." I'm led to her casket where she lies inside a border of banked flowers marked with a single sign: FOR MOM, WITH LOVE. YOUR CHIL-DREN. Her face shines pinkly, emptied beneath the lights. For a moment she seems so alive that I'm certain she's going to sit up and say, "Nass boy." Then my father touches her cheek. His eyes fill; his lower lip quivers.

I mumble a prayer, in silence: *Hail Mary, full of grace* . . .

Aunt Catherine walks in through the door, stomping her feet, brushing the snow off the shoulders of her long cinnamon-colored coat. She speaks in her usual cheerful, tough voice, preoccupied with who's bringing what to lunch after tomorrow's Mass, when she spots the unlikely casket across the room. Her knees weaken, buckle. Her face contorts. "That's not her!" she cries, as Joe and Francie hold her up by the elbows.

A block in Willowdale, the development next to where we live in Cherry Hill, starts to crumble. The houses are too spacious and expensive for anyone to use the word "slum," but driving down Heartwood Drive with our mother at the wheel, we spot the unweeded flower beds, the crusty gold rags in the dirt behind the bushes. Paint is flaking off the trim boards. Storm windows are ajar. But it's not the only block in Cherry Hill that looks like this: there's Strathmore Drive in Point of Woods, Collins Drive in Holiday Estates, Latches Lane in Candlewyck, Chaucer Place in Downs Farm. And while these streets were apple orchards less than ten years ago, the houses on them seem to be tired already. *The mask is falling. Our owners can't afford us. We've had enough of trying to pretend who we aren't.*

Maybe the families who live inside these houses are changing and their children don't feel the pressures that their parents once did. ("Yes, it's good to be Jewish,

Italian, Polish, Greek! Watch us now. We're just as good as the rest of you!") Although there are different kinds of pressures—odder, more complicated pressures. Someone I once saw in the lunch line of my school cafeteria stabs his mother over and over in the family living room, a story that seizes the attention of the Philadelphia/South Jersey news media for weeks. Someone else flings a vial of sulfuric acid on a special-education student's back as she wanders across the front lawn of Cherry Hill High School East. Richard Dubrow, a boy in Bobby's homeroom, stands in his closet one October morning, steps off a milk crate, and hangs himself with one of his father's blue neckties. In house after house, the kids simply fall silent, holing up in their bedrooms with their doors closed, or hanging out in the parking lot of the 7-Eleven. Anything to stave off the oppressive, persistent boredom. Until they get out. *But it's all been for you,* think their parents. *You've tread on the names of your ancestors.*

Weren't you the reason we were born?

One day after school, I'm lying on my stomach, trying to work out a proof for geometry class (in which I got a D on my last test, to the horror of my mathematician father), when the sirens outside wail and fall, wail and fall. Why is it so dark inside my room? I walk through the front door, and then one by one, people run out onto their wide green lawns with their heads raised. A sooty bank of smoke covers the entire sky, blocks out the late afternoon sun. "What's burning?" I call out to a neighbor.

"The racetrack," says Mr. Coticone. "It's going up."

43

A parade of funerals. Every few months there's another sudden, unexpected death in Allentown. Someone goes to work and feels pins and needles in the chest, a numbness in the jaw. A crack, flash of fire, and … Anna. Steve. Catherine's husband, Joe. We go to so many funerals in a such a short span of time that we're getting to be in practice now. We're careful of what we say to one another. We clench our shoulders every time the phone rings.

We mill outside the St. Catherine of Sienna Cathedral as Joe's silver casket is carried down the front steps by eight of my older cousins. A flock of doves scatters about us with harsh, beating wings.

Aunt Mary turns to my father. "You're next, Tony," she says.

▲▼

Our car idles on the eastbound shoulder of Route 70. My brother Michael aims his camera at the lighted billboard against the winter blue sky: TOTIE FIELDS. *LAST NIGHT TONIGHT: THANK YOU FOR TEN YEARS OF PATRONAGE.*

▲▼

The meat at the Bonanza Restaurant is tough, chewy, a little hard to swallow. I'd like to eat at the new restaurant on the old Hawaiian Cottage site (another arson), but this place has become so familiar, so much a part of our family ritual on Sundays that it would seem wrong to go anywhere else. And besides, it's inexpensive, so we won't have to feel anxious later about my father's cracks about the extra side salad one of us asked for and didn't finish. All five of us sit at those long, dreary wooden tables, beneath the red wagon wheels suspended overl when another family of five sits down beside us. I close my eyes. Don't I just know what my father's going to do? Isn't he going to talk too loudly? Isn't he going to ask the waitress for her first name, flirt with her within sight of my mother, before he asks for a refill? Isn't he going to make some observation about the length and style of my hair? All the ingredients are here: the audience of strangers to his left and his faltering son before him.

"What's the matter, Paul?" he says casually.

I shake my head back and forth.

"Paul?"

I lift my head. "Nothing."

"Can we have some of that A.1?" says the other father, leaning in over my plate.

I pass the bottle to the man. We've been talking about my lousy scores in the math segment of the PSAT, what we can do to raise them before I take the SAT in the fall. I wonder if I should just come out and say that I'm not interested in college, that I'm not obsessed with money like he is, that I don't want to build cities in South Florida anymore. All developers do is pollute and destroy. All developers do is rip people off. I'm going to be a musician and a composer. I'm going to live a life that isn't measured and determined by how much money I have in my bank account. And if I'm poor, so what. At least I won't be worried and miserable all the time.

Still, I keep all these thoughts to myself.

He's going on and on about the possibility of hiring a tutor or sending me to some remedial class that meets at 8:00 A.M. at the high school every Saturday morning.

Just as we're ready to leave, he produces the sheer, plastic doggy bag patterned with blue and red asterisks he's picked up from the dispenser next to the cash register. "Come up, kids," he says. "Fill 'er up. Make Taffy happy."

Obediently we fill the bag with gristle, bone, fat—all of which will be emptied into our little collie's bowl, even though she almost choked to death on last week's scraps.

His face is calm, expectant. He glances at the family to his left, at the cast-off pieces of steak on their plates. I know that look; his eyes shine as if he's been possessed of some idea.

NO! I think.

"Would you mind if we took your scraps?" he says to the father of the family.

A wave of dread rises from my feet to my face.

He says it again. *Would you mind if we took your scraps? NO!*

"You can't do that," I murmur.

My father glances up at me.

"You can't. You can't, Daddy. It's just not done."

"Oh, it's perfectly fine," says the other mother in a hard voice. "I'm glad someone else has the sense to ask for it. Here," she says, and scrapes the food off her plate into the outstretched bag with the edge of her steak knife.

Where *am* I? I exhale, exasperated, shaking my head back and forth.

"These kids," says my father with a smile. "Always worried about what other people think."

"You mustn't worry, son," says the other father. "We're certainly not offended."

"Don't be a snob," says the other mother. "Think about your puppy."

I look toward to the door. In twenty-five years, I'll recognize him in my duty to work hard, to extend myself past my limitations, and beyond, in spite of resistance, fear—the possibilities of transformation he's offered to me! A rush of love: I thank him. But right now I can't see beyond this moment. In 1976, the whole story comes down to this moment.

My father doesn't stop. One by one he goes to the un-bussed tables of the Bonanza, filling up Taffy's bag with whatever he can find—biscuits, fried chicken wings, lukewarm baked potato skins.

"Time to go," I call.

"We're going out to the car," says Michael.

My father walks to another table and starts a conversation with another family, all of whom find his request infinitely charming. My head pounds behind my eyes; my cheeks burn. Soon enough he finds more to add to the bag.

Is our embarrassment the very thing that's egging him on?

What on earth is he trying to teach us?

"Stop," Michael calls.

We cower by the front door of the restaurant.

"You're the chairman of the Cherry Hill Planning Board," says Bobby.

"You have two master's degrees from an Ivy League university," says my mother.

"We're so much better than this," I say.

But he keeps at it, determined, cheerful, until the bag is full, ready to burst from all it contains.

FAMOUS BUILDER 1

*The early American Village has achieved enthusiastic
acclaim for quality, dignity, and colonial charm by
the 400 families now living here.*
    ▲▼ Bob Scarborough, Barclay Farm brochure, 1962

In a deep socket of an empty acre lot in South Jersey, a
wiry boy with dark eyebrows, burnished blond hair, and
thick lenses in his glasses clears pathways through the
milkweeds, trying to preserve as many of the leafy, muscular stalks as he can. He works harder than he's worked
in weeks, so hard that he doesn't even hear his father's
car engine in the distance, or his mother ringing the
cowbell for him to come inside for dinner. This is Telegraph Hill: the first community he's built that he's genuinely proud of, from the curving of the cul-de-sacs as they
wind through the woods, to the discrete street names
he's penned in meticulous, Early American script on
scraps of faux-antique wood he's pilfered from his father's workshop: Saybrook Road, Weston Drive, Laven-
ham Court, Henfield Road. No wonder his fingers are
cracked and cut, his toes sore from using the front end
of his sneaker as a tool.

The wind rustles the weeds. He's about to back up

the slope, to look out over his first fully wooded community. His belief is so deep that he can practically see the lanterns trembling on, the hushed couples stepping up the sidewalks toward The Northfield, the most recent two-story model (vertical rough-hewn siding, copper-hooded bay window). Then Tommy Lennox, his neighbor, walks toward him with a football tucked beneath his arm, the faintest suggestion of a smirk around the corners of his lips. "What's that?" Tommy says.

A ripple, a blush to his skin. The boy's pleasure has been so private, so intimate, that he might as well have been making love to the land. He can't even raise his eyes. "A development," he says finally.

He swelters inside his shirt. The boy imagines Tommy stepping through the community casually, knocking street signs aside, crushing the tall can that stands for the silo at the entrance. Sweat drips down the center of his back. But when the boy finally lifts his head, he's surprised to see the animation in Tommy's face, the quizzical expression that suggests he's waiting to be shown around.

In no time at all, Tommy is building his own development, Willow Wood, in the open land beside the single pine along the back of the lot. He's out there every day, just as the boy is, digging with his mother's garden shovel, replanting tablets of moss until the knees of his pants are soaked through. But why doesn't this feel right? The boy doesn't have the heart to tell Tommy that straight streets intersecting at right angles went out with 1949. And what to make of the names Tommy's assigned to them: Motapiss Road, Vergent Court. They practically carry an aroma, suggesting all sorts of things no one likes to talk about: flesh, death, the mysteries of the body. At least Tommy's sister has the good sense to know that she should pay attention to what's attractive. Although Cathy Lennox's "Green Baye" is entirely misnamed (what bay? what water?), the boy cannot help but be impressed with the added *e*, and with the skillful way her streets meander down the slope.

Still, neither of their projects can stand beside the elegance and understated good taste of Telegraph Hill.

Today all the neighborhood children roam the field, some down on their knees, others carving out streets, all squinting, foreheads tightened in concentration.

The boy looks up at the houses across Circle Lane where he and his friends spend their time when they're not in school or out here. Of course, it would be their misfortune not to live in a real development, but in a neighborhood in which all the houses are decidedly different from one another, with no consistent theme. Although his mother tries to invoke the word "custom" as often as she can, he's not having it. Most of his fifth-grade classmates live in the newest developments, places where the wood-plank siding is coordinated with the trim (sage green with aqua, barn red with butter), always that pleasing sense of order and rhythm. Truth be told, he frets about living in a place with no name. Just to say "Timberwyck" or "Fox Hollow East" or "Wexford Leas" and be entirely understood! His dilemma even seems to bewilder that substitute teacher with the kind face and the gray, washed-out hair in whom he confides one day.

"You don't live in a development?" she says. "How could you not live in a development?"

Flushed, he turns away.

"Have you talked to your parents?"

He shakes his head. He steps back from himself, watchful, distant. Silent boy, ghost, so weightless and emptied he barely has a body.

What would she say to the story the *Philadelphia Bulletin*'s just written on him: BOY, 12, LONGS TO BE FAMOUS BUILDER? He imagines her unfolding the newspaper at her kitchen table, spreading orange marmalade on a burnt piece of English muffin as her teakettle whistles on the stove. Would he be real to her now? Although the article tells of the 600 brochures he's collected from developments all over the country, and of the fan letters he's written to Bob Scarborough, whom he wants to work for someday, it frustrates him, if only because it's written in that cheerful, yet patronizing tone that suggests his work is mere play, that he'll come to his senses in a few years. Hard not to wince when he sees it tacked to his principal's green bulletin board. How he hates being on display like that, lying on his stomach in the photograph, marveling at that brochure in his hands (is it Charter Oak?) as if he'd never seen one before. He'd like to tell the substitute it's an ineptly written piece, a foolish piece, but he's as guilty of the lies as anyone. Why did he simplify himself when he talked to that reporter? Why did he allow her to think there was something less than profound about the binders of street names he'd collected? Here he was, hiding the ferocious depths of his passion inside something harmless and benign, when all he really wanted was to move her, to show her he was in love.

When he looks up from his reverie, both Tommy and Cathy and all the others wander back toward their houses, the sky charcoal above the rooftops, the trees.

He gets down on his knees. He shivers inside his

jacket, which he zips, chucking the skin of his throat, but he'll work long after the street lamps have blinked on, defying his mother's cowbell, ignoring his long-division assignment, the piano scales—all those dull, grinding duties that suggest his life has nothing to do with pleasure, the warmth of this soil in his hands.

NAMING YOU

I.

Beads, cones, pears, amber nets of foil-wrapped chocolate coins tied at either end. January 8th, and I'm placing ornaments inside the sturdy dividers of their boxes. My hands work faster. Enough of Christmas already! No more dull, obligatory parties. No more last-minute runs to the post office. No poignantly ugly sweaters (snowflakes, argyles) doomed to feed moths at the bottom of a rarely opened drawer. But this isn't like me at all. Point out the first sign of an end—a red, crinkled leaf of poison ivy in late July—and that's it: brooding. Maybe I'm developing a better attitude, coming into a saner, smarter relationship with time. But just when I pull the tree out the door, some needles fall to the floor with, *what?* The sound of a shaken, blown-out bulb. I stop myself, blinking. 1938, the Christmas tree of my mother's seventeenth year. Lights glow as her twin brother's model train clicks around the track at its base. A gate raises. Signs shudder. Although it isn't the holidays anymore, but February: Valentine's Day cards scattered on the table. Something has happened; I can't remember what it is this time, but my grandmother, Anna, has given in to Paul's request to keep the tree up for one more week, because it's cheerful; isn't it? I think, *silly boy*. And I drag out the dried-up spruce through the door, its pitch gumming up my palms.

2.

My mother's twin was killed not long after the winter of the February tree. I think I should know the exact date on which her family car was broadsided by a drunk driver in a municipal truck, but to do that I'd have to make a phone call, and when I think of my mother watching the canal from her sixth-floor balcony (bells ping, drawbridges open), I think: spare her.

Although I wish I could speak with authority. I never heard his jokes or his laugh. Never passed the salt to him at a dinner table, never hugged him with that stiff, halting quality one only reserves for saying good-bye to a sibling at the holidays. Never went crabbing with him, never showed him New World or my other planned cities, never pretended to enjoy a hockey game he bought me tickets for. I've never seen more than a dozen images of his face. (Inside the picture frame on our family piano he wears a sepia-tinted sport coat and tie, both painted atop his T-shirt by a photographer.) He's blank space. I don't have much to go on here. I'm clearly having trouble, though I need to conjure him up, at least to try, even if the effort feels about as possible as building a thirty-story temple out of struck matches.

A few essential facts:

1. He wore white, size fourteen sneakers on which he drew portholes and the words S.S. Homan—his

and my mother's last name—with a laundry
marker.

2. Lanky, six foot four, he spent entire afternoons
   hurtling a basketball toward a hoop nailed to the
   side of the barn.

3. He had a cat (name?) who slept in bed with him.

4. He had more than a few friends, all drawn to his
   wit, cheer, and magnetic nature.

5. He often ate an entire box of cereal at a sitting,
   spooning soggy cornflakes from a silver mixing
   bowl.

6. When he learned that his father had shot himself
   in the front room, after a long period of estrange-
   ment from the family, he wept openly and hard,
   as his older brother and twin sister fell silent.

3.

My mother is quick to be silly, with a warm, endearing
sense of humor about herself. Her face tightens yet
glows when my brothers and I make fun of the expressions she used when we were children: "Hell's Bells,"
"Christmas," "Tough apples." Or when we imitate the
traces of her South Jersey accent: "Delawhir" for "Delaware." She's not the kind of person who appears to be
marked by grief. She looks and acts a great deal younger
than her age. She knows more about Britney Spears and
Jennifer Lopez than I ever will and is an avid fan of ten-
nis and classical music. She has a light mezzo-soprano
voice, which she lent to church choirs and recitals for
years. "If anyone ever said anything unflattering about
her children," my father has said, "they better watch out.
She's a lion."

But she couldn't have always felt the will to rise from the bed, to comb out her hair, to roll on a coat of lipstick. As early as I can remember, she spoke of Paul with such force and feeling that I couldn't but turn my head, an admission I feel ashamed of as I write it. Was I jealous? I could never mean as much to her, could never do anything to bring that ring to her voice, even though I did everything I could to earn it. She'd say: Of the two of us, he was the one with the friends. She'd say: Of the two of us, he was the one who was kind. I didn't yet know that this is the way we talk of the dead, the people we've known whose mouths, hands, and eyes fade from memory over time.

More than once she said, "He would have lived in our house." I'm sure she didn't mean that literally, didn't mean to suggest he wasn't independent enough to strike out on his own. Maybe she was doing the best she could to make him real for us, to create a future for him in which he'd brush out the mats of our dog's tail or sit beside us in a dark movie theater, face blued by the light of the screen. But for years I pictured a casually handsome man with a warm gaze—a blurrier version of the photo on the piano—standing in the bathroom doorway with a towel, the slightest hint of goofiness around his smile.

4.

How not to poeticize the unspeakable? How not to heighten for dramatic effect the thing that resists being written? I cannot fill it out, cannot give it color.

The day is entirely unremarkable, without drama. My mother and Paul are in the backseat, my grandmother and Uncle Alfred up front. Alfred is behind the wheel.

They're on the White Horse Pike in Collingswood, on their way to school or to work. It's winter. Someone in that car might be thinking about Easter, the green of the crocus pushing through thawing soil. A truck veers out from a side street—or does it cross the white line? Flash forward: my young mother steps out over the body of her brother, whose head has been cut open by the sheer force of the impact; someone's leading her out, away from the car. People stand at the curb, hands to their mouths, faces silent. Someone whispers a prayer. There's a metallic drop on the tip of my mother's tongue. Then, waiting for the medic to attend to the cut above her right eyebrow, she turns to a stranger. "That's my twin brother."

5.

Only recently have I noticed how I tense my hamstrings, if slightly, when I'm a passenger in the front seat of a car. If the car ahead comes to an abrupt stop, brake lights blaring, I instinctively glance in the mirror to my right to see whether I should brace my feet against the floor. I'd be exaggerating if I said I hate to drive, but when I'm in a car, I'm always pulling in my breath or cursing those cars passing on the shoulder, swerving in and out through the traffic.

My first car, a used, poppy red hatchback, was like a first love. I might not have been making mortgage payments or living in some basement studio with a single barred window at sidewalk level, but I owned a car. I might have been thinking these thoughts, proud that I'd finally mastered the stick shift—watch me work it through the gears—when another car flew through a stop sign as I was traveling east on Kresson Road and broadsided my front end.

I wasn't hurt. (Well, a little: within hours, my hand, which had been broken, swelled up to the size of a tiny oven mitt, the skin a shiny, lurid pink.) Still, I stood out on the street and yelled. I yelled and I yelled, forgetting who I was, forgetting that there was another person on the other side of my words, a man who put a tentative hand to my forearm, as if to cool down my skin.

6.

"Let's go for a ride," she said.

Bobby turned off the *Channel 27 Noon Report,* Michael latched the jalousie door, and soon enough, my mother drove the four of us up the Garden State Parkway through the wetlands, across the bridges, the smell of scrub pine, charred wood, and bay mud in the air. I opened the flapping map across my lap. How I loved her sense of possibility, her eagerness to keep us interested, excited. More often than not, she let us choose wherever we wanted to go. Lakehurst, with its airship hangar, so towering and vast the clouds inside formed tiny lightning storms. The tip of Cape May, with its concrete, cylindrical lookout towers from World War II. Loveladies, Strathmere, Brigantine, Manahawkin, Forked River Point—and model home after model home. Our destinations couldn't have been further from typical ideas of beauty or worth, but my mother went along for the ride, in a manner of speaking, and taught us, without being entirely aware of it, to crave difference, otherness, the *world out there.*

It's hard not to appreciate the negotiations she must

have made in order to sit behind that wheel. The farm markets along the road, the dark green spartina of a flooded marsh: she took in everything she could as she whipped the car around the curve, pressed the gas pedal deeper into the floor mat.

7.

In the years following the accident, my mother and her mother went roundabout ways to their jobs in Philadelphia and Camden, determined to avoid that particular stretch of the White Horse Pike. When they finished work, they went to the cemetery every day, even if it was too dark to see, and they'd kneel before the gravestone, before the headlights, damp grass seeping through their knees. Sometimes they'd say part of the rosary. Sometimes they were absolutely silent. I'm not sure whether my mother fully approved of these rituals, but she did it for Anna, whom she was devoted to, and who, by this time, must have felt that she was being tested. (What could it have felt like to lose the two people closest to you, your husband and son, to suicide and car accident, within three years?)

Then a respite. Just as my mother's high-school classmates were marrying and having babies, my grandmother sold the dairy farm, which had become too much to handle, and moved to a duplex in suburban Collingswood—only a few miles from the site of the accident. It's hard not to wonder whether my mother would have stayed on had the unthinkable not happened. If you've lost your twin, then what do you do but look for another, even if that twin happens to be your mother? How else to feel closer to whole again, to make

PAUL LISICKY

yourself real, if he was the outgoing one, and you were the shy one, and the outgoing one has left for good? No other way to fill up that *lack*. And certainly Anna probably couldn't have made it easier for her to pack up her things. (I used to think, if she knew what was best for her daughter, she'd have sat down with her on her bed, placed a hand on her back, said, "Go, make a life for yourself.") But love can't ever be entirely un-threaded from dependence, guilt, and need. And, fi-nally, my mother probably wasn't ready to marry or to set up housekeeping on her own. Although it could not have been easy, she stayed on fourteen more years with her mother, who kept a watch on her boyfriends and huddled in the dark hall at the top of the stairs.

"Time's up," she'd wail, when things got a little too frisky.

8.

My father thinks that my mother shouldn't dwell in the past. He thinks she should keep a firm eye on the here and now. I'm not sure whether that's so much about an unwillingness to empathize, as much as it is about his relationship to his own past, which, like all pasts once we reach a certain age, must be full of regrets and missed opportunities.

Or maybe he's only telling her what he'd been told himself. It goes without saying that both of them grew up in hard times: Depression, World War II. My mother has told me stories of a hearing-impaired, middle-aged woman with a brittle voice who showed up at their front door in 1936, valise in hand, after she'd lost everything: children, husband, house. She moved into their back bedroom and became a part of the family until she died in her sleep one night. The way my mother tells it, their taking her in wasn't some act of self-sacrifice. Rather, they let the woman share their soup and scrub her forehead with their washcloths, because with a missed payment or two, there they'd be, a mother and three children, knocking on some stranger's door.

So how would my mother's grief have seemed larger or more urgent than any of the other griefs surrounding them? *You have to forget,* said a friend. *We all have it hard.* And she murmured those words to herself long into the night, curled upon her side, tearless, rigid.

9.

The driver drove a maintenance truck for the borough. It's always been a deep brown in my mind, with splashes of mustard-colored water behind the tires. Or is it road salt? I think of him taking that last drink—in the bar, in the bathroom of the borough hall, wherever he was— in those numbed minutes before the accident. I hope it meant something to him. I hope it did for him what he wanted it to do. When I think of all the people who are finishing up drinks right at this moment, putting their glasses to their lips, swallowing those last clear drops as they fumble in their pockets for their car keys, I want to keep them still for a minute. I want to sit them on the curb until their heads clear, until the pavement steadies beneath their shoes.

10.

To name your firstborn after the twin you lost is an extra-ordinary act. How strange it must have been to say it again—Paul—to feel, all at once, your lips meeting in the center of your mouth, the depth of the vowel where your throat hits your nose. To connect that name to the baby in the playpen, who pulls himself toward you, on his stomach, in his diaper, with his pink, dimpled arms.

I wonder sometimes whether the particular quality of our relationship might have been different if I'd been a Duncan or a Craig. How could she not have been more fearful of losing me than she was of my younger brother, Bobby, born sixteen months behind me, who pitched and reeled a full mile down the shoulder of busy Kresson Road, at five, to visit some imaginary friend? (As challenging as he was, it must have been hard not to admire his chutzpah.) Of the two of us, I was the "good" child, so good, so desperate for approval, that I couldn't, in retrospect, have been anything but a trial. What had I been thinking? Refusing to cross the emptied Cranford Road without the assistance of an adult. Voluntarily turning over to my father my beloved bottle of rubber cement after I'd been brushing the stuff onto strips of blue construction paper for six months, because I'd read the label one day: Not Recommended for Children under Eight. It couldn't have helped that I caught colds more frequently than my classmates, and like the little Proust, was subject to fits of nausea at the slightest prospect of excitement. Too anxious to eat a real lunch in the school cafeteria, I'd eat a single sandwich on Pepperidge Farm party bread brought from home in a brown bag, until my habit caused a bit of a stir among my classmates at the table: "Look at that little sandwich!" Which was not what I'd wanted at all. Which was simply to eat it as fast as I could and disappear.

Silly boy.

Was I my mother's little twin? The question gives me a twinge. Could we have created this dynamic together without even being aware of it? Was it even avoidable? Growing up, I couldn't bear to be separated from home, and what's home when you're that age but *mother*? I sat at my fourth-grade desk, pretended to be absorbed by the pressure of my pencil on the paper, when all I wanted was to save her: to sit at the kitchen table, to hear her chatting, cheerful, phone clenched between her chin and her shoulder blade, as the eyes of the dead—her brother, her father, then her mother—watched from other places in the room.

II.

"Bye, dear," she says.

"Good-bye."

I'm standing outside the car, bending toward her in the passenger's seat. She pats the top of my head. A kiss. And there it is again: that tap, that crack to the rim; the light comes in. The white separates from the yolk, almost, not quite. Something gluey loosens and pools, collects into the bottom half of a household cup.

I clench the suitcase handle tighter, until my knuckles go white, just to make sure I haven't disappeared.

I clear my throat, smile, then hurry toward the doors of the airport.

LUCK BE A LADY

We drive through Panorama Shores, Florida. Although it's 1992, it might as well be 1962; the houses have been meticulously preserved right down to the jalousies, the pylons, the alarming geometry of oblongs and fins. Mint greens and pinks and ice blues and saffrons: it's hard not to fall a little in love with the town's Palm Springs atmosphere, whatever you think of midcentury design. My brother, Bobby, is practically in heaven. For most of his adult life he's been entranced by the architectural charms of the era, the sweetness and optimism, its faith in a decent populist esthetic. We turn north onto Mahogany Drive. Amid the travelers trees and the coffee shops and the neatly tended motor courts are bars, more bars than I could have imagined in such a pretty little beach town. I imagine stylish lonely widows lurking behind their gates. I think of the older Joan Crawford. Or else, the aging Vivien Leigh, who's worrying the pearls around her neck, dressed in that inimitable color that could only be described as *champagne*.

We pull out the address from the glove box. We're surprised that Mrs. Fox isn't presiding over one of the fancy houses on the causeway. We make a few more turns and soon we lurch up some side street, and then

67

an alley barely wide as a Lincoln Town Car. Palm fronds swipe the windshield. It's obviously not the clipped, constructed paradise from which we've just emerged. There are trash cans and tomcats and stacks of weathered lumber in the yards. Not that there isn't a ramshackle allure to the place (I can't help but think of Key West), but it's on the edge of something seedy and exhausted.

Number 16406: the Sting Ray Motel, outside of which a skinny woman with starved eyes smokes a brown cigarette, exhaling through her nose.

Number 16408, not two feet to the north. The sign clues us in: *The Foxes: Time Out.*

The house itself is an L-shaped rancher, a narrow affair, which appears to have been specifically designed with a problem lot in mind. A forbidding garage wing extends toward the street. The walls are blinding white, the roof tile is blinding white. Oddly enough, it's the only yard on the block without a scrap of vegetation. Only a bed of white white stones where the grass might be. It's so white that it's hard to look at; our eyeballs ache, blue, then throb.

But that's not really what startles. To the left of the garage, we see a wrought-iron gate through which circular stepping stones lead to the front door. And the color of that wrought iron? Orange. Not a subtle, cheerful orange, but an alarming orange like the color of a traffic safety cone.

Who would paint wrought iron orange? The thought is so disturbing that I'm certain that Bobby, an architect and designer with intractable standards, will press his foot on the gas.

Instead, he shifts the car into park and opens his door.

"What are you doing?"

"We're going to see Mrs. Fox."

"She won't even open the door." And I remind him of the incident twenty years ago when, with our parents, we made a surprise visit to her house in Huntingdon Valley, Pennsylvania, and she refused to answer our insistent knocking, even though we saw her frozen silhouette through the curtains.

"Oh, stop it. We'll just say hello, then leave."

"No!" And I'm a bit startled by the tone of my own voice. What am I so afraid of? Is it only that I'm worried that I haven't measured up in her eyes, and I can't deal with the possibility of her censure or indifference? But she's in her eighties now. Her husband has been dead for ten years. Might she be touched by the fact that we've remembered her, that we've come to pay homage?

Bobby folds his arms and sighs, plainly annoyed by my paroxysm of shyness. I haven't yet relented. But his eyes fall once again on the safety-cone orange as if it tells him something he doesn't want to take in, and he swings back behind the wheel and drives north.

▲▼

It was a matter of accident that we ended up spending our summers next door to her. My parents must have seen something—a newspaper ad? a billboard?—prompting them to take a detour from Ocean City, New Jersey, where they'd spent the afternoon pushing me down the boardwalk in my infant stroller. It was nearly 5:00 P.M., August 1960. Sunburnt, thirsty, they pulled into Anchorage Point past strings of snapping pennants. WATERFRONT WONDERLAND. MODEL HOMES FROM $12,990. They drove around and around the single completed loop, gazing at the spinnakers on the bay, the humble skyline of Ocean City. Soon they were talking to Isabel Falone, the developer, with whom they stood outside the landscaped model home. The future glittered before them: yacht clubs, restaurants, shopping centers, marinas, beaches. Three thousand homes, the most extensive waterfront development in the state. I have no idea how Isabel Falone might have appeared then, but I've given her a black French twist, dark eyeliner, and seriously red lips. She's a force to be reckoned with, a hybrid of Bill Levitt and Jacqueline Susann.

Before 6:00 P.M. my mother and father had placed a $1,000 down payment on the single model available, The Sea Breeze, a waterfront three-bedroom rancher. If only he'd known that Isabel Falone's Anchorage Point Development Company would file for bankruptcy not two days later. For years I imagined Isabel Falone literally running from continent to continent away from my screaming father. I'd decided she'd made off to Buenos Aires where she ran down the boulevards, hiding her French twist with a sheet of clean newspaper.

In retrospect, I'm surprised that that bit of lousy luck never prompted my father to forgo his dream of owning a summerhouse. His dedication to the pursuit of pleasure is certainly not in character. Why didn't he turn his attention toward something harder, more demanding? But he was fierce, optimistic in those years. The son of Eastern European immigrants, he'd made a little money, and he wasn't going to let anyone turn him away from the door. And he genuinely loved Anchorage Point. He couldn't forget the color of that lagoon. Freshly dredged, it was a rich Caribbean beryl, an enormous outdoor aquarium through which you could see all eight feet down to its clean sandy bottom. Minnows, sand sharks, blue claw crabs: every few seconds they flashed up to the surface, scuttled away, then flashed again. And the water temperature was just to my father's taste, cool enough for swimming laps. So my parents bought one of the existing forty-four houses—one not that much different from the one they'd hoped for and lost—next to a middle-aged couple from Huntingdon Valley.

I'm a little troubled by my parents' relationship to the house. It seems to me they don't take it seriously enough. It's not that they don't take care of it, but their work goes only as far as cutting the lawn every two weeks, sweeping beach sand from the floors. All around us, however, our neighbors stamp the once-identical houses with their signatures. The Bertmans, for instance, put up a basket-weave fence enclosing yucca, sunflower, dusty miller, and prickly pear. Two houses, down the Brunos side their house with raw textured planks resembling California redwood. The Ansteys even talk about adding a second story in order to take advantage of the views across the marshes and bays. Hammers start banging at 7:30 A.M., followed by the shredding circular saws. People have forgotten how to relax. No one seems to remember that these are vacation houses. Boats stay fastened to their docks, squeaking and rubbing as they go up and down with the tide.

Could it be that the house is entirely too modest for my father, and he's cultivated a relaxed attitude? On one level, its sheer austerity—pebbled roof, vertical wooden trim, its two modest double-hung windows facing the street like two expressionless eyes—must not fit the bill. He'd prefer something bigger. But bigger costs money (they've already given up on Seaview Harbor, the more expensive lagoon development closer to the ocean), and my father obviously wonders whether it would be appropriate to take on a larger monthly payment. Aren't all his brothers and sisters working overtime? And isn't his mother getting older, less mobile, waking up in the middle of the night to talk about her fears of the "poor house"? So he makes a pact for us to live simply. The house will embody one thing alone: we're not going to be something we aren't. Which is finally more difficult than you'd think: who *are* you if you've essentially recreated yourself?

The Foxes, who have struck up a friendship with my mother and father, gently encourage them to take a look around. They stand at the property line and point out our crabgrass, commenting breezily upon the punched holes in our screened porch. The chain-link fence, which encloses our entire yard, seems to be a particular point of contention. I'll be ashamed of its grave practicality myself a few years into the future and cite several reasons for it to be replaced, but my father has installed it so he won't have to worry about finding Bobby or me floating facedown in the lagoon.

It's interesting to me that my parents don't seem to mind the Foxes passive-agressive jibes. I can't tell whether they just don't hear them, or don't care, consumed by problems of their own. The work goes on next door. One day several dump trucks spill enough bleached stones to cover the yard six inches deep. On another the wooden picture window is replaced with a sleek two-panel sliding glass door. "Custom," Mrs. Fox assures us. This in addition to redwood planters, a cupola/weathervane, floodlights, a patio, stepping stones, a short pier into the lagoon. Inside, the work has been even more extensive, the stuff of neighborhood myth. They've filled it with sleek, understated furniture and have installed appliances that indicate they've taken the house seriously, quite seriously, in fact: a pale pink refrigerator, a front-loading washer, and most intriguing to me, a General Electric wall oven in which Mrs. Fox allegedly never cooks anything. Not that I've seen any of this. Children aren't allowed in the Fox house. Not even her own grandchildren, Jonah and Jonathan, who must stay with their parents at the Port o' Call Hotel in Ocean City.

Nor is Mrs. Fox's mother, for that matter. Well, she's allowed, but not welcomed. During Mrs. Halvorsen's single weeklong stay, she sits all day on the carport and stares morosely at the lagoon. Mrs. Fox makes no secret about her feelings for her mother. She calls her "Muz," which my own mother finds particularly disrespectful, though forgives. Mrs. Fox tells my mother about the time when, as a teenager, she came home to find Muz naked in bed with another man, a man she'd met in some bar, and how they kept at it ("fucking," she whispers), while she went into the bedroom to scratch holes in the wall.

"*Whoore*," she grimaces, twisting the pronunciation to sound like *sewer*.

My mother's mouth falls open.

"That's right, Annie. I'm not afraid to say it. My mother, a *whoore*."

"What's a *whoore*?" I say later. I stand with my mother in the tiny kitchen, high on my tiptoes, and stir chicken Rice-A-Roni while she empties a brick of frozen peas into a saucepan.

73

"Whore," my mother says, correcting me.

"Whore."

"A woman who sells dances," she says without missing a beat.

I cock my head. Selling dances: I cannot think of anything more delightful.

I love our seashore island. Its elevation, a mere six inches above the high waterline, both alarms and mesmerizes me. I love nothing more than those new moon nights when the lagoon actually spills onto the yard for a few hours and leaves behind piles of cordgrass that we must rake, gather, and deposit in the trash. But there's more to my enchantment than that. Surrounded on three sides by flooded green marsh, Anchorage Point's topography satisfies my desire for solitude and separation. Or could it be that fluidity of land, water, weather, sky? There's nothing better than returning to our house after we've spent a hectic week in Cherry Hill, the suburb that we're supposed to like, but actually don't. Far from the brutal playground, far from Sister Miriam Veronica, who humiliated me before my second-grade class because I had a Go Port folio instead of the required Pee Chee brand—all our petty anxieties disperse once we hit the bridge and pass the Coppertone billboard. (That pigtailed girl and her round white butt always elicits a song from us: *Get the fastest tan that anyone can. . . .*) To the east: the beaches of Longport and Margate. To the west: the bustling marinas, the bright blue generating station, the shining expansive water. No more claustrophobia, no more repetition and rigidity.

Walking through the back door, I breathe in that re-assuring closed-up house smell (mildew? crawl space?) and creep into the room I share with my brothers. Bobby and I lie in our respective twin beds, with Michael on the folding cot in the middle, thirsty and pleasantly carsick from the 55-mile drive. We rest beneath screens beaded with moisture. Sleep never takes long. I press my scalp into the damp flat pillow and try to name what I hear: rose vines creaking in the breeze, a line chiming against a mast, the moaning of the drawbridges as cars pass over their grids.

And Mrs. Fox's rituals and rites are a part of this ex-perience. The next morning I wake to the suck-slam of her jalousie door, to which she has added a device that plays a jingle when it opens. I crouch on my bed, chin pressed to the sill, and revel in my role as spy. She's working hard today, but not any harder than usual. Down on her hands and knees, she scrubs down the as-phalt driveway with a bucketful of Tide. She's in her regulation day uniform: tight tight shorts, candy pink tube top, and a white sailor cap with a turned-down brim. She scrubs harder now and peppers her exer-tions with soft grunts and a curious utterance that I've learned to imitate: *ish*. She glances up at a cabin cruiser, breathing in the dim smell of spent fuel.

Early on, I know that Mrs. Fox's struggles are com-pounded by the fact that she doesn't drive. It's two miles to the Somers Point Center, and she'd rather stay at home than be seen walking along the shoulder of Long-port Boulevard. No wonder she's always sending my mother on some little errand, a loaf of Arnold Bread, some Taylor Pork Roll. More often than not it's for a six-pack.

"Which brand again?"

"Piels," she says, passing the five-dollar bill over the fence rail. "Buy the boys some candy with the change."

The request inevitably comes on an occasion when Mr. Fox is away in Huntingdon Valley or out on the boat fishing. Since he's due in at midnight, she consumes all six cans in quick succession, "tinkles," as she puts it, then takes herself to bed.

My mother bristles at these requests, but complies anyway. For some reason, she always stops at the closest place and leaves us in the car. It's not quite a package store, but a taproom in which she must walk past the older men at the bar, most of whom fall silent upon her entry. Only a few nights ago she sat behind the wheel to inform us that one of the men had called her "stacked." I couldn't tell whether she was delighted or appalled, or some combination of both.

"Be back in a few hours," says my mother.

My brothers and I walk to the car and dream about what kind of candy to get with Mrs. Fox's change: a Tootsie Roll pop, some Pixy Stix, Fleer bubblegum. But as I turn around at the gate, I see Mrs. Fox pinching and twisting the skin of her palm, as if to say *hurry*.

We watch *Exercise with Gloria*, which comes on every morning at nine following the *Today Show* with Hugh Downs. Although the program's clearly designed for women and their special needs (the opening segment features the svelte Gloria and her seven blond daughters in black leotards), Bobby and I exercise with our mother anyway. We thrust our fists from side to side, scoot our butts across the rough beige rug until we get carpet burns. We're all panting and gasping when we hear a tapping sound on our front window. It's Mrs. Fox, a look of anxiety and boredom on her face. She's been spending far too much time in the sun, and she's getting so dark that Mrs. May recently mistook her for someone's cleaning lady, something she'd never in a million years repeat to Mrs. Fox.

"Annie," she calls. "Annie? Are you inside?"

"Oh, Hell's Bells!" My mother has made it quite clear that she prefers to be called Anne, but Mrs. Fox persists.

I pull up my mother by the arm, then follow her outside. Bobby totters behind. Her flash of rancor fades to relief. She likes the company, after all, even if Mrs. Fox manages to say something patently offensive, which she does without fail. My father's RCA job requires voracious amounts of overtime, and when we do see him now, on the occasional brief weekend, he seems nervous, embarking on the latest in a series of projects—jacking up the sinking porch slab, tarring the roof—endeavors only an engineer could love. Years later, we'll call them home destruction projects, if only because they remain unfinished for months and never involve the pursuit of beauty.

I love to listen to Mrs. Fox. I rest my brow on the warm fence rail, the summer heat boring deep down into the roots of my hair. Much of what's discussed goes over my head, but it has the luscious zing of gossip. It underlines all our neighbors' gestures and celebrates community life, inadvertently making all of us feel significant.

"The Sendrows are away," she says conspiratorially.

My mother's eyes dull. Mrs. Fox has been consumed lately by the aesthetic sins of her next-door neighbors to the south, and my mother's probably not so sure she wants to open that door.

"Let's get a look."

Together the four of us walk across Mrs. Fox's stones and stand right up to the Sendrows' picture window, cupping our hands around our eyes. Inside, there's a rocking chair with roosters stenciled across its back, a gold braided rug over the pink speckled floor. No front-loading washer, no pastel refrigerator/freezer. I can see why such beach-house minimalism might bother Mrs. Fox, but I don't mind, if only because I like the Sendrow daughters with their sassy blond hair. These girls are wild. More than once Mrs. Fox has caught them sneaking their boyfriends in through the bedroom windows. In a few years I'll pick up the *Courier Post* to find out that Pam Sendrow has been arrested for the possession and distribution of LSD, a fact that will thrill my imagination for days.

"How can they live with themselves?" mutters Mrs. Fox.

My mother says nothing. She knows very well that our own house isn't much better.

"I mean, is this a fishing shack?"

We walk back to our respective houses. My mother seems largely unfazed by this latest demonstration of Mrs. Fox's belief that we're living in a slum. "Mmmm," she says. "Mmmm." If only to indicate that she hasn't nodded off. She's tired, I can see it in the shadows beneath her eyes. We've been wearing her out. And late to marriage (she's thirty-eight when I'm born, but it's not till I'm twenty that I learn she's ten years older than I'd thought), she must be struggling silently with something. Having this kind of time on your hands can be a little dangerous, can swallow you whole, but she's grateful to be in a place that so much resembles Stone Harbor, twenty miles to the south, where as a girl she was happiest.

"What's the matter, Mommy?" I step into the living room one afternoon, hand clutching my elbow, afraid that it's something I've done. If I'd only been a better child she wouldn't feel this way.

She's lying on the rattan sofa, left arm crooked over her forehead. Wavelets of light reflect off the lagoon, shimmer above her on the gold-flecked walls. I stare at her elbow, its intriguing roughness, so unlike my tender brown skin. Is this what happens when your elbows get old?

"I'm down in the dumps," she says with a sad, apologetic smile.

"It's okay, Mommy." I sit beside her on the floor and peck her inside the wrist.

Someone who does get along with Mrs. Fox is my aunt Goldie, my uncle Francie's wife. Aunt Goldie is tall, slender, and exotic, with a deep whispery voice. In the broadest of terms she bears a vague resemblance to Jackie Onassis. Someone at the electric company, where she works, has pointed this out in the cafeteria, and she's played it up ever since, teasing out her dark hair to give it extra volume and wearing huge round glasses that hide half her face. I adore Aunt Goldie. Not only is she my godmother, but she takes a naughty glee in my imitations of Uncle John, her brother-in-law, a red-faced, always smiling, sweet-natured man who speaks from a small wet spot at the back of his throat. In addition, she likes the way I play the piano. Hearing me perform "Aquarius" from the rock musical *Hair* (in which there are reportedly many nude scenes), she virtually shivers with pleasure, pressing her fingertips to her collarbone to say *unh*.

And she's pretty good at mimicry herself. One Thanksgiving we walk into her house in the Allentown, Pennsylvania, suburbs to see that she's modeled her living room on our Cherry Hill house, right down to the sculpted gold carpet, the burgundy sofa, and the Queen Anne highbacks. A serious student of style, Goldie is always looking for the newest, the brightest, the best. Once, driving Bobby, Michael, and me to Atlantic City, Aunt Goldie spots a carriage house on Ventnor Avenue with green-and-white-striped awnings, geraniums in the window boxes, and a painted wooden carousel horse on the front porch. Without warning, she slams on the brakes, turns before oncoming traffic, parks, then breezes up the front walk. The door opens. She tells the owners "I *love* your house." Such enthusiasm earns her a tour of the place while my brothers and I sit for an hour in the sweltering car.

But there's a darker side to Aunt Goldie, a side which I find both irresistible and a bit threatening. She's prone to excessive emotional outbursts that might come out of nowhere. Within my father's extended family, she's known as "sensitive." During one Easter dinner, she gets up from the table and throws herself facedown on the bed after Aunt Myra asks whether there's dressing on the salad. (There is, of course, but it's subtle. A tangerine vinaigrette.) On another occasion she nearly faints in her kitchen when one of my cousins remarks on the frequent roar of jet planes overhead, the way they shudder the dishes in the china closet. (After all, Goldie and Francie live across the highway from the Allentown-Bethlehem airport's newest runway, but we don't talk about that.)

Despite what the family might think, it's Aunt Goldie's sensitivity that earns her an invitation to tour the Fox property. Mrs. Fox is different with her than she is with us. She knows she has a captive audience in Goldie, and is more sedate, almost abashed and overwhelmed by her own capacity for good taste. I peer behind the shed to watch. Fingertips are extended; every meticulous detail is commented upon in a whispered hush. The tour starts with the Coupe de Ville convertible, then progresses to the lagoon-front patio, then moves finally to the custom sliding glass door. I crawl out into the open, astral-projecting myself into those rooms, stunned by the sheer proximity of all that beauty, that longing to be more, better.

When Goldie finally returns to our house, she seems different somehow. I look around at the battered tile floors, the turquoise and chocolate brown sofa cushions, the old Zenith TV with its sad flag of aluminum foil attached to the antenna.

"How was it?" I ask.

I want her to tell me everything. I want her to say the world is not what we thought, but someplace better, where vitality and hope are indeed possible.

But she hangs her head. She seems both breathless and sick.

"Play 'Aquarius,' Paul," she says. *"Please."*

And I do it over and over, if only because it seems to be the thing to set things right.

▲▼

Before long, Bobby and I have conspired to fix up the place. We're sick and tired of waiting for our father to do something. We've gone so far as to draw up little blue-prints with pens we've purchased from Stainton's de-partment store. Once every two months my mother worries that we're spending far too much time with her, that we have no playmates our age in Anchorage Point. (The average age of our neighbors must be fifty-five.) If there's anything good to come out of this perceived predicament, it's that we know how to entertain our-selves. Part of our imaginary development can be attrib-uted to the fact that we're living in an abandoned subdivision, and we can't help but imagine how things might have been, which prompts us to come up with our own solutions. There's an empty lot across the street, crowded with bayberry, spartina, discarded pilings, and swampy blond puddles in which tadpoles breed. I've built a miniature waterfront development in a secluded section. I've called it Ocean Harbour and have named the streets appropriately: Barkentine Drive, Clipper Cove, Spar Buoy Lane. These tiny cul-de-sacs are surrounded by intricate canals—wide as an ice-cream scooper—filled with actual puddle water in which I hope the tad-poles will navigate.

A humid and torporous morning, with low sluggish clouds and a tangy wind off the sea. Bobby and I are ready to explore the site of our lost house when we spot the Caceeses' old signpost pulled out of the ground, lying in the trash. The skin of my arms tightens and hurts. Before Bobby and I have even expressed our shared interest, we run down the street and lug the weighty signpost back to our front yard. We get the shovels. We dig the hole. Soon enough the sign is leaning like Pisa, but we like it, at least we think we do, even though the Caceeses' house name—Summer Place—is still spelled out upon the crossbar in cursive black letters. We shrug. We dig smaller holes around the base, into which we transplant portulacas from the lagoon side, the same portulacas that were given to us by Mrs. Fox, who disapproved of our marigolds. But something's missing. Cedar chips! We give ourselves permission to steal some from the Remetas' backyard. Soon we run up and down the block, carrying splintered wood within the bowls of our cupped palms. We're intoxicated with the pleasure of creation. We pant, sweat. We take on much, much more than we can rightly handle. But our work will be worth it finally, for once we're done, the neighbors will be sure to take notice: certainly we'll be popular and very much loved.

My mother walks out into the front yard. She's been taking a nap; she's groggy, the pattern of the pillowcase still imprints her forehead.

"Surprise!" we cry.

We look up at her with delirious smiles. To our surprise, her forehead's ridged with worry. She looks around at the piles of dirt and the tilting post with the vaguest sense of bewilderment.

"Where did you get these things?"

We tell her *down the street,* and point to the Caceeses' yard. "Don't you like it?"

She shakes her head hard. "Why didn't you *ask?*"

Bobby and I squint. In our wildest dreams, we never

thought she'd be anything but pleased. Maybe she doesn't feel well. She's had a terrible pain in her neck for months, for which she does grueling exercises that require her to strap her chin into some horrifying contraption involving pulleys and weights and a metal hook over the door.

She nudges the base of the signpost with the tip of her sneaker. The wood is soft; it yields to her pressure like balsa. At once a procession of bugs climbs upward from its damp interior core.

"Termites!" she cries.

Waterbugs, I'm about to say, but I don't think I should correct her now. She hasn't been this upset since the time she asked for the paint scraper when I was all of three, and I mistakenly tossed it at her forehead. Once she recovered, she pulled down my pants and spanked me, and I ran out into the side yard, leaping and hopping at the scarlet red pain.

I feel just awful, misunderstood by the woman who I thought would always want the best for us. Doesn't she know we want the best for her?

"You better fix this up before Daddy sees it." And she walks back into the house to get a start on dinner.

Bobby and I begin to do what we're told, before slowing down in the hope that Mrs. Fox will open her back door to see what we've done. Surely, she will appreciate our efforts. She won't be so inscrutable. But it's dark now, and the smell of spaghetti sauce is drifting out through our screens. A lone gull bleats like a sheep. A cricket saws inside the inner branches of the hydrangeas. With heavy hearts, we fill up the hole and drag the signpost back to where we found it.

▲▼

Our parents have agreed to take us to the Anchorage Point Civic Association dinner. I can't imagine anything more exciting. The prospect of attending literally changes my demeanor, and in the days leading up to the event, which I imagine to be as glamorous as the Academy Awards ceremony, I walk around with my chin held just a little high, practicing an expression of drollness.

The dinner takes place at the Bali Hai, a restaurant to which I've attached an enormous amount of significance, not only because we drive by it twice a day, but because it's Mrs. Fox's favorite restaurant. As she never cooks anything in her General Electric wall oven, she and Mr. Fox go there practically every night, reportedly ordering the same meal: chopped steak. I have no idea what chopped steak actually is, but I imagine it as rarefied and impossibly elegant until one night, when I'm discussing Mrs. Fox's interesting habit with Bobby, my mother cries, "It's just *hamburger*, dear." I refuse to believe her. Every time we pass the Bali Hai—with its twenty-foot tower topped with a red flashing light—I can't help but imagine her at her table, where she closes her eyes and brings a delicate piece of charred meat to her lips.

A crowd has already assembled inside. A pianist named Nick Nickerson plays old standards on the baby grand in the corner, and there's Mrs. Sendrow and Mrs. Caceese, shy in their black cocktail dresses, holding martinis. I see Dr. Bruno, Mrs. Vanderslice, Jean Russo—everyone's dressed up, cordial, and delighted with themselves, grateful to be seen. I wander away from my parents to seek out Mrs. Fox. For a moment I'm convinced that she's not coming, that she's stayed at home to scrub out an unexpected spot on the driveway, when I see her off to the side in an silver sequined dress. It flings shimmers all over the black walls. She holds herself apart from the crowd, but she's also *of* us. She's so beautiful that I swear her presence alone sets off a small explosion of bluish green light behind her.

In minutes she moves to the center of the room, where everyone grants her her space. Mr. Forte, our other next-door neighbor, asks Nick Nickerson if he could play for a moment. Nick steps aside as Mr. Forte swings his legs over the bench and cracks his knuckles with a flourish. Before he moved next to us Mr. Forte worked as a counterfeiter, for which he was sent to Allenwood Prison. But he's a law-abiding citizen now, as far as we know, in spite of the persistent rumors we hear about mob ties. I think of him as the Philadelphia Frank Sinatra, and soon enough he launches into one of Old Blue Eyes's favorites: "Luck Be a Lady Tonight." Miraculously, he knows all the words. His phrasing is supple and taut, and I love it when he blows into his fist and pretends to warm imaginary dice.

At once, Mrs. Fox steps forward. Holding a tall clear cocktail, she stands beside Mr. Forte and snaps her fingers. She doesn't sing or dance, but her sheer presence is enough for us. I love her shining platinum hair, her expression of uttermost sophistication. Her head bobs slightly with the rhythm. The flashes come more quickly, more brightly. Perhaps a photographer has stopped by to record this illustrious moment. I turn around and hope I will be caught—foxlike!—in the flashbulb's glare. And then I have a revelation: *this* is where Mrs. Fox belongs. Not picking weeds, not scrubbing her driveway at six in the morning.

Mrs. Fox belongs in Hollywood.

I lean against my mother's chair. She smiles, far from her troubles, giving herself over to the whole glamorous scene. More bright lights. My eyeballs thrum. My mother turns around and looks at me with a squinched forehead for what seems to be an extraordinarily long time.

"Are you okay, dear?"

I nod feverishly. I have never felt more energized and engaged in my nine-year-old life.

"He looks funny, doesn't he?" she says to my father.

My father places a cool palm on my blistering forehead. My mouth is dry. "He's hot. You better take him to the bathroom."

The chair screeches back. The green lights flare, the floor buckling and sloping dangerously beneath my feet.

My mother whisks me past the crowd, down the hall into the ladies room. (The ladies room? What on earth am I doing in the ladies room?) But then I'm down on my hands and knees, throwing up into the cold white porcelain. My back is rubbed with circular motions. "Are you finished yet?" says my mother nervously, but it scorches my throat, this sluice, this orange bitter grit, until there's nothing inside me. I'm dying, I'm sure of it; I'll have to be taken by the rescue squad to the hospital. And yet, I feel as if I'm living for the very first time, pulled toward a new world of style, artifice, and self-invention.

I am ushered to the car. It is all too much for me. I spend the night dreaming of being blinded by the fabulous spangles of Mrs. Fox's dress.

▲▼

(Could it be our name? Would Mrs. Fox like us better if we were the Wanamakers? I have to admit there's something undesirable and odd about Lisicky. No wonder we're made fun of, my brother and me. *Robert Lisicky sucks his dicky.* Which sends my mother right to the doorstep of Mrs. Gold's house after she learns that Brian has said these words to Bobby on the Bret Harte school playground.

I'm in my thirties when I finally learn the Slovak translation of Lisicky. It's Fox. Actually, son of a fox.)

▲▼

On the *Channel 6 News,* Francis Davis points to the whirling comma off Cape Hatteras called Tropical Storm Doria. We've spent the day in preparation. We've stocked the cabinets with Campbell soups and snacks; we've filled the yellow bathtub with water. I'm practically vibrating: the drama, the helplessness, the sense that we're at the mercy of a hostile, indifferent force. The wind picks up right on schedule. The lights go dimmer. The rain comes down so hard that it leaks through the windows, spilling over the sill. The rafters sigh. I rush into Bobby and Michael's bedroom (now that I'm getting older, I have my own room, which I've painted amber and blue, though it looks too much like a Sunoco station.) I watch them sleeping. Finally, I declare that we have to evacuate, that the tide is rising through the floorboards, that we must act quickly if we are to live. "Get up," I cry. *"Live."* I treasure the look of abject fear on their blinking, disoriented faces. Once I smile, they're not only relieved but amused by my warped little prank.

We all crowd before the front window. The rain is horizontal now, pinging the glass like sleet. The mimosas thrash and weave in the floodlights. Within minutes it becomes clear that the braided blue ropes holding the Foxes' 24-foot cabin cruiser, *Time Out,* are fraying. "That boat's going to break loose," says my father. His concerns are not entirely altruistic. Our boat, the 17-foot *Anney Ho Ho* (a play on Anne Homan, my mother's maiden name), is docked due north. Already I imagine our beloved boat smashed, the fiberglass floating like matchsticks on the frothing black water.

My father raps repeatedly on the Foxes' jalousie door. It's two in the morning, the lights are off. Unlike everyone else in Anchorage Point, they haven't prepared at all for the storm. Basket chairs, pagodas, tiki torches, a mirrored ball on a pedestal—all wait like potential artillery if the predicted winds of 100-miles-an-hour hit.

In our raincoats my mother and I huddle in the tiny passageway between our houses, where we watch my father. Mr. Fox answers the door with a look of drowsy indifference. They've been sleeping soundly, in spite of the shrieking winds and emergency sirens. Above, the power lines churn and lash the trees.

"Your boat—" my father cries.

Mr. Fox gazes out at the transformed lagoon with a grave expression. His visage says: *There's nothing to be done about this.*

"I'm out of rope," my father says. "Do you have any rope?"

"Wait here," says Mr. Fox. And he shuts the door to leave my father saturated in the soaking rain.

He returns after five minutes. Once he has his rope, my father races across the yard and, to my mother's horror, jumps upon the deck of the heaving cabin cruiser. I don't know whether he's acting sensibly. Is this just another occasion to prove himself, and he's thinking of Humphrey Bogart in *Key Largo?* "Christmas," says my mother. "Why did I ever get married?" But after a few minutes he does manage to tie the boat to its moorings, and the wind lets up, just enough to allow him to jump onto the raft in safety.

"That should hold it," my father says. He's coughing; he's out of breath. He hands over the portion of unused rope to Mr. Fox and wipes his stinging eyes with his fist.

"Big storm," replies Mr. Fox.

Blue lightning over Ocean City. My father nods, and Mr. Fox walks back into his house without a suggestion of a thank you.

The next day the yard is spangled with roof shingles, wet newspaper, torn branches, assorted trash. Mud has swamped the end of the street. Our Russian olives have blown over. In fact, all the trees have been stripped of their leaves: winter vegetation three months ahead of schedule. But it's oddly sunny and cool and dry. Pleasant, really. I'm humming "Shout from the Highest Mountain," a song that I like from folk Mass, when I spot the Foxes' cupola lying on its side by the lagoon. Obviously, it has blown off the roof and I stare at its battered louvers in a kind of horror. I can't help but think of Charlton Heston and his hysterical, femmy outburst after he's seen the wrecked Statue of Liberty at the end of *Planet of the Apes*.

My father sits cross-legged on our dock, tightening the bolts with a wrench, when Mr. Fox spots him. I'm glad that he's finally decided to say thanks, even though my father has already decided to forget about it.

He beckons my father with crooked finger. "Tony."

He wants my father to help with the cupola. But it's a demand, not a request. My father complies without hesitation, and in that single moment I see him perhaps more clearly than I've ever seen him before, someone suspended between the two worlds, professional and workman. And in Mr. Fox's gesture, I see how the Foxes see him, my mother, us, how they will *always* see us. We're beneath them. Although I'm peeved at my father's acquiescence, I'm more peeved at Mr. Fox for taking advantage of his eagerness to demonstrate his worth. I turn, trudge back into our yard, and start raking up cordgrass.

In the wake of the hurricane, things shift ever so slightly between the Foxes and the Lisickys. Maybe we're more confident now. Bobby, Michael, and I are far more likely to imitate Mrs. Fox's cleaning rituals, to make gentle fun of her behind her back. Even our mother joins in on the play, and we love her willingness to parody her friend. We've grown tired of her impetus to control. When she says of our freshly painted shutters, "Are you keeping them blue?" we're appalled. And there's something mildly distressing about her jibes at the community, the latest of which includes putting a sign on the Sendrows' front yard, beneath the heavy limbs of the mimosas: FOR SALE, CHEAP.

But we've truly always known what Mrs. Fox was made of. Recently she's professed to touring the model homes at Rossmoor Corporation's New World, a subdivision on the outskirts of Cherry Hill, and she claims to have loved the faux Mission-style ranchers, the fake Tudors, the "luxury modern French Provincials." We're perplexed. Everyone in my school knows that New World is bad taste, as embarrassing as the replica of the 1964 World's Fair Unisphere that marks its entrance. We wonder if she's secretly making fun of us. As summer draws to a close, I write a short song about her: *Grunting and groaning, gasping and whining—that's Mrs. Fox. Sort of a cross between Moms Mabley and Wally Cox.*

Our relationship with Mrs. Fox reaches its nadir just before Thanksgiving. Bobby and I are helping our father transport panels of unused sheetrock to Cherry Hill from Anchorage Point. We're on the Black Horse Pike, halfway through the Pine Barrens, when guess who we see pulling into the passing lane? Bobby and I hide our faces with our hands. We sit in the back of the open station wagon, weighing down the panels to which my father has tied strips of red rags. To make matters worse, the muffler is broken, roaring. Oh, Tobacco Road. We're traveling twenty miles under the speed limit, and because the water's been shut off for the season, we haven't showered in two days. Still, we wave and cry, "Hey, Mr. Fox. Hey, Mrs. Fox." Their eyes look determinedly forward, deliberately obliterating us.

We talk about their dismissal endlessly for weeks. We enumerate the times they've behaved poorly, though we can't help but be mildly entertained by the flamboyance of their bad behavior. Over the next several months I contemplate enacting a similar form of disacknowledgment, until something else happens. Early June, the night before trash day. In bed, lying awake, I listen to the causeway traffic, the distant boat engines, and . . . what? The melodic clinking of glass. I peer over my windowsill. Mrs. Fox carries what must be a trash bag full of beer bottles. She walks out beyond the edge of the yard to place it alongside the Garbers' trash, then tiptoes back to her own yard, her shoulders sagging.

▲▼

Sometime during the school year, while we're back in Cherry Hill, the Foxes' house is sold to Don and Anne Naughton, a retired couple from Millville, New Jersey. We're not entirely surprised. The Foxes have owned another house in Florida for the past two years, and they've grown dissatisfied with their New Jersey neighbors—so many falling outs with former friends. The completeness of the transition doesn't hit us right away, and though we're a little sad, I'm still young enough to see change as essentially a good thing.

The Naughtons clearly don't share the Foxes' aesthetic commitments. They do everything possible to decimate the place, as they're hell-bent on making the house maintenance-free. Vinyl soffits, vinyl siding, vinyl doors: how quickly beauty festers and fades. "They want a fishing shack," my mother says sadly. The cupola is chopped up for firewood; the stepping stones are pulled out of the ground, stacked like concrete dinner plates beside the back door. Each week another piece of Mrs. Fox's prized furniture from W. & J. Sloane is hauled out for the garbage man, and Bobby rescues and refinishes what he recovers. "Look what I have," he cries one night. "The swag light. I have the Japanese swag light!"

Soon enough our house is beginning to look more and more like the Foxes'.

For a while we attempt to stay in touch. My mother writes a few letters in which she tells Mrs. Fox that the place just isn't the same without her. They're never answered, but we don't quite mind. Then my mother sends a Christmas card. Three weeks into January we receive a postcard of a travelers tree on which Mrs. Fox says that she's never been happier, that she has a pet heron named Lulu who perches on her dock every afternoon.

93

This is the best thing we've ever done. We should have moved out of that dump years ago. Love to Jack and Bobby. "Jack?" I say aloud. "Why would she call me Jack?"

▲▼

In Mrs. Fox's absence we become friendly with the Dashers, who live directly behind the empty lot in which I once built my Ocean Harbour. They've installed a flag pole with a flashing red light on top, in imitation of the Bali Hai, which puts me off, if only because I've internalized Mrs. Fox's taste. (One thing if it's a restaurant; quite another if we're talking about a private home.) We don't know what to make of the Dashers. We are intrigued as much as we are appalled by them, and we probably wouldn't have paid them much attention had Dolores Dasher not made a concerted effort to win over my mother, by pausing at the fence one day with a flounder wrapped in foil. They have a son named Timmy, who's almost Bobby's age. The Dashers are big people. They're not exactly fat, but they're trunky, like sequoias. The Dashers have density. They're prone to making such statements as "We're big salad eaters," which Bobby, Michael, and I find particularly amusing.

Dolores Dasher and Timmy come over to our house frequently for dinner. By this time our living room has been walked totally uptown. In a matter of months, the entire place looks even better than Mrs. Fox's, thanks to Bobby and his restorations. Initially I'm a bit surprised that my parents encourage Bobby's work, but it coincides with his doing well in school. Never a committed student, he's now getting As, and my parents attribute his scholarly success to his interest in design. And he's never seemed more self-assured. At one point, he even asks Ann Naughton for Mrs. Fox's beloved Danish armchair—he's been looking for it every Sunday night in the trash—and amazingly she just offers it to him. "Oh, we'd probably just get rid of it, anyway," says Mrs. Naughton with a benign, clueless chuckle.

The Dashers seem both resentful and in awe of our house, which we're quite proud of by now. When they have us over for dinner, I can tell they're a little embarrassed. Timmy's G.I. Joe hangs by the dining-room table, and when Dolores catches me staring at it, she leaps up from her chair and yanks it off the wall.

Then something strange happens when we come back the next summer. Over the winter months the Dashers' house has been completely remodeled. Not only have they purchased expensive kitchen appliances, but they've enclosed the porch and installed shag carpeting, which they rake dutifully every morning after breakfast. Even stranger is what they've done to themselves. Mr. Dasher, who's six foot seven, has taken to wearing bell-bottom dungarees, while Mrs. Dasher has developed an attraction to bikinis into which she sews side panels to accommodate her hips. Everyone these days is talking about Anchorage Point's most arresting vista: the newly blond Dolores Dasher weeding her petunia bed in a jumbo bikini patterned with black-and-white psychedelic swirls. The Dashers appear to be happier, but there's an odd strain between us, which I can't quite pinpoint. We still go to the beach and boardwalk together, but these mostly pleasant excursions are interrupted by occasional flashes of anger from Dolores. This anger comes to a head when Bobby, in a breezy, sardonic tone, informs Timmy that our Cherry Hill house is a "city-block long." Mrs. Dasher, who's spent much more time in the city than my brother, having lived in the same northeast Philadelphia row house for twenty-seven years, finds this observation patently offensive, and tells my mother about it. In sight of Mrs. Dasher, my mother tells Bobby that this isn't true, that this isn't nice, though she doesn't sound entirely convinced. "So it's *half* a city-block long," Bobby says, and rolls his eyes. And Mrs. Dasher jerks Timmy home by the arm.

Two weeks later we're driving down Bay Avenue in Ocean City. Pointing to a dull Colonial under construction, Bobby says, "yuck." To which Mrs. Dasher, who's driving, wrenches back her head and says, "Robert Lisicky, I'd like to see the kind of house *you* live in someday." It goes without saying Bobby is appalled. The Dashers accuse him of being competitive, stuck-up, but within months they sell their Anchorage Point house and move into a two-story contemporary in Seaview Harbor, the more expensive lagoon development down Longport Boulevard, which my father had turned his back on sixteen years before.

We're the last of the old guard in Anchorage Point. All the others—the Foxes, the Fortes, the Caceeses, the Muscufos, the Sendrows—have either moved south to Delray Beach or simply died. With the passage of casino gambling in Atlantic City, a half hour away, the houses are occupied year-round now. Newer residents, mostly casino executives and their families, are drawn to the waterfront property, now in high demand because of EPA rulings restricting the dredging of wetlands. Many of the original California ranchers are all but unrecognizable. Second stories are thrown up overnight; huge landscaped pool decks extend toward the water. Some houses are entirely torn down, replaced with floodlit bunkers. Ronald Reagan is president, and size seems to be more significant than modesty or understatement. One teardown is reportedly on sale for $325,000. The strangest thing about these developments is that we're virtual strangers in our old neighborhood. The DePalmas or the Denelsbecks don't appear to care that we've been here since the early 1960s, that we've stuck it out through tropical storms, water problems, difficult days when the post office refused to deliver our mail.

Still, Mrs. Fox isn't quite forgotten. As late as 1986, a dozen years after her departure, we hear an anecdote from Joan Britt, who happens to run into us at the Acme. Joan is the kind of senior citizen we'd all want to be: attractive, alert, and perky, all undercut with a pleasing subversiveness. She's one of those people who makes you feel grateful that she likes you, because you know that she just doesn't give it away.

My mother and I draw closer once Jane starts in on her story. 1961, and Mr. and Mrs. Britt are dining with Astrid and Warren at the Sandpiper Pub, a once-exclusive oceanfront restaurant that has since become a nightclub with an ominous reputation. (Two years ago a college kid was stabbed repeatedly behind a Dumpster.) As Mr. Fox leaves for the bathroom, Mrs. Fox places both hands on the table and leans forward.

"I hate my life," she whispers.

The Britts smile uneasily. After all, the couples aren't close. Isn't this just one more instance in which Mrs. Fox is dramatizing her circumstances? They don't know what to believe. They ask themselves, *Has she been drinking?*

PAUL LISICKY

"I hate my life. Are you listening to me?"

"Astrid, *no*—" says Mrs. Britt.

"Some days I just want to throw myself into the lagoon."

Then Mr. Fox returns to the table, and she's once again talking in a cheery voice about replacing the carpet with Karastan rugs.

This tale, which we repeat over and over in the subsequent days, examining every detail for meaning, doesn't bring us any closer to her, or shed any light on the utter mystery of Mrs. Fox. We can't place ourselves at a safe distance from it, though, and we feel guilty when we chuckle. After all, didn't Mrs. Fox instinctively know that the sanest way to make it through a life is to attend to the particulars? She found a method to transform her sadness, funneled all her energy, chaos, and anger into form. She knew the sheer pleasure of revision. She stamped her prints into materiality and tried as hard as she could to get things right. Wasn't that enough?

Famous Builder 2

It didn't matter who you were or where you came from but how you lived your life. Mr. Levitt enabled us to have the good life.

▲▼ Daphne Rus, Levittown, New York, resident
The Levittown Tribune, February 4, 1994

You're so crazy about Levitt, let me ask you something. Where is Levitt now?

▲▼ W. D. Wetherell, *The Man Who Loved Levittown*

And there he is, pacing the terminal of the airport in Brookhaven, Long Island, in a marine blue sport coat, light slacks, and fawn-colored oxfords. He taps out another cigarette before he's finished the one already in his mouth, its smoke curling up into his face. He pats down his lapels, smoothing back his gelled, wavy hair, but the truth is, he's a wreck. He looks as if he's lived into every one of his seventy-six years. The San Juan casinos, the Scotch, the sparring with his brother Alfred, the lenders, the wives—all of it has marked his face like a plat map of his nearby Strathmore at Stony Brook development. Even his oxfords, once impeccably buffed and shined, now look like they could have been bought off the rack at the Huntington Goodwill.

So there's no reason that the boy, his ardent admirer, should be hiding behind a column, five feet from his idol, so burdened with intense feeling that he thinks he might need to be rushed to Dr. Boguslaw. That's the least of his problems. Why does he still have the body of a twelve-year-old when the calendar above the rent-a-car desk says 1986? How did he get here from there? And why is he still wearing that same awful pair of dungarees from E.J. Korvette that scratch in the crotch, that ride too high in the waist? It occurs to him that he might be dead, struck by a car on one of his determined bike rides to Point of Woods or Cambridge Park, developments five or six miles from his house. Once he shakes out his arm, though, he can tell he's as alive as the rest of the people fidgeting about the tiny airport. Certainly his mother must be in the car outside the terminal, where she waits for him to walk out the door with maps and brochures, the beautiful news of how streets get their names.

But enough dawdling. He sniffs, stiffens his neck and walks forward, extending his hand to Bill Levitt. Instantly the famous builder claims every inch of his six foot frame.

"If it was for a penny less than $92 million, I'd walk out right now."

The boy is too scared to blush, whimper, or hyperventilate.

"One more stunt like this," Bill Levitt says, "and I won't do business with you again."

The boy steps backward. He thinks of running out to

his mother—of course this was a mistake; of course he should have stayed safely back in 1972. But as he's about to give up, he tells Bill Levitt that he was the one who wrote the fan letter, the boy who saw his first model homes at nine and hasn't stopped talking about them ever since.

"Ah," he says. "I thought you were a little young to be in S&L." He sits down with a sigh, patting the seat on the bench next to him. "Cigarette?"

The boy shakes his head no.

He squints, draws in some smoke until the tip flares orange. "Paul Lipstick?"

"Lisicky."

Gratitude and awe flash through the boy's cheeks. Bill Levitt *remembered.* In the distance, a bulldozer pushes a bank of torn-up potato vines into an enormous mound. Beyond that, workmen hammer up two prefab walls.

"So what makes you want to be a builder, honey?" Bill Levitt says.

He shifts back and forth on the bench. His eyes burn and tear from the smoke. *Honey?* Impossible to answer such a thing. Could Bill Levitt? Even if the boy said, "I want to build the kinds of developments that make people happy to be alive," he wouldn't exactly be telling the whole truth. His feelings run deeper and colder than Long Island Sound. They mean more than any single component: an imaginative street name, the pleasure of redesigning a Colonial as a Contemporary, the swirl of feeder roads, color codes, and cul-de-sacs on a master plan.

"I want to do what you do," he says finally.

Bill Levitt's smile is tinged with remorse. His eyelids

look heavy. "Here's my only advice." He leans in close until his mouth brushes the boy's ear. "Beg, borrow, or steal the money, then build, build, build."

And then he spills every drama from the start of the year. The sums borrowed from family charities, the down payments spent from Florida's Poinciana Park development—how was he to know that a single stake hadn't yet been driven into the sand? Or that his third wife would have such expensive tastes, expecting a present every month on the date of their anniversary? All the failed ventures—Nigeria, Venezuela, Iran (Levittshar!)— all the money lost, and now he can't even afford to pay for treatment at North Shore Hospital, the hospital he paid millions of dollars to build decades ago. He's sold his chateau in Mill Neck, the Rolls Royce, the 237-foot yacht once docked beneath the Brooklyn Bridge. He doesn't even have a dime to call a cab. And if those bastards from Old Court Savings and Loan don't show up in five minutes—he taps the face of his Cartier with an elegant forefinger—there's going to be hell to pay.

"Miniature Lane," the boy says, his eyes welling. "I hope you're going to have a Miniature Lane in Poinciana Park."

Bill Levitt stubs out a half-smoked cigarette in an ashtray. His eyes fix on the carpenters in the potato field.

"Tardy Lane, Italic Pass," the boy says. "You took the time to be inventive, original."

"Those workers?" he says, pointing in the distance. "They're Union. But we couldn't have built Levittown with Union. Those assholes tried to shut us down."

"The altered setbacks," the boy continues. "The see-through fireplaces, the village greens."

"We kept our profit margin low. 17,447 houses in 5

years. Our own lumberyard, our own roofers. And that's how we slaughtered the competition."

"You gave style to the masses, things only rich people could have afforded before."

"And blacks," Bill Levitt says. "The minute you let the blacks in, the property values dive. I mean I have nothing at all against the blacks; some of my best workers have been blacks, but look what's happened to Willingboro. Or Belair at Bowie or Winslow Crossing. I had every right to keep the blacks out, but you couldn't do that after 1964. And look who suffers but the homebuyer."

A calm in the terminal. The air tastes grittier, more troubling on the boy's tongue—is that sawdust blowing through the open doors? No, something else: he feels it in his eyes, tastes it high in his throat. He knows things he'd rather not about Levitt. Not just that he restricted Jews from the high-end Strathmore-Vanderbilt or black people from the three Levittowns, but sins of a lesser sort. Flooded conversation pits in Monmouth Heights' Contempra; "streamfront" lots in Cambridge Park that bordered a concrete culvert. And, then, of course, his ties to Joe McCarthy or any corrupt individual he thought could be of use to him. "How can I be racist," he replied years later, "if I'm Jewish?" The boy can't begin to understand such things. Nor why Bill Levitt is not the least bit interested in the poetry of building rather than the making of money, which doesn't matter to the boy at all. Here they are, seated side by side on a bench, a cornucopia of detail waiting to be exchanged between them, but right now he feels vague and unsatisfied: Massasoit trying to hold a conversation with Miles Standish.

"The masses are asses," Bill Levitt murmurs to himself.

The boy gazes out at the development burgeoning in the potato field. Hammers swing, nails pierce. Piece by piece the neighborhood comes into being. Nothing that Bill Levitt says is going to sour his morning. He thinks about what's sure to come a few months in the future: the signs in refined script posted outside the exhibit homes, the copper beeches leafing out along the strip of grass between sidewalk and street. Inside "The Ardsley," the Luganos stand in the foyer, looking up the staircase at the light fixture overhead, before Richard, Lori, and Kate rush forward, imagining themselves into the next ten years. There they are with their cousins, tangling their arms and legs together on the Twister mat on the dining-room carpet. There they are, just the five of them, trimming the arbutus, planting pink geraniums around the patio in grateful, pained silence, taking in the news that Mrs. Lugano's treatment has been successful, her illness in remission. And yet as much as the boy tries to hold onto his vision of a kind, perfected future, in which no one is hurt or stunted and all longings are satisfied, he can't stop seeing an overlay. 1996, and the children have moved away, resentful, bored, though not quite knowing why. Mr. and Mrs. Lugano stay put, wary of strangeness, difference, suspicious of the two black men who come to deliver the new sofa one day. A tree hasn't been planted in years. Unclipped limbs rub and shadow the bay window, and no one on Hornblende Lane gestures when Mr. Radwin, a neighbor, walks past. The traffic crawls. The sprawl takes over Middle Country Road, and . . .

"Look what I've done." Bill Levitt's voice is full of forced authority, as if he's talking to an S&L guy again. He pulls out at least a dozen clippings from his pocket, all taped at the seams, and presents them with quivering hands to the boy.

Nothing new here: the 1950 *Time* magazine cover story; later articles announcing ventures in Paris, Puerto Rico, Madrid, Frankfurt. The boy pores over the stories and pretends he hasn't memorized them in a carrel of the Cherry Hill Library. And for some reason he knows that Poinciana Park will essentially remain a tree farm during his lifetime. Although he hasn't nearly fallen out of love yet—that takes longer to acknowledge than a fizzy, unsettled feeling inside the body—he can already sense that his own future will be more complicated and alive than he ever could have imagined.

How to live without the dream of making, building?

"My mom's in the car," the boy says, in distress. He stands up, and pats the shoulder of Bill Levitt's marine blue sport coat.

"Listen," Bill says, tapping out another cigarette. "One thing you'll promise me."

"Yes, sir?"

"Don't call your first Lisickytown."

The boy is silent. Not that he ever had such an idea, but didn't Bill Levitt get to rename his first huge development in honor of his family? Would Island Trees have ever gotten the publicity of Levittown?

"That kind of thing's out of style. Why do you think the schmucks from my New Jersey project changed it back to Willingboro?"

"What do you suggest?"

"I don't know. Green Park?"

The boy feels the corners of his mouth pull. "Whatever happened to your imagination?"

"Ahh," he says, waving smoke away. "That was

Alfred's department. Give me eighty bucks at the craps table and I'll turn it into two thousand." Bill Levitt steals a glance to his left, waiting to berate the lender he's convinced is still coming to meet him.

The boy steps backward. With a nod, he turns around and heads for the door.

"Paul?"

He stops midstep. "Yes?"

"Get yourself some decent pants, for Christ's sake."

The boy looks down at his dungarees from E. J. Korvette. A blush fires up from the soles of his feet, scorching his scalp until his hair feels damp.

"Don't be hurt. Here's some money," he says, and offers a bill. "Here, take it."

"I thought you were broke."

"Try Brooks Brothers. Get yourself a decent suit."

The boy takes the fifty that's extended to him and inadvertently shakes Bill Levitt's hand. His palm is dry and vaguely cold, as if he's already thinking about the life to come, the grander developments he'll build in the next world.

"And one other thing. Don't judge me, all right? And don't feel sorry for me. I've lived."

The boy slides the bill in his back pocket. "Would you like my mom to give you a ride somewhere?"

But before Bill Levitt can respond, the boy has vanished, back to the tyranny of the linear, the parameters of time that have been dealt to him.

WISDOM HAS BUILT
HERSELF A HOUSE

Sweetest of sweets, I thank you: when displeasure
Did through my bodie wound my minde,
You took me thence, and in your house of pleasure
A daintie lodging me assign'd.

▲▼ George Herbert, Church-musick

I sit before the choir, playing through a dense chromatic passage in Richard Proulx's "Look for Me in Lowly Men," when Marcia Mackert pushes her vibrato, shakier than ever these days, up and over the other sopranos. I try not to laugh. It's far too sad: the desperation, the flamboyance, the need. I lock eyes with Kate Papagallo, who steels her expression, trying to sing and stay composed. My lip quivers. My mother, standing to Kate's left, catches the mischief in our eyes. Then all three of us snuffle, turning redder in the face, while the congregation looks back at us with an appreciative interest.

Soon enough the whole choir is in tears, with the exception of poor Marcia Mackert, who's oblivious anyway, caught in some private fantasy of herself. But no one's ashamed; such casual behavior seems to be oddly in keeping with these surroundings. Even though we're celebrating the Fifth Sunday in Ordinary Time, we, like most of our fellow parishioners, love to flout tradition and convention, to push out the parameters of acceptable behavior. It's a decade after the Second Vatican Council, just before the deeply conservative Pope John Paul II puts a damper on the party, and we're enlarging our sense of what being Catholic means. We receive Communion in the hand years before we've been given the Bishop's green light. We hold our collective breath as dancers pirouette and bow in the sanctuary. We sing the latest works from the Composer's Forum for Catholic Worship; we struggle through bootlegged hymns from the radical Dutch church. I'm particularly drawn to their translation of Psalm 13, which is entirely absent of direct references to God, the Lord, or any higher power: "Even then I'll cling to you, cling to you, cling tight to you, whether you want me or not." There's even time for the occasional rock Mass. One languid May morning, beneath the willows on the rectory's lush lawn, Blue Danner—barefoot, sixteen, longhaired, with frayed bell-bottoms—grasps the fingers of his girlfriend, Tina, as they receive Communion to the electric strains of "Peace, My Friends." Perhaps our audacity is best embodied in the design of our church. (Correction: Parish Center.) A starkly modern, circular affair, it features a sunken sanctuary, not unlike the conversation pits of our township's splashiest living rooms. Abstract banners in every conceivable size and color—fishes, wafers, lopsided chalices—hang from the industrial black ceiling. To our delight, there's not even a kneeling bench or a crucifix in sight. In no time at all the brand-new building is the object of much speculation in our predominately Jewish community ("It's a nightclub." "It's a spaceship"), and when I attend an ecumenical service at the boomerang-shaped Temple BethEl on Chapel Avenue, I can't help but feel relieved we've outdone them.

We are the new Catholics: rebellious, ironic, sophisticated, sexy.

Mass ends. I play an instrumental as Kate clutches her sky blue choir folder to her chest. We look at each other for a second longer than we intend to. There's something sly in her face, an expression that's both a smile and a pout. *"What?"* I say. But she's silent. She walks up the steps, her lustrous blond topknot swinging behind her.

I'm surprised that I get along so well with Kate, given that I'm fourteen and she's thirty-two. One wouldn't think we'd have very much in common (she's married, after all, the mother of two school-age children, Holly and Sean), but we took to each other immediately. It's not that I don't have friends my own age. I do, but, like me, they're on the margins, too oddball to claim the attention of our teachers and peers. There's Craig Cole, for instance, who appreciates my creative compulsions without judgment (lately I've been writing a play, *East of Canaan, North of Scranton*—about a glamorous terrorist who longs to be a movie star—which cracks him up). I'm entirely at ease with Craig, but there's a little problem: he has the alarming habit of pretending his father's still alive, even though I'm almost positive that he died the previous summer while I was away. I've gone so far as to look up the obituary in the records of the county library. Why has he kept this from me? A minor omission that's gotten out of hand? I know for a fact that he wasn't close to his father. Frankly, I'm too embarrassed to call him on his stories; we're not on such intimate terms. But he's been getting more extreme. When I ask what he's doing one Saturday night, he replies, "I'm going with Dad to the Flyers game," a declaration so ghastly that I refuse to fully process it. So it's no surprise that I feel closer to Kate than I do to Craig. She recognizes my potential. Once, unprompted by any occasion or incident, she puts her arm around my shoulder, pulls me close to her, and tells me that I'm charming. Her perfume smells of lilacs. The blush burns hotly in my face. Later I'll turn her observation over and over in my head, both honored and humbled, yet convinced that she's confused me with another boy.

Could it be that she sees something of her younger self in me? At six foot one, unbearably nearsighted, with braces and prominent features, I'm certainly awkward beyond belief, and I can see no way out of this predicament. I wasn't always this ugly. I blame it on a protracted fever I'd had in fourth grade after which my eyesight deteriorated dramatically. To help matters, I purchase wire-rim aviators and a expensive shirt from Bamberger's (patterned blue rayon with a knitted black band around the waist), though no one remarks on my intended transformation. What I need is a vast overhaul, a new head, an entire new self. I stand before the bathroom mirror, twisting and pinching my face, and ponder plastic surgery: an ear tuck, a nose job. Maybe even a chin reduction. (Years later, after I've finally been fitted with contacts, grown into my features, and put on a little weight, my younger two brothers will love to show home movies in which I appear, pointing to my unruly hair and painfully skinny limbs, slapping their thighs until they fall out of their seats.) On more than one occasion Kate has talked about her junior year at Chevy Chase High when her life drastically changed, when all at once she had so many boyfriends she had to turn them away. She attributes her achievement to stripping her hair and dying it blond, but my mother suspects she's holding something back. Kate's father, Peter, whom we've met on several occasions, has a schnozz that virtually dominates his face, and there's something unlikely about Kate's pert and shapely nose. Every time she turns her head, I gaze and gaze at her nostrils, looking for the nicks and scars, the telltale signs of the knife.

But if it's indeed true, it's curious that she withholds such information from me. After all, this is Cherry Hill, and a goodly percentage of my Jewish and Italian classmates come to school decked out in bandages, practically flaunting their Sweet Sixteen birthday presents. "Brides of Frankenstein," says Craig.

▲▼

Quite by accident I end up being the accompanist for a church choir. One Sunday morning, when I'm distracted and ill at ease, my mother's friend, Janet Margot, introduces me to the director. I'm not sure why I agree to play. Am I just afraid to hurt everyone's feelings? Isn't everybody already depending on me? It distresses me to think that I'll be on display before some of my more savage classmates. The choir is positioned right beside the altar, illuminated beneath a set of black can lights, and I can already imagine John Pompo, who hasn't let me forget the time I used my hands in a soccer game, smirking at me from the congregation, arms folded across his chest. I practice defending myself in my head. *So I'm a church-music geek. So sue me.*

But as far back as I can remember, I've loved music. I study piano with Leon Roomberg, who with his wife, Jacqueline (pronounced Jak-wah-*leen*), run the Jacqueline Studio of Music and Dance in the paneled basement of their Imperial Estates rancher. I'm not sure what to make of Mr. Roomberg. He dresses in tattered black and wears a pair of thick chunky glasses that are forever sliding down his nose. He never pushes me to sight read, and is far more likely to assign Burt Bacharach's "A House Is Not a Home" than Chopin's Nocturne in D minor. All I need to do is play, and when I come upon a passage in which I can't make out the notes, I simply make it up. "That sounded better than the original!" he cries, shaking his mop of graying hair. I can use the compliment, of course, but the compliments come a little too easily to him.

Still, the improvisatory techniques come in handy. My ear is getting sharper. It's been happening for years actually, even before Mr. Roomberg was in the picture. I think back to Barbara Brewer, who sang and played guitar in the early days of our parish when we still attended Mass in the chapel of the Diocesan nursing home. She led the congregation with such authority that we often burst into spontaneous, hearty applause, forgetting that the place smelled of bouillon, that senior citizens kept wheeling themselves, senile and lost, through the overheated sanctuary. She wrote and performed her own songs, which she later recorded on her own record album—imagine a liturgical *Ladies of the Canyon*. The second I came home from church, I sat down before my grandmother's old upright and played Barbara's latest melody from the song sheet my mother had stuffed conveniently inside her purse for me.

I'm surprised by how much I get along with Nancy Fallon, the music director, especially after disliking her for such a long time. (Is it the way she introduces new songs to the assembly? That hint of condescension? *Louder, please. Now repeat after me ... Priestly People. Kingly People. Holy People.*) But she's kinder and sassier than I'd first expected. She's friendly with the wildest priests in the diocese, having directed the music for their ordinations, and I love the way she calls them Vince or Joe, something which, no matter how open-minded I am, seems delightfully transgressive. She's immersed herself in the world of liturgical music, attending the leading workshops of the day in places as far as Los Angeles and San Antonio. She's a close friend of Joe Wise and the Dameans, all major figures in the movement, and once, driving me home from choir practice, she tells me about another composer, a former Scientologist and current lay Franciscan, who has a boyfriend on the side.

Like me, Kate seems to be a little in awe of Mrs. Fallon's worldliness. She's deeply committed to the choir and actually tapes our rehearsals on a high quality reel-to-reel that she lugs around in her station wagon. It's no surprise that Mrs. Fallon takes a particular shine to her. I cannot help but wonder whether she's also impressed with Kate's fancy house and CPA husband, given that she lives in a sad little bungalow on the outskirts of Camden. No one's surprised when Kate is offered all the descants and solos, even though her voice tends toward the shrill on the high notes. Marcia Mackert is clearly not impressed by this turn of events. She stops showing up for Mass, finds more and more excuses not to come to practice, until one day we learn that she's directing her own choir at Mary Mother of the Church.

I've become a veritable archivist of contemporary liturgical music. I embark on my task with all the ardor I once gave to the design of suburban developments, which after almost five years has lost its allure to me. Occasionally, annual reports from Levitt and Sons, Kaufman and Broad, and the Rossmoor Corporation still arrive in the mail, but I cast such things aside and rarely bother to open the envelopes, and even if I bother, the houses on the pages inside look feeble, dull, lacking in vision. Instead, I give myself over to a project in which I can excel today, not ten, fifteen years from now. I write to all the major music publishers for catalogs; I spend Saturday afternoons alone in the dank music library of the Blackwood Catholic Center, sitting cross-legged on the orange-gold carpet, where I listen to scratchy, already outdated recordings like *The Mass for Young Americans,* while my classmates hang out at the Echelon Mall, looking for dates. I'm more driven and centered than I've been in a long time, and it relieves me that I've finally happened upon something into which I can channel all my jumpy adolescent energy.

It takes me about two weeks to realize that a lot of this music was written quickly, published impulsively. There's a hunger for the new out there, primarily because there isn't much available. Aside from some chants, psalm tones, and a few musty standards, the American

Catholic Church doesn't have an established musical tradition. We need the goods, and the three publishers currently in operation are determined to produce as much as they can until the fad runs its course. There's money to be made, but there's a strange upside to all this capitalism: some of the music is so tepid that I find it oddly encouraging. Listening to one album, I think: Maybe I could do that.

A few weeks after my revelation, I start humming a tune while an old episode of *Bewitched* flickers on the TV. Before Aunt Clara has committed her third and final blunder involving Darren, I've written my own liturgical song. It's in 3/4 time, in the key of C, and though I know it's not very accomplished or original, it gives me a certain physical pleasure. Especially when I transfer it to paper. I love to copy the notes onto the staff. I love to sketch the clefs, even though my eyes hurt from the squinting. Such meticulous precision! I come home from a hard day at school to see the upright with the green-gold antique finish looming in the family room. *Oh, God, do I have to do that now? Can't I have a life like other people?* But I fix myself a glass of chocolate Nestle's Quik, sit, and soon enough my fingers are playing disconnected chords, attempting to find some pattern that's pleasing, while my mother makes chow mien in the kitchen.

After two months have passed, I've filled my spiral music notebook with thirty songs, to the detriment of geometry, in which I have a D average. What is it about proofs and truth tables? My mind refuses to struggle toward finding the inherent patterns there. Is it that I don't believe in a single Truth with a capital T, and I think the whole thing's a sham?

I take the next test insouciantly, without bothering to study.

▲▼

Mrs. Fallon has found out about my songs. Has Kate told her? Most likely, because she's spending as much time with Mrs. Fallon as she's spending with me, and I must be the topic of some of their exchanges. Lately I've been baby-sitting Holly and Sean, and though I don't feel any particular connection to them (they seem bratty, needy, and out of control), I like to stay at Kate's house. Last week, while sitting on the sofa to watch *The Carol Burnett Show,* the eight-year-old Holly pulled off my glasses and ran away with them. Frantic, defenseless, I lurched through the big rooms, bumping into the coffee tables, as Holly giggled behind a living-room chair. "No-neck monster!" I mumbled.

At any rate, the terrors of the job seem oddly worth it. On an upper shelf in the huge master-bedroom closet sits a stack of magazines that includes recent issues of *Playboy, Penthouse,* and *Playgirl.* I don't come upon them through snooping. Kate, in fact, has mentioned casually, in conversation, exactly where they're kept, so I think, of course, she *wants* me to take a look. After Holly and Sean have taken their baths and are soundly asleep, I tiptoe up the stairs and lock the bedroom door. I spot them right away: they're stacked two feet high in a crisp pile atop a silver hatbox. They practically shimmer beneath the glare of the exposed bulb. And just as my hand reaches for the top issue, Holly pounds on the locked door. "I have a tummy ache!" she cries.

"Oh, sit on the toilet!" I answer, making sure the door's still locked.

▲▼

After Mass, after all the people have filed out to the parking lot, I play "My People," my setting of a Good Friday response, for Mrs. Fallon. It's probably my best composition to date. I'm shy and overly self-conscious as I negotiate the odd chord changes of the verses. Why are my fingers so sluggish? They feel as if they're attached to someone else's hands. I make a few mistakes in her presence. Still, my song sounds better than it does within the confines of my parents' family room, and after it's over, I sit there, sweating, swallowing.

A pause from Mrs. Fallon. I expect her to be proud, grateful that she's had some sway over my efforts, but she doesn't say a word. She seems tired, dull-eyed, a little blue. Why did I ever do this? I think. I'm just not good enough.

"We'll use this for Lent," she says finally.

Across the sanctuary the violets of the banners ripen and flourish. And before I've had the chance to process my excitement, she looks at me with a fatal gravity and says, "It's time to introduce you to India Wills."

▲▼

India Wills lives in nearby Cinnaminson Township, in a barnlike house built around a pipe organ. It's a good fifteen miles from Cherry Hill, and as I'm two years shy of seventeen, my mother must drive me to my Tuesday-afternoon lesson during rush hour, a task that must seem like a chore, even though she's quite good-natured about it; she shops for dinner at the Clover around the corner, waits at the curb after ninety minutes have transpired. Like Kate and Mrs. Fallon, my mother, too, must inherently believe in my possibility, though she doesn't tell me about it too frequently, lest I get a swelled head.

Mrs. Wills's house is completely unlike the French Provincials and California Contemporaries of Cherry Hill. The vaulted living room is a veritable temple to the art of music: it's virtually bare but for a harp, a music stand, and the alarming rosewood console, which shines beneath overhead spotlights, its pipes actually built into the walls. And of course, there's the ironing board. It's always left out, something I'm puzzled by, if only because Mr. and Mrs. Wills's khakis are perpetually wrinkled. She's set up a program of study for me that includes the Bach fugues and Hindemith's theory lessons, both of which I undertake with a certain dutiful reluctance. What does this have to do with *my* music? In my naïve yet arrogant, fifteen-year-old way, I could not care less about tradition and the laws of composition. Laws. Who cares about laws? Laws are made to be broken. I want the new, I want to shake things up, and when Mrs. Wills points out and admonishes the parallel fifths and doubled thirds in my theory assignments, I bristle. To Mrs. Wills's mind, the laws of composition are as indelible as the laws of quantum physics, and when I point out a doubled third in a piece by Brahms, she's shocked to near speechlessness (even while I detect some admiration for my obsessive eye).

But I wish I could like Mrs. Wills more. I appreciate her, I guess, but she's an awfully strange duck (even Mrs. Fallon has assented to that), standing beside me with a toasted sandwich and a cup of English Breakfast tea.

And her breath's a little funny, scented with chestnuts and patés and various organ meats, which I try desperately not to notice. In addition, she's more than a little patronizing about the musical tradition I come out of. "You *Romans*," she says, shaking her head, after I finish Lucien Deiss's "Wisdom Has Built Herself a House." She invariably finds unabashed fault with the Catholic liturgical songs I occasionally bring to my lessons and hopes to convince me of their compositional ineptitude. Bah! she says. Amateurs! She, on the other hand, is anything but a Roman. As music director for the First Presbyterian Church of Cinnaminson, she uses the music of Bach and Brahms, along with twentieth-century composers like César Franck, Gabriel Fauré, and Flor Peeters. All of this I find a little stodgy, even though I'm reluctant to admit it to myself. Frankly, I'm grateful to be Catholic. *We* use guitars and electric basses. *We're* smart enough to know that the old forms are falling away.

"How did it go?" my mother says.

"Oh, fine," I say, slumping down in the seat.

She puts the station wagon into gear. "You don't sound too fine."

I look at the dark gray house with its severe barnlike roof. "She's so . . . *Presbyterian*."

One afternoon Kate and I walk through Talk of the Town, a supermarket in our neighborhood. We load up the carrier with fruits and vegetables, preparing for a dinner to which both our families are invited, when, lo and behold, we spot a new magazine rack down the center aisle. The selection is various and thorough. *Paris Vogue* and fancy auction catalogs, publications we've never even seen in a regular supermarket. We pause beside the other browsers. Kate's eyes intensify as she spots something on the lower shelf. "Ooh," she says, leaning over to pick it up.

She flips through the latest issue of *Playgirl.* I try to divert my attention as she pauses at the snapshots of readers' boyfriends. A bead of chilled sweat rolls down my side. I look from the page to the ardor and bemusement in Kate's eyes. She pages forward. She stops at the centerfold, which features a muscular man in a caramel-colored leather vest. He's buck naked in a hayloft with a weed between his teeth. His thick, sizable dick lazes against his furry left thigh as if it's just waiting for someone to wake it up. Above the photograph, a name floats: WOODY PARKER.

I cannot stop shifting my weight from foot to foot. I scratch at my lower back. The Muzak goes sluggish for a long suspension.

"What's the matter?" Kate says.

"Ew," I say.

She looks up at me. "Ew?"

"It's *disgusting,*" I say, without the authority I'd hoped for.

She laughs softly through her nose with affectionate exasperation. "Boys," she says cryptically. She places the magazine back on the rack.

I cannot get the photo out of my head. Nights later I wake, wide-eyed, to see Woody Parker standing at the foot of my Early American twin bed. With a sexy smirk, he whispers gruffly that I'm a good for nothing runt. My pulse rate quickens; he's going to wake up my brothers! And though I squeeze shut my eyes, I cannot fall back asleep.

Later, when I open my eyes again, he's still standing in my room.

I wait a few more days. While my mom fills a bag with bagels, I wander off in the Talk of the Town by myself. I make my way down to the magazine rack, check to see if anyone's looking, then gently pull the centerfold from its staples. I stuff Woody Parker underneath my shirt as the coolish paper singes my hot, hot skin.

I subscribe to a magazine called *Folk Mass Today*. It features articles on the liturgical renewal and cheerful bright drawings in the style of Sister Corita Kent. It's all rather pleasant, but that's not what really interests me. The center section of each issue includes new songs written by the major liturgical composers of the day (Sister Suzanne Toolan, Brother Howard Hughes, and Mike Joncas), and though it's not their best work, I'm intensely, energetically interested in every acclamation and responsorial psalm, and I play their melodies over and over until I know them by heart.

One day I show the issue to Mrs. Fallon after choir practice.

"Why don't you send them your songs?" she says.

Certainly, she can't be serious. Certainly, I am no Sister Suzanne Toolan. I'm both honored and confounded by her suggestion. Still, it only takes me a few days to gather my nerve, and I pick out my five best pieces. My father Xeroxes the pages for me at Semcor, where he's worked since he left RCA a few years ago. I staple the upper-left corners. I lay the beautifully brown envelope in the bed of the mailbox, watch from the front window, and wait for the postman to take note of the brilliant red flag.

I hear nothing for days. The mail is boring: electric bills, oil bills, tax statements, *Newsweek,* the weekly issue of the *Cherry Hill News.* Then weeks go by. I've assumed a funereal air; my schoolwork suffers. Truth tables are a disaster. I shouldn't have done this; whatever possessed me? I'm far too young and inexperienced, far too clumsy. And just when I've given up on my wild, presumptuous, self-defeating dream, I get an envelope from Lawrence Nilsen, the music editor of *Folk Mass Today.* I'm far too agitated to read the whole message in its entirety, but one sentence leaps out from the page: "We'd like to use your song 'Easter Acclamation' for our January issue." After some statements on copyright, this pronouncement: "You're no doubt destined to be one of the major figures in modern liturgical music."

I run through the house, leaping through the rooms like a deer with his feet aflame. I yell for my parents. I yell for my brothers. I kiss our dog, Taffy, the only sentient being in sight, upon her downy white forehead. My life is finally changing. Look at me now. Certainly, I'm well on my way to superstardom.

Our choir is playing the cathedral! It's Holy Thursday, the Chrism Mass, and our choir, as one of the most accomplished in the Diocese, has been asked to participate along with other musical groups from as far away as Cape May. Mrs. Fallon, unfortunately, isn't able to join us, having already committed herself to visiting her daughter, Shawna, in Long Island for the weekend.

Instead, Jim Schaffer presides over the occasion. It's hard not to be overwhelmed by Mr. Schaffer. A former priest and former musical director for the Diocese of Trenton, he combines Mrs. Wills's musicianship with Mrs. Fallon's liturgical know-how. His reputation is impeccable. When I learn that I'm to be the sole accompanist for the occasion, I blanch, though I'm excited and honored to have been asked. There's an emptiness in the pit of my stomach for days. "You'll do just fine," Kate assures me with a touch to my shoulder.

I sit before the behemoth of a pipe organ, which hasn't been maintained in years. Some notes are out of tune; a few keys stay silent when pressed. We're in downtown Camden, after all, one of the roughest small cities in the country (think of Gary or East Saint Louis), and the tiny faithful congregation can't afford such luxuries. So it's all grand, but a little sad. When a grizzled homeless man wanders up into the choir loft just minutes before the church bells ring, the ladies from Cherry Hill are put off by his awful stench. Puzzled, he makes his way back down the steps.

Someone signals from the front. Mr. Schaffer raises his baton, counting four beats. I begin the processional hymn, try to subdue the trembling of my shoulders. The choir sings: *Hail thee Festival Day. Blest day that art hallowed forever.* Through the rearview mirror above the organ, I can see the pink-faced bishop with his miter and fancy red robes advancing up the aisle with his many attendants. I am not going to make a mistake. I must be perfect for Mr. Schaffer. I must be perfect for the Bishop. Our choir's reputation is at stake. When I make it through the hymn without so much as a missed note, I look over at Mr. Schaffer and see that he is just as relieved as I am. We're going to be okay. He looks back at me with a formal but consoling smile.

I play through the Responsorial Psalm, the Preparation of the Gifts, the acclamations of the Eucharistic Prayer, and the Communion hymn. The choir has never sounded better; they perform with a bracing grace and precision that takes us all aback. We have become something else, something elevated and other, transcending our limitations. We're celebrating all that's good and right about the world, all that's possible. The stakes get even higher with each new piece. And the assembly joins us with a full-blooded vitality that would win even Mrs. Wills's respect. When the Bishop—aloof and curmudgeonly, not especially known for his personal warmth—gazes up at us as he processes out of the candlelit cathedral, we know that, together, we have made a beautiful thing.

Already it's gone from us, our well-wrought notes drifting off into the ether.

"Thank you very much," says Mr. Schaffer to me as he packs up his octavos. And I am too humbled and shy to say anything back to him. I nod, just once. Then he makes his way down the steep, dangerous steps.

Two days later Mrs. Fallon, Kate, and I meet at the Country Club Diner over bagels and quiche to discuss how it all went. Mrs. Fallon says she's heard nothing but wonderful things from her priest friends; she's disappointed to have missed it. And more than a little jealous. She discusses Mr. Schaffer, how he can't find a decent church job in order to support himself, how he's thinking of leaving the music ministry altogether. "I don't understand why he's moving in with that *guy*," says Kate about the gentle black fellow who sat in the corner of the loft, who looked up at Mr. Schaffer with something like awe. Kate and Mrs. Fallon trade knowing glances. Mrs. Fallon says, "It's time he settled down."

I knock into my coffee cup. The thin blond liquid washes over the lip and pools inside the saucer.

On an unseasonably cold April afternoon, with periods of sleet and driving rain, an envelope with a Santa Clara, California, return address arrives. I shiver beside the huge black mailbox. I stick the envelope inside my coat, protecting it from the elements, and sprint down the narrow black driveway. Inside I sit at the kitchen table while my mother, father, and brothers hover at my back. Even Taffy gets into the spirit of things. She lies beside the sink on her small braided rug, which she thumps with her big plume of a tail.

The issue is beautiful. I pause briefly at the cover, a sketch of an angel over brilliant blue splashes, then page forward to my "Easter Acclamation." It's on page 47, alongside a piece by Sister Maria of the Cross. I'm still excited, though I can feel my intense connection to it already diminishing, if only slightly. It's already itself in the world, a child I've sent off toward kindergarten on its thin, hobbling legs.

My eyes graze over the notes of the third measure. "Oh, no."

"What's the matter?" says my mother.

"There's a mistake." I tug on my finger. "There's a mistake in measure 3."

My whole family looks nervous. They don't know what I'm going to do. I leap up from the table, then page through my music notebook on the piano. To my shock, there's an error on my own staff paper: How could I have missed this for so long? An A natural instead of a G sharp! To make matters worse, the editor has changed the chord symbol above the melody to jibe with this unlikely cadence, to make it look like the whole thing was *my* idea.

They have bought and published my song with a mistake in it!

"You stupid," I say, wagging my fist at the overhead light fixture. "You stupid, stupid, stupid."

"Play the mistake," demands my father.

"No!"

"Play it, dear," says my mother with a softer voice.

I play the refrain once through, then play it again. They all look edgy. I wait for somebody to say something. "*Say* something."

"Now play it the right way," says my father, with a solemn nod.

I do as I'm told. As I finish, my father says, "I like it the wrong way." Although he doesn't sound entirely convinced.

"It's not so terrible," my mom assures.

When I bring it to choir practice, I've all but forgotten the high drama of the afternoon. By this time I've played the printed version over and over so many times that I've gotten quite used to it; I've convinced myself I even like it that way. The choir members are as excited as I am. "Let's do it next Sunday," cries Mrs. Kapischke. And as the whole choir concurs, Mrs. Fallon falls silent, blinking behind heavy black glasses. She clenches her forehead. She tries to smile through her tension, but she fails to conceal her true feelings. She's never seemed more false or less assured. "Okay," she says, tapping the top of the piano. "We have a lot to do. Page 23, 'Where Charity and Love Prevail.'"

Rehearsal wraps up. Kate strolls across the church classroom and takes the magazine from my hand. Mrs. Fallon laughs finally, immersed in a conversation with Mrs. Martone, whom she privately can't stand. Is she trying to avoid me?

"What did I do?" I whisper to Kate.

My mother joins us. "I don't like what just happened tonight."

"Oh, don't take it so seriously," says Kate. "She had an argument with Shawna." She stops paging. "Oh, God, isn't this *rich?*" She almost hoots, pointing to an ad for a new music collection. *Announcing Antoinette Napolitano: The Bright Gleam of a New Star.*

Antoinette Napolitano lives in a rural town outside Cincinnati that I imagine to be dominated by the cooling towers of a nuclear power plant. She plays a Gibson 12-string guitar and directs an inner-city folk choir comprised of about fifty teenagers. According to the ad she has extensive performing experience, having played for "church, concert hall, and cabaret," in countries as distant as the Netherlands and Brazil. But that's not quite what compels me about her. I'm especially attracted to the brochure of her collection, which arrives in the mail two days later. It's a curiously clumsy affair printed on dark orange paper, featuring all sorts of inept pictures of Antoinette. There she is, standing before the dismal stone front of the Saint Thomas à Becket Church, with glasses, stringy, unconditioned hair, and a horsey overbite. There she is, all four foot ten of her, hunched over her huge guitar, dwarfed by the gargantuan folk choir behind her. She looks like a female version of me, actually, albeit shorter, and when my dad laughingly points this out a few weeks later, I'm outwardly insulted, but silently grateful. Kate and I make raucous fun of Antoinette, analyzing her awful taste in clothing (those checked leisure suits, those slacks), though I'm reluctant to tell Kate I'm looking forward to hearing Antoinette's work. It's the first album from UIA in almost five years— they've recently been rescued from bankruptcy by a missalette company—so it must be something extraordinary.

One night I show up at Kate's house for another baby-sitting assignment. It's not so rough anymore. Holly and Sean have settled down a bit, and they're far less likely to steal my glasses or to bang on the locked door. Just as Kate and John are ready to head out to the garage, she hands me a flat package wrapped in silver paper with a gray-green bow.

"For you," she says, watching what must be the puzzlement on my face.

Tearing off the paper, I see the now-familiar cover of Antoinette Napolitano's album. Kate laughs with a naughty glee as I turn it over to scan the liner notes. My palms moisten. She has no idea how genuinely happy I am. She kisses me lightly on the lips, winks, and glides on her black pumps out the door.

With an immeasurable care, I bring *Together We Sing* to the turntable and sit before the speakers. Antoinette's voice is surprisingly good, a rich, controlled contralto, that makes up for the silly songwriting. (What a gap between the performance and what's performed!) The lyrics are especially clumsy and unsophisticated, even cornball at times. "Watch for those who share. Who care . . . for the lowly ones." Or something like that. Still, there's something appealingly eccentric about its particular fusion of liturgical folk music and slick Nashville pop, and though I know I should have better taste, I'm swept away by Antoinette's undeniable individualism.

In only three weeks the grooves of the record will be so worn out that I'll have to send away for another copy.

I walk up the stairs. Holly and Sean have taken to their respective beds, and they're both fully dressed on top of their covers, fast asleep, mouths parted. I head back for the stairs, hoping to catch the opening of *Saturday Night Live,* my favorite new show (how I love that Laraine Newman: another skinny person, just like me), when I stop at the master bedroom. The closet door's ajar. I shut my eyes. I shouldn't do it, I *know* I shouldn't do it, I am a runt, I am a dirty good-for-nothing boy, but before I can harness my surging faculties, I lock the door. I stumble toward the closet, reach for a *Playgirl.*

I lie on Kate and John's king-size bed. Trembling, I open the magazine, stop at the page featuring the readers' boyfriends, and indulge in a little self-gratification. It takes all of ninety seconds. When I'm finished, I'm hot and chilly at once. My breaths stick like a crust of bread in my throat. Is that knocking? *Holly?* Oh, God. *Please don't tell on me, Holly. Please.* I wipe off my stomach with a Kleenex. I put the magazine back exactly where I found it, then, to my relief, find her snoring softly on her Marimekko bedspread.

After church the next day, Kate seems cheerier than ever. She and John have had a lovely dinner in Center City with John's new boss, Tom Pacquin, who has huge plans for the firm. There's even talk of a new office outside Princeton, though that's a couple of years in the future. Kate gazes at me for an exceptionally long time. There's a peculiar sheen in her eye. I look away. *"What?"*

"So how was Antoinette?"

"Good," I say. "It's kind of awful, but the production's good, very good."

More silence. A few feet away my mother is chatting with Mrs. Fallon. Although Mom's decided that she doesn't trust her anymore, she's outwardly polite and jovial. Kate takes a step closer to me. She smiles. Her eyes narrow slightly. "I know what you did," she whispers.

My forehead tingles and numbs. I smell her perfume.

"You looked at the magazines. You looked at the dirtiest one and left it out on the bed."

Instantly I blush from the tips of my toes all the way up to the roots of my hair. Do tears spring to my eyes? Why don't I have the wits about me to deny it?

She smiles now, warmly, genuinely, reaching out to touch my face as if she's sorry she's embarrassed me. She's sorry. Over and over she tells me that she's sorry. When I find out later that day that this was all a prank, I can't help but wonder whether I did indeed leave the magazine out. Did I want to be caught? Did I just *imagine* putting the magazine back? I thought I'd placed it four issues from the bottom, but who knows?

(Years later, what I want to know is this: Was I more distraught than I knew? There was the day, of course, when after fantasizing about my next-door neighbor, Mr. Aslanian, a short hairy bull of a man old enough to be my father, that I stated to myself, quite directly: "Your desires are homosexual." I sat still for a second and pondered its implications. I could live with that. Then I strolled out into the kitchen and made myself a peanut butter and jelly sandwich.

It would take me almost two decades to make sense of that self-definition. But how could I fault my younger self for my initial, glib embrace? I was Catholic, after all. The church was changing; the world was changing. If priests someday could marry, if, in fact, women could someday be priests, then couldn't I be understood and loved by the world around me?)

I write weekly to Antoinette Napolitano. I send long handwritten letters to her office at the Diocese of Cincinnati, where she manages an office called Folk Liturgies Express. These messages are full of gushing admiration for her work and for her willingness to expand the form. I have convinced myself she is to be the next Ray Repp, and I bring her name up incessantly to Mrs. Fallon, who's clearly not so impressed. No one has yet thought to hybridize the forms, to create something both contemporary and classical, high and low, at once; at this particular moment, there's a vast schism between traditional church music (organ) and folk music (guitar). In spite of her friendships with Joe Wise and Lucien Deiss, Mrs. Fallon clearly posits herself in the former camp, and though I appreciate the complicated harmonic structures of the organ-based music, I've decided that organists and traditional choir directors are stuffy, conservative, and just plain old. All the forward-thinking types play guitars, and here I am stuck behind this blowsy old organ like a middle-aged matron who's broad through the beam.

To my surprise, Antoinette sends me long letters in which she talks about her folk choir and an upcoming engagement at a downtown nightclub. In only a few short weeks she's traveling to Nashville to record a demo tape of what she calls her "secular" music. She wants to break into the country field, or "hip country," as she calls it. She's just joined ASCAP. She's started a publishing company and has begun work on her own four-track recording studio in her elderly parents' basement. I love the idea of attracting a larger audience for my music— maybe "church" just isn't enough anymore. Clearly, Antoinette Napolitano is determined to broaden her world.

When she tells me she's using one of my songs for an upcoming Lenten Mass, I'm more than a little moved. I tack up her letter above my desk and stare at it at least twenty-seven times a day.

I wish Mrs. Fallon would be as appreciative of me. She seems to have deliberately stopped using my music, though we've never spoken directly about her decision. My feelings are hurt, and I'm tense and uneasy in her presence, perpetually making statements that she takes the wrong way. What is her problem? Why can't she be like Mrs. Wills? Thrilled by the spate of my recent publications, she's taken up the folk guitar, of all things, and has scheduled my song "Let All the Earth Cry Out with Gladness" for the service this coming weekend at the once-stodgy First Presbyterian Church of Cinnaminson. Parallel fifths? Doubled thirds? Bah!

Choir is on hiatus from June through August, and our family is at our summerhouse. The days are long, unhurried, and relaxed, and in between going to the beach or taking the boat up through the Great Egg Harbor River, I fill pages and pages of music notebooks. It's not immediately apparent to me that I've left behind the intricate movements and structures of my earlier songs in favor of the basic, the broad, and the direct, but I tell myself it's good to try something different, to search for the one right chord that lifts the whole sequence above the quotidian. When we attend Mass at the local church, I'm stupefied by the flat-footedness of the ritual. Ancient pole fans oscillate throughout the sanctuary, working to cool us with their feeble whir. The grim monsignor trudges through the Mass. We're all thinking about the beach, hating our sweat-drenched clothes, dreaming of a chilly wave breaking against our chests. I stare up at the unlit chandeliers. It seems to me that the vernacular liturgy is fairly dull without music, that the *other* can only be embodied through the agency of art, and when several young women faint, one after the next, in the back of the church, I know it's not from dizziness or dehydration. They're simply in dire need of some music.

Kate drives down for a visit. She wants to see me off before my trip to Wisconsin, which is six days away. I'm off to participate in a one-week music workshop sponsored by UIA Library, Antoinette's publisher, and while I'm excited about getting to meet her, I'm considerably nervous. I find it harder and harder to finish all my meals. Still, Kate's presence helps to placate my troubles, and we spend the days waterskiing or talking on board our docked boat, where we clutch beaded glasses of sun tea.

That night Kate drives the five of us to Atlantic City to give my mother a rest. I'm not sure why we're not going to the more benign Ocean City, which is five minutes across the Bay, but we must be tired of its overly polite family atmosphere, its restrained rides. We crave the exotic, the wild, the new. Although casino gambling is already in the works, the place has never been in sorrier shape. Big brick hotels—the Traymore, the Claridge, the Marlborough-Blenheim—slump beside the boardwalk. Little blue jitneys sputter and fill the streets with exhaust.

We find the city parking garage on New York Avenue and begin our walk toward the ocean. Pink and blue lights pulse and twinkle. Ahead there's a crowd and we're not sure what to make of all these people standing amid the ruin. Their voices are hushed, furtive. A man in a leather vest walks by. And then another in a black Harley-Davidson cap. This one smirks, then slinks down an alley toward a basement door: CLUB BATHS.

We're walking through what must be the gay neighborhood.

I steel my arms, face, and feet. I step harder, more solidly inside my shoes. We pass a bar called the Lark, outside of which dozens of men pose in their chaps and their harnesses, all menacing, arrogant, consumed by their lust. Don't they have other lives? I'm far too young to understand that this is all play, that these men are most likely salesmen or accountants by day, that they're all enacting whom they'd want to attract. But now it just seems ghastly; I want no part of it and try ferociously to look away, annoyed by the fact that they all seem to want me.

(None of us know that a goodly percentage of these men will begin dying, one after the next, in less than five years' time.)

"Hold my hand," I say, anxiously, reaching out for Kate's wrist.

"What?" she says.

"Hold my hand. *Please.*"

She doesn't comply. I'm not even sure what I'm asking of her. Am I so pulled by what I really want that I need to be tethered to something? Or is that I'm trying to demonstrate that I'm purely off limits, a straight boy who's with his girlfriend or sister? I don't want them to read me, that much is certain. Kate shakes her head, then screws up her face. Unlike me, she's largely bemused by the display of all that fragrant male flesh, and soon she passes me up the ramp to the boardwalk, where she stops to tie Sean's sneaker.

The incident is forgotten. We do what visitors do. We ride the rides, we stroll the aquarium, we buy the popcorn and toss burnt kernels to the plump, shiny pigeons.

We sit on the benches of a pavilion. Holly and Sean are sagging; my brothers are off to Fralinger's, where they buy a box of salt water taffy for our mother. The ocean murmurs at our backs. Distant screams from the roller coaster. I think about persuading Kate to take a different route back to the car when a toothless man appears before us in a pair of soiled white jockey shorts. He cups his hands, pleading for us to give him some money, a hamburger, but we look away, shaking our heads. We're alarmed; we're frightened by his smell. He isn't the only profoundly desperate person we've encountered during our stay. The whole place seems to be a magnet for the nameless, the defeated, and we feel distinctly out of place (and more than a little guilty) in our scrubbed, suburban attire.

We watch him cup his hands before somebody else.

"If you ever tell me you're homosexual—" says Kate.

I just look at her. For some odd reason, there's a hint of a smile on her face.

"I mean I don't know how I'd talk to you anymore."

A nerve makes my eyelid jump. Does she know something?

"Think about what they do. I mean, I just can't begin to think about what they do in bed."

"Don't worry," I say at once, patting her on the knee. I stretch, pretending with all my might to be casual. We stand. I don't belong here—not with the homeless. Not with the lusting, the hopeless, the crushed.

And this time I walk back down New York Avenue past the bars and dark alleys with my straight-ahead gaze.

▲▼

I'm on the plane to Wisconsin. It's the first time I've ever flown anywhere by myself, and I can't even eat the beef tips dinner the flight attendant places before me. Suddenly, a dip and a shimmy, and in unison, all the passengers scream. We're flying through violent thunderstorms, tornadoes, says the pilot, and we need to reroute over Omaha. Consequently, I miss both my connections, and I arrive in the sleepy hail-ravaged burg of La Crosse at 4:00 A.M.

Although I'm supposed to stay in the men's dorm of the small Catholic college, I can't find anyone to help me. Inside, the halls have that sacred, parochial-school scent: candle wax, chrism, Palm Sunday leaves. Everyone's been asleep for hours. There's a letter on a table inside that directs me to my room, but I must first pass through an outer door. I jiggle the knob. Locked. I knock and I knock; I hope someone will answer, but no such luck. I press my forehead into the smooth blond wood. I consider butting it down with my head, but I'm too afraid to break something. Lightning flashes out a tall thin window. I pull out a T-shirt from my suitcase, ball it up into a makeshift pillow, and lie down on the carpet.

I stare down the darkness toward the exit sign, basking in its soothing red glow. My heart's sluggish, warm inside my chest. Rain on the roof. *It's okay. Everything's going to be just fine.*

I wake to find a young man with long hair and a downy moustache standing over me. "Hi," he says.

"Hi," I say. I shove myself up with my elbows. Could it already be morning? My mouth is stale; my forehead tightens above the bridge of my nose. "I'm locked out."

His entire demeanor is a figurative demonstration of the expression *duh*.

"Sorry, man." His gaze empties. Then all at once he proffers a dazzling, thousand-watt smile. "I'm a heavy sleeper. Sorry you had to spend the night on the floor. "

I nod shyly. Somehow his stupidity doesn't seem to matter so much anymore.

Wisconsin is green, like no green I've ever seen. Ocher bluffs mellow and glow in the late afternoon sun. The Midwestern-ness of it all is a little overwhelming. Such blondness! Is there a toxic dump nearby? How far to the nearest refinery? In addition, the participants at the conference seem oddly regional, friendlier than I'm used to, and with the exception of the troop from Bowling Green, Ohio (many of whom include nuns with habits), they all talk in flat, wide-voweled accents that mimic the openness of the surrounding prairie. Oddly enough, they all think *I* have the accent, and they look at me as if they can't stop asking themselves: What the *hell* is this fifteen-year-old doing at a conference full of nuns? I'm continually treated to horror stories of nasty people back East while I attempt to cut my cube steak in the cafeteria.

I'm in the college chapel on the second afternoon of the conference when I first see Antoinette with her huge 12-string guitar behind the podium. It's hard not to feel disconcerted. She's much more attractive in person than I'd imagined, her hair cut in a stylish wedge à la Dorothy Hamill, though she's *tiny,* an overgrown tot, a grown woman trapped in a Lilliputian's body. How skinny her arms! The guitar is as big as she is! But I get past my bewilderment soon enough. Before Mass, she leads us through the antiphon of her newest song, and it's fresh and quirky, her alto soaring through the rafters. She joins Neil Witt, another liturgical folk composer, and they're a great team. They trade off guitar riffs, sing reedy, gender-bending harmonies in which Neil's voice is actually a third above Antoinette's. Light cascades through the stained-glass windows of the saints, pooling blue, red, and yellow on the floor. I hold up the portable microphone of my tape recorder until my hand aches. My face burns. I'm on fire. Without a doubt, it's the most engaging, innovative Mass I've ever been to in my life.

After Mass, I step forward to the altar, where Antoinette eases her huge 12-string in its case. She chats with Neil Witt. I stand paralyzed for a moment and take in a deep breath. "Hello, Antoinette. I'm Paul," I say in a quick and jerky tumble.

She cocks her head and gives me the most direct, genuine smile. "Hi, Paul," she says, extending her hand to me. "It's so good to finally meet you. Do you know Neil?"

I shake my head. Do I know Neil? Do I know the *Pope?* "I'm Paul Lisicky," I say.

"Hello, Paul," says Neil.

"He's very, very good," Antoinette says to Neil. She looks at me and grins. "Listen, I want to spend some time alone with you. I want to hear what you're working on. Are you free any time this week?"

"Oh, sure." I nod avidly. Why is my throat so dry?

"Well, we'll play it by ear." She turns to Neil. "*We're* off to dinner. See you, Paul. I'm so happy that you've come to the conference."

I walk back to my dorm, strolling beneath the limbs of the Wisconsin pines, as alarmed and gratified as I've ever been in my life. I'm so excited that I forgo dinner to sit alone on my narrow dorm bed, where I stare at the aqua cinder blocks with my fond and pleasant thoughts.

Which is what I do for the remainder of the week. Oh, I go to several scheduled events for sure, but it's all too much for me. I attend a couple of seminars in which Antoinette introduces new songs from her forthcoming collection (how much her work has grown!), and I hold up my microphone, already looking forward to playing the cassettes when I have my wits about me. Antoinette and I exchange simple greetings as we pass each other on the grassy quadrangle, and her warm and direct "hi's" are all I seem to need.

On the last night of the conference, I run into Antoinette in the dorm lobby. "Hey," she says, "what are you doing tonight?"

My face must be pink. I look down at the floor. "Nothing."

"Why don't you meet down here at eight? Me and some others are going to share some new songs." Share. I just adore the way she uses the word "share."

"Okay." I run back upstairs and pretend that I've forgotten something.

And in two hours I'm on the lounge's blue tiled floor as Antoinette introduces another new number, this one a children's song: "The Lord Is on His Way.'" It's in a call and response format, and the group echoes Antoinette in robust fashion. My fingers tingle. My foot is prickly with sleep. After what seems like hours, Antoinette asks me to sing something of my own. What should I do? I'm not much of a solo singer, and I'd don't play the guitar, at least not well enough for a performance. Disappointment flickers in Antoinette's eye, but she's not going to push me to do something I'm uncomfortable with. I'm ashamed of myself. This might have been my big moment. One of the nuns from Bowling Green (thank God, she's taken off that habit) looks at her watch and announces it's time for bed. But before she leaves, Antoinette says to the assembled, "You guys should check out Paul's music. It's really, really good."

"Oh, thanks," I mumble, abashed.

"Take a look at his 'Easter Acclamation.' But tell me, Paul," she says, looking down at me, "is that a mistake in the third measure? I've played it over and over, and I just can't get it to *sound*."

"Yes!" I cry. "Yes!" How brilliant and sensitive! Of course Antoinette would be perceptive enough to recognize my intentions.

"I thought so!" she says exultantly. And then we both laugh longer than necessary.

I take myself to bed. The week has been wonderful, more than I ever could have hoped for. And I'm so looking forward to seeing everyone again. I'm not even scared to fly through bad weather tomorrow. Even if the plane gets spun up inside a tornado, it'll be okay: I'll have died a happy boy.

I'm still awake two hours later. From the next room, the rustling of the blond guy, who must be packing for his trip back to Bloomington. After a half hour, he's still closing drawers. I pull up the covers to my neck and squeeze shut my eyes. First, it's Woody Parker who's standing at the foot of my bed, and then it's Mr. Bloomington. Although Mr. Bloomington is not making fun of me or calling me dirty names. He moves to the bed, straddles me, then pins my wrists above my head. His tongue moves deeply, achingly in my mouth. It tastes of smoke, death. We smear and nip and push against each other, our hearts burning in the fires of our mutual love for Antoinette Napolitano.

▲▼

"You're so skinny!" cries Kate as she meets me at the airport. My parents, attending one of my cousin's weddings in Allentown, won't be home till tomorrow night, so Kate's agreed to let me stay at her house. I hug her hard, so hard that it seems to take her aback. But she's thrilled to see me. I talk her ear off as the station wagon races through the swamps, refineries, and junkyards of southwest Philadelphia's Penrose Avenue. The air is muggy, hot, wafting with chemicals. The pine-scented forests of Wisconsin couldn't be farther away.

Three hours later, at eleven o'clock, I'm still talking.

I've eaten not two, but three servings of her eggplant lasagna. Calmer now, I'm clearly making up for my involuntary starvation of the week before. I tell her all about Antoinette, about the radical growth of her music, her public endorsement of my work, and her deft recognition of the mistake. Kate looks and listens with the keenest expression, though I can't help but notice the furrow above her speckled brown eyes. Am I talking too much? Am I simply too excited? Am I making her feel bad in some way? Enumerating Antoinette's many virtues, I get the strangest feeling—both thrilling and awful—that I'm moving away from Kate, though I have no idea what that might mean. *I am here,* I tell myself. *I am sitting on Kate Papagallo's sofa on August 1, 1976, and I am alive in the world.*

After eleven o'clock, we walk into the living room, where we sip tea from fancy Italian mugs. I am totally exhausted and dehydrated from spending so much time in the air. My excitement is finally catching up with me, and every so often, when Kate's not looking, I close my eyes. I drift off. My head falls forward like a puppet's. Is that my chin pressing against my collarbone?

I'm not even sure how we've gotten where we are, but she says something like: "I just think she's jealous of you."

"Who? *What?*"

She grimaces and smiles all at once. "Nancy," she says. "Mrs. Fallon. *You* brought her up, Paul."

"Oh."

"Anyway, she wouldn't be talking behind your back if she didn't feel so threatened."

My eyes spring open. "She's been talking behind my back?"

Kate nods, her eyes filling up with concern. Among other things, she tells me that Mrs. Fallon doesn't want to use my music anymore, that she never really liked it, that I'm simply getting a little too big for my britches.

My forehead's hot now. Of course, I've sensed all these things for months, but it's something else to hear them confirmed. "I'll show her," I say in a gruff whisper.

"She's lonely, disappointed. She hasn't gotten what she wanted in life."

I roll my eyes.

"Paul—"

"I'll show her," I say in the calmest voice I can muster. "I'm going to go to music school just like Mr. Schaffer, and she's going to be sorry she ever said anything bad about me."

She laughs. "Mr. Schaffer?"

"Mr. Schaffer." I redden. What I really want to say is that I want to be like Antoinette, playing in church *and* playing for a larger audience, but that sounds too immodest.

"Mr. Schaffer's a nobody," she says. "He makes $12,000 a year, and he can't even afford the rent on his apartment. What kind of life is that? You're better than that."

I'm mute. All along I thought that Kate had fully supported my musical aspirations. She knew I was going to music school. What does she think I've been doing with my life—playing?

"So what do you expect me to do, be a CPA like John?"

Kate gets up from the sofa. She walks into the kitchen, where she runs the sink and latches the dishwasher. The water jets and churns, the motor loud as a tractor. I look about the living room with its antique grandfather's clock, its bright Venetian glassware. I think, Is she really so happy here?

When she comes back, her face is softer and kinder, closer to the Kate I've always loved. She sits down beside me on the sofa and hands me a foil-wrapped chocolate shaped like a fish. "I've been meaning to tell you—" she says.

"What?"

"We're moving to Princeton. John's been promoted."

My throat tightens. "No way."

"We've already picked out the house. We're leaving in a few months."

On September 15th, the choir is back in full swing. We sing "Wisdom Has Built Herself a House" for Communion, but there's a chilly vigor to our performance that makes me long for the days when we were a little less polished, when a shaky alto part transmitted a certain humanness. Maybe it's just that our heads and hearts are still somewhere back on Long Beach Island and we're not ready for the enormous commitment that weekly choir demands. Has something changed? It feels as if we're collectively afraid of something, and though we're still honoring the purpose of our group, our protective distance is keeps our harmonies from actually *gelling*.

My mother makes no secret about how she feels about Kate. She tells me Kate had no right to dampen my enthusiasm after my return from Wisconsin, that I didn't need to be told of Mrs. Fallon's cruelty. My mother finds Kate's behavior appalling, and she wonders where her loyalties really lie. I'm a bit baffled by the depths of my mother's pain. I know that she doesn't want to see me hurt, but her reaction seems to be about . . . is there something I don't know? When I try to defend Kate, when I say, "She only tried to help me," she shakes her head; she doesn't want to hear it. Has she been a little jealous of her old friend's sway over me? Their mutual tension quavers across the aisle. They stand on either end of the row of six sopranos, too full of feeling to speak to each other.

After Mass, on Kate's last day, she hands back her choir book to Mrs. Fallon with a tentative embrace. Mrs. Fallon pushes a piece of Kate's blond hair behind her ear and they laugh with downcast eyes, promise to stay in touch. Princeton is only an hour away, and they declare that they'll be seeing a lot of each other, even though Kate will be singing in a brand-new choir, this one directed by—who would have guessed it?—Mr. Schaffer.

Kate turns to me. I walk her to her car, where Holly and Sean punch each other on the backseat. We don't have much to say, and there's still more than a little uncertainty between us. Something ineffable has happened; how are we to behave toward each other? When she reaches out to hug me, I break down, to my shock. I bury my face in Kate's hair and can't stop the sobs from coming up my throat. "Oh, *God,*" I say. Some people have stopped to look, and I hug her, hug her harder than I thought possible, and she hugs me back, says, "Oh, honey, I'm sorry, I'm sorry." I don't even know what has happened between us, and it all seems too complicated for me to untangle. She holds me for the duration of my sobs, stroking the back of my head, and she doesn't let go until I'm quiet, until I'm almost breathing normally again and my cheek is resting against her hot wet collar.

She backs out of her parking space. We wave to each other. I swipe my nose with my forefinger and laugh. I am laughing through my tears. Is it only that I already know that she'll be the last woman I'll ever fall in love with, and I don't want to be homeless, and it scares me that I don't know where I'm going next?

On a raw overcast morning, in late 1997, the infamous Reverend Fred Phelps, of "Godhatesfags.com" fame, marches with his "family" outside the town hall of Provincetown, Massachusetts, my off-and-on home for the last seven years. We've been buzzing for weeks; their expected demonstration is anticipated with as much horror and dread as the KKK's arrival in Skokie over ten years ago. It goes without saying that Provincetown has enormous symbolic value to many as a zone of safety and refuge. Hundreds of men and women have spent their final years here, and in spite of its reputation as a gay amusement park, it's a kind of Benares to some. How many have strewn the grit of their lost loves in the marshes outside of town? Sometimes when I'm alone, when I'm out on the fire road with our two retrievers, I imagine all those souls watching me from the other world with their calm and curious eyes.

I arrive at the designated time on my bicycle to see the family Phelps sing their hymns on the green in front of the Bas Relief. As much as I think I've prepared myself for the demonstration, nothing quite readies me for the sight of all those ghastly slogans. There's something psychologically toxic about the Day-Glo colors of their placards. This isn't any accident; they know exactly what they're doing. Some of my friends, too cynical and weary to get worked up about the whole affair, will find the sheer exaggeration of the signs (AIDS=GOD'S GIFT TO FAGS, complete with two male stick figures entangled in a sex act) flat-out comic, unwilling to admit that the world outside Provincetown, South Beach, West Hollywood, and Chelsea might be darker than we're willing to admit. But as I look around at the collective grief written on the faces of the townspeople who've gathered here (straight and gay, drag queen and fisherman), I feel only the deepest rage.

I pick out one of the demonstrators and shoot him the finger.

Then I cringe. I'm doing exactly what he wants me to do.

The guy focuses on me, mumbling his stream of hate as if he's speaking in tongues.

He thinks I'm the rabble-rouser. He thinks I'm going to be the one to get things going. *Sorry, pal. It's not going to be me. But, Lord, how I wish someone would fling a rock at your head.*

I'm exhausted, bludgeoned. It drizzles; my melancholy deepens when a young man, face ravaged by illness, approaches with his dog tucked underneath his arm, looking toward the demonstrators with an emptied incredulousness. He shouldn't have to see this. When Mark, my partner, pedals up to me on his bicycle, eyes glistening with amazement, I'm seized with an irrational need to protect him, though I stop; he can certainly take care of himself. He shouldn't have to see this either. We put our arms around each other, calmer and probably more shaken than we're willing to admit, before he pedals off to buy some bread at the Cheese Market.

Just as I've decided I've had my fill, a therapist in town, an older woman in a long gauzy dress, who's lost dozens of her dearest clients to AIDS, wanders up from Ryder Street. She approaches me with waving hands. "What are we doing here? What on earth are we all doing here?" Someone with a yellow armband tries to subdue her (after all, we're not supposed to get too stirred up), but it's not much use. She doesn't want to admit that there isn't a simple answer to this question, and when I attempt to think aloud about it, explaining that it's probably some combination of things—voyeurism and duty, witness and activism—my language crumbles. She won't have it. Perhaps it's just too slippery to talk about. Then, out of nowhere, she says: "How do you know they're not using your songs?"

I just look at her. I'm about to say "too musically complicated, too theologically uncertain," but that sounds too self-serving. I shuffle my feet, angry with myself for keeping silent.

"How would you stop them from using your music?"

Well, I couldn't, could I?

She walks away. Our gestures mean nothing. Although Phelps leaves town to the jeers and gibes of the townspeople, it's hard not to feel a sense of deepest defeat.

▲▼

Is it only because I've always imagined such judgment about my work that I've redirected my artistic lens toward other creative tasks?

The music I wrote in my teens and early twenties still

appears in hymnals and songbooks all across the country, and more than once, wandering into church while
visiting my parents, I've heard a choir struggling through
one of my responsorial psalms. It's like a visit from a lost
side of myself. I've kept this aspect of my personality
hidden from my friends, some of my very closest friends,
for reasons that are not quite clear to me. Is it only that
I've wanted to present a coherent version of myself, and
that facet of my personality is in contradiction to everything else that they know about me? It's probably more
complicated than that. After all, it's over thirty years
after that brief, fleeting period in which there was so
much hope and possibility about the church, before
the institution settled back into its fearful, conservative
ways. Lately I've been thinking about working on some
new music, but how can one not feel a huge ambiva-
lence about Christianity in this day and age? How can
one ignore charges about colluding with the enemy? Organized religion has never seemed darker or more de-
structive. And while it would be simplistic to implicate
all Christian denominations by pointing to Fred Phelps,
I sometimes think his tawdry protests merely distill and
intensify an all-too-pervasive point of view.

But I can't help but think that I've all but killed a certain aspect of my creative life, that my decision to turn
away from music has come at a cost. Today I tell myself
this, How compelling to celebrate all that's potentially
wondrous about the world: hope, mercy, justice, good-
ness, light. How compelling to name what we'd *want*
God to be, even if He or She remains elusive and intractable, resisting our definitions. I'm told that Bach
and Brahms were ambivalent about writing for the
church, that many of the most accomplished liturgical

composers were gay men. Not that I'm placing myself in the camp of Britten and Poulenc, but I'm grateful that they kept on working. You'd have to be foolish to think otherwise.

I haven't talked to Kate in ten years. She began a long series of moves that took her to Bryn Mawr, then back to Princeton, then on to Greenwich, Connecticut. She and John are likely very rich now. I suppose she still sings in a choir, but she probably performs Handel now rather than the Dameans. Nor have I kept in touch with Mrs. Fallon or Mrs. Wills, though I assume they continue to meet their respective ensembles every Tuesday night. Antoinette Napolitano lives in Nashville, where she writes and publishes country music; I've seen her name on the liner notes of various CDs. And Mr. Schaffer? Mr. Schaffer was one of the first people I knew to die of AIDS, all the way back in 1981.

Sometimes I imagine Kate standing in the sanctuary of her stylish, mossy brick church in Greenwich. Does she ever think of me? If, coming upon one of my responsorial psalms in her parish hymnal, would she still pore over that fusion of melody, harmony, and text? Would she try to sing it to herself? What if she knew the truth about me: that I'm happy, that I've spent years living with a man whom I'm just crazy about? Would she return the book to its rack? I can't ever know the answer to that, but I'd like to think that she'd surprise me, linking us across space and time, through all those lives.

Renovation

The Anchorage Point house smells weirdly lemony inside as if a can of latex paint had been left open and allowed to sit for weeks. The electric baseboards tick; kerosene fumes permeate the atmosphere. Although it's bone-chilling damp, Bobby and I sweat through the layers of our shirts, working harder to keep ourselves warm. Outside, the lagoon is already turning to ice. The phragmites on the opposite bank have browned, the marsh grass in the distance flattened like a tatami mat. The sky above the bay looks swollen, as if it's actually inhaling all that freezing salt water, but somehow we wouldn't want to be anywhere else. So what if the heat doesn't quite work, that our father drained the pipes for the winter months ago.

I walk inside the laundry room to pee inside an emptied coffee can. When I come back to the living room, Bobby's already at it, slamming the plasterboard with a crowbar. Powder settles on our lips and lashes. Powder settles on the gray-beige carpet, the sofa from our old house in Woodcrest, the dried palm tray from the Florida Keys that my mother allegedly hurled at my father during a fight a dozen years ago—an incident which they periodically refer to with quiet, gleeful affection. I reach for the nearest hammer. Bobby and I know that we could have covered everything with tarps from the boat (it's up on sawhorses in the driveway), but the operation must be achieved efficiently, swiftly, so that it's too late to turn back. Our father hasn't quite said yes to Bobby's plan to switch my bedroom and the kitchen around. Maybe he doesn't quite believe we're going through with it. Or else he's too wrapped up in his To Do list to take our plans seriously. But we're trying to get as much messy work out of the way first, to prove to him how beautiful the house will be before he has the chance to resist.

Which he inevitably will.

Bobby's sixteen; I'm seventeen. This is how the two of us plan to spend our weekends for the next four months.

The wall between the living room and bedroom is already half down before I strike it with my own hammer. My wrist hurts. We whoop, holler. I strike again, and then again. We laugh. Take that, I say, to the outrageous nervousness inside my gut. Take that, I say, to cheapness, control, the cold deep whirlpool that wants to take everything down inside it—what Mrs. Fox knew too well. Take that. We work through a storm of grit, a fierce white blizzard that's transforming us into snowmen, but we're entirely involved, committed to our project, even though Bobby hasn't finished drawing up his plans, and doesn't know how to manage the wiring, or how on earth he'll get a sink to run water where my bed once stood. He yanks nails from the wood, the exposed studs sighing (how human, vulnerable they sound), as if he's pulling out the house's back teeth. Take that, death. We're already fighting weariness, the inevitable second thoughts, but the truth is we haven't felt this energized since that Mischief Night many years ago. Forbidden to paper trees with the Lennoxes and the Perozzis, we offered to guard our house, only to pull out bars of soap and write FUCK THE LISICKYS, THE LISICKYS SUCK DICK at the foot of our driveway, before we summoned our parents to witness the crime. "Who could have done such a thing?" we said, exasperated, speechless.

Then the storm door creaks in its frame. Bobby and I fix our eyes on each other—no, absolutely not. But I know the weight of those footsteps down the hall. I see a vision of myself dropping to my knees, picking up crumbled plaster from the carpet, though I know it's too late. I stand perfectly straight and hide my hammer behind my back.

"I thought you were staying in Cherry Hill," I say.

My father's eyes go pure, blank, as if he's come upon a murder. "My house."

"We're making it better," Bobby says.

"My house," my father says, more quietly now. "What are you doing to my house?" And then he's down on his knees himself, pinching plaster in his fingers.

"Trust us," I say, trembling inside.

"We're making it better," Bobby says. And with a steady pressure of the crowbar, something else gives way.

CAPTAIN ST. LUCIFER

Show them you won't expire
Not till you burn up every passion
Not even when you die

▲▼ Joni Mitchell, "Judgment of the Moon
and Stars (Ludwig's Tune)"

We're grouped around the battered piano in the dorm
lounge. Although outwardly we're working out the harmonies of Ann and Nancy Wilson's "Dog and Butterfly,"
we each perform something else on our private interior
stages: Bernardine picks her 12-string Gibson to Pure
Prairie League's "Amy"; Kevin perfects his monotonic
nasal stupor to "One More Cup of Coffee for the Road";
Grace's vibrato comes from a deeper, more womanly
place (she has to stop listening to *Streisand Superman*).
And I'm doing my own music, a romantic, violent mish-
mash that borrows fiercely from Laura Nyro and Joni
Mitchell. In our best moments, the four of us are capable
of bringing a rowdy crowd of undergrads to reverent,
bewildered silence (see them rest their beer bottles on
their tables, their eyes filling, blinking), though when
we're off, we're really off. No wonder the two fratboys—
our audience—wince every time Grace raises a splayed

palm toward an imaginary spotlight, suggesting in no uncertain terms that her feelings are the most important ones in the room.

Once we've gravelled our vocal chords, Bernardine asks to hear "Long Train Comin'," the song I finished while I was home at my parents' last weekend. I slide onto the piano bench, shoulders falling forward, feigning indifference, though my brain's screwed so tight I might as well be running a fever. I start the first verse, my eyes squeezing shut as my throat strains for the high notes. My fingertips stick. No focus. What's that outside? Dog? Church bell? I think of the big, ponderous bell swinging left, right, left, right, pushing back the air on either side as if it's massive, heavy as water. By the time the rhythm shifts, though, and the key changes to B minor, E, then back to B minor, I'm entirely inside the music, throwing my head back, stunned by the lights above until my eyeballs ache. When did I become this person? I'm still trying to get the hang of it—the authority others give up to me, this unnerving privilege and power. Life was never like this when I wrote and sang Catholic folk songs or performed at nursing homes with my high-school madrigal group in those foolish black tights. What would people think if they knew my history, the hidden me? It all feels cagey on my part. Surely, one of these days I'll be found out. Someone will come across one of my psalm settings in the college chapel missalette (I've published a dozen since tenth grade, and more, to my embarrassment, are on the way), and I'll be tossed overboard.

But should I care? Let whoever finds out spray me with a cold hose, wash off the mud, the seaweed. I don't see any real point to being in this group, or any group for that matter. I don't listen to bands; I don't even like bands. There isn't even a single band that I can think of—not the Rolling Stones, the Beatles, Pink Floyd, Led Zeppelin, The Clash—that can match Joni Mitchell's harmonic structures or Laura Nyro's beautiful, murderous intensity. Bands are too damn casual, bands are too damn fun. All that collectivity, all that willingness to merge, submerge, give up the self. Isn't it all about group love? Don't you wish you were us? Don't we fuck more than you do? Posing, posturing: white people tossing about their fried hair, throwing out words like "ain't," or "don't" for "doesn't." Perhaps it has something to do with my father (his work ethic, his distrust of anything lazy or lax), but to my mind certain kinds of collaboration come too close to cheating. Performing should scare the shit out of you, turn you inside out, hang you upside down from your toes, take you within a hair's breath of your death. "The lights go down/ and it's just you up there/ getting them to feel like that," sings Joni, and that's exactly what I want. I tremble inside a splash of light, trying to stay on pitch. There's a burnt, electrical taste in my back fillings, and somewhere, deep in the darkness, a match flares; someone with a starved heart is calling out my name.

Then one voice, two, three—Kevin, Grace, Bernardine. What's going on? The three of them are harmonizing, working their way through the last verse, mulching, fertilizing the melody until it pops, bursts into a layered garden: irises, tulips staining each other with color, light. A breeze blows. The air scents. We're moving, alive, a wholeness. Throats are dusted with pollen. Tiny hairs tremble on the backs of our necks. And what would a single flower mean?

▲▼

"So what kind of recorder do you need?"

My father's bent over the open hood of the sedan, loosening a nut on—is that the carburetor?—with a wrench. I'm home from school for the weekend. Beyond the open garage door, rain pours down into the driveway drain, wetting the birch clumps, the veined leaves of the silver maple, the spreading junipers leeching across the licorice root.

"Daddy," I say. (How I hate to say "Daddy," but what else to call him? "Dad" sounds like someone you'd throw a football to, and "Father" sounds like it's from the last century.) "We don't have to do this today, really." And I absolutely mean it. While I leapt at his offer to buy me a four-track recorder last week, I feel differently today. Don't I already hear him in the kitchen yelling to my mother late one night about the checks written to Clover, the local supermarket; the small iced cake we had for dessert last night?

He turns his head to the left. "Hand me those pliers."

I pick out a wrench before delicately putting it back. I wish I had the aptitude for car repair (wouldn't my help mitigate this boredom, this dizziness?), but my father and I mutually gave up on my mechanical abilities when I started playing piano at age six. Not that he expects me, or my brothers, for that matter, to be him. If anything, he wants us to live lives that are bright, extraordinary, that spin off and away, and laugh at how simple his own was: the way he took backroads to bypass toll bridges, or wiped doorknobs with a pink

T-shirt each time he locked the house to help catch the burglar who never seemed to arrive, but who would certainly take every last thing we had when he crashed an ax through our front window. Still, that doesn't stop my father from marshaling us to his side when he puts on roof shingles or digs trenches in our enormous front lawn to lay pipes for sprinklers. If we can't truly be helpers, then we can be witnesses, provide company. And a little suffering can be good for the soul, can toughen it, can't it? Too much pleasure, too much of the easy life, and before you know it, you lose your brain cells, slouching on the couch before the TV, eating, well—cake.

"I don't have the right tools. Ah, shit." He rubs his face vigorously with both palms then holds them there for a second, breathing into the torn up skin. "Let's go get your machine."

"I think we should reconsider."

"Listen," he says solemnly. "You need a four-track recorder to make demo tapes. That's what you told me, right?"

"Yes, but—"

"You want to be famous?" he asks more quietly now.

The question literally stops my breath. Famous? The way he says it is absolutely sincere, with only the slightest intimation of force; he doesn't hear anything embarrassing above, beneath, or suffusing the word. He believes in my possibility with such steady, practically holy conviction that I'm moved and strengthened by it, though I'm reluctant to admit it to myself. Yes, I do want to be known and recognized for my work; I'd like to sing back to Laura and Joni, to enter the conversation. But admitting to a desire for fame sounds shameful—

and as moral, frankly, as bulldozing acres of Arizona saguaros to sell lots.

"You have to earn a living," he says.

"I know, but—" This doesn't seem to be the moment to talk about claiming self, about creating something that resists the problem of death. Anyway, I don't have the language for such thoughts. "If I was after money—" A delivery truck drives by, flings a wave of puddle water on the flooded lawn. "There are probably more efficient ways to earn a living."

He faces me, shoulders relaxing backward, neck lengthening until it makes a tender crack. We sigh at once, together. It still startles us both that I've turned out to be six inches taller than he. We smile tentatively, then glance away. "I'm going to change these clothes," he says.

A single yellow chrysanthemum blows across the floor of the garage and hits one wall, catching somewhere on the undercarriage of the car, absorbing the scent of the back tire. It occurs to me that if I'd stayed back at school, I'd have finished the new song I've been struggling with for weeks, not to mention those French conjugations. But, in spite of the agitated particles in the air, the sense of constant motion, the occasional blowup, the stifling routine of things, I love it here. (Where else can I sit and read the newspaper or work on my songs in silence and not feel the burden of presenting myself in an acceptable way? Where else but in their lamplit kitchen, with my parents attending to their tasks in other rooms, can I be absolutely alone but together with people at the same time?) Is something wrong with me? Sister Mary Jonathan, the school therapist I see on Tuesday afternoons, thinks so. She's suggested more than once that I'm too attached to my family, that it's time to separate, that I'm not giving the luminous Loyola College, a school I've come to loathe more than simple three-chord pop songs, a chance. The problem is that she's so convinced of the school's intrinsic value that she'd never let me go. Two months into my first semester I can't figure out whatever possessed me to choose this small Catholic school with a heavy concentration of business majors and no established traditions in the creative arts. Was it only that they made a fuss over me when they found out about my work in music? Or was I so sick and tired of hearing my parents' worries about my desire to put off college, their fears that such a decision might turn out to be "low-class" that it was easier to give in to the first school who'd said yes? (Didn't my brother Bobby do that when he signed on to four years at L.S.U., prompting the whole lot of us to weep silently for hours after we left him off, as we drove back north through the swamps of southern Louisiana, devastated?) Whatever it is, I've gone wrong. And time is running out: I need the nerve and audacity to get myself the hell away from school, from home, to fly out to Los Angeles, to rent a little apartment, to perform at Doug Weston's Troubadour, to pound the streets, to work myself ragged, to get my tapes into the right people's hands.

"Ready?" My father's changed his T-shirt, but he's still wearing the same pants he wore while working on the car.

"You're wearing that?"

"What's wrong?"

"There's a spot on your pants."

He looks down at the hem, squints his left eye, and

rubs it—protein? blood?—with the tip of his thumb. He shakes his head. "You worry too much."

Within minutes we're inside a cramped electronics store across from the Cherry Hill Mall. In one corner: a taped-up photo of the Ayatollah Khomeini with three red circles superimposed over his face. In the opposite: a potted mother-in-law's tongue that hasn't been watered in weeks. There's a stale smell baking: cherry lozenges, the slightest suggestion of cigarette breath. The sales-people, all with bushy, black mustaches, stand with their backs to the register counter. They trade jokes, though they're sending out signals—I swear I'm picking them up—like hammerheads who haven't smelled human flesh in weeks. (How tasty we must look to them. Who's buying luxury electronics during an oil embargo and hostage crisis?) We paddle out between the displays, try-ing our best to look like energetic, capable swimmers, only occasionally grasping onto a raft before we swim on. How to tell the difference between one machine and another that costs a thousand dollars more? I know I should probably care more about the mechanics of popu-lar music, but it's as comprehensible to me as the dusty wires inside the hood of my father's car. To me an ampli-fier is an amplifier, and I'm inwardly distrustful of those who'd give as much credence to the sound system itself as to the quality of a performance. Perhaps this has to do with my years of playing guitar in 1960s-era Catholic churches, where we had to make do with a humble mi-crophone attached to a blond lectern embossed with an abstract fish. At such moments I feel the grave tug that I should offer myself up to the realms of church music forever—that this obsessive need to turn myself out to the world, this wanting, wanting, is simply going to do me in. Look up to God, I think, but such thoughts are almost unbearable right now: a lifejacket with weights sewn inside the collar.

A salesman with brass-colored freckles moves in our direction. Suddenly my father folds his thick arms over his chest with the instinctive distrust he holds for anyone who's out to take something from him. My headache pounds. "The youngster here," he says, before the fellow has the opportunity to extend his hand, "is a singer/songwriter."

"Is that right?" The salesman's gaze goes right to the tiny spot on my father's pants, then fixes on a spot on his own. "We get a lot of young singer/songwriters in here. We just talked to a composer from Juilliard."

My father's features settle into a harder, more brutal version of his usual expression. Looking at him, you'd never know that he tears up, in public, at most movies, regardless of their content.

The salesman glances up, rubs his mustache with a ringed finger. "How can I help?"

"He needs a four-track recorder."

"A four track recorder—okay. And mikes, and stands, and headphones, and—?"

My father nods once, firmly, with emphasis.

"The whole nine yards," the man says somberly.

He leads us down a passageway. I try to hold myself together, but second by second, my edges are melting, flowing. I'm all over the floor now, a cold clear puddle of ammonia that could make your nose run, or scald the skin of your hand if you let it linger in me too long. Why should it make me so uncomfortable to receive something? Of course, my father spends the better part of each weekend working himself to death, but he's choosing that, for God's sake. He's an electronic engineer; he has two graduate degrees; he's certainly not as cash-strapped as he makes out to be. And yet, such thoughts are not enough to lift me off the floor, to take away this smell, which can only be described as guilt, guilt, the domain of the lazy, the muddle-headed, a state of being that was supposed to have gone out of fashion with Vatican II. I'm a solid, coherent adult at Loyola: no "youngster." Why can't I be that here?

We stand next to a small tower of boxes.

"A songwriter," says the man. He looks at me directly in the face for a second, for the first time since I've entered the store, then turns away again. (Is there something about me that scares him, and him me?) He says these words with a brisk casualness, a lifted corner of the lip, as if such declarations are familiar from the mouths of ambitious Cherry Hill parents and their misguided offspring. A part of me wants to tell him, you don't know who you're talking to, but I keep my mouth shut if only to further things along.

The salesman reaches for a box marked TEAC. "Who do you sound like?"

I pause. It doesn't occur to me that he doesn't expect a complicated answer, that I should probably just say "John Cougar Mellencamp." Instead, I choose to pose the truth as a question: "Laura Nyro?"

The corner of his eyelid pulses. I'm not sure he's ever heard of her or not, but whatever he thinks of my answer, it's wrong. He tears open a box and gingerly removes a bright machine with simulated walnut on the sides and two 12-inch reels. A bar is clicked to the right. Wheels turn with a satisfying *sshh*, like tide moving through a marsh. He holds up a mike. "Test, test."

"Sing something," my father says.

I roll my eyes, glare.

"Come on," he says softly, with a hint of flirtation. My father turns to the man, a kinder, more relaxed expression softening the set of his nose, the length of his upper lip. He makes a slight nudging motion, even though he's a full four feet from the man. "He's bashful."

"Daddy."

"Go sing one of your church songs."

The man hits the rewind and plays our conversation back for us. Church songs? What to do? Sing Psalm 150 in a public space for someone who'd have to pretend he'd appreciate my performance. Or worse, disappoint my father. But wouldn't he love it, though, talk about it for years, just like the way he talked about my brother Michael when he played "Day by Day" on the piano in that restaurant in Mexico, with the ocean through the window behind him, to the applause and cheers of everyone at the tables—one of the many things that Michael had done over the years to lift my father's gloom.

Fortunately, the salesman must know what's on my mind. Or maybe the thought that we might be fundamentalists or fanatics of some sort, rallies his attention. (But you don't understand, I want to say: Catholic folk songs. Guitars! Liturgical dance!) He quotes us a price that's at least a $150 under list, so shocking my father that he's entirely disarmed: he's stunned that there could be something like luck or good fortune in the world.

"You're sure you're not selling me something returned?" My father squats, runs his hand on the surface of the machine for nicks, scratches, dents.

"You have my word, sir. It's in tip-top shape. It's just last year's floor model."

My father turns to me. He lifts his brows until his forehead wrinkles; the corners of his eyes squint. "And you're sure that's what you want?"

I nod.

"You're not making this up. You want this, right?"

I put more effort into my second nod, though I think, well—too much is depending on this, no object in the world should ever carry so much meaning and possible defeat. But when I switch the knobs to the left, right, and imagine myself with the headphones on, my lips barely touching the spongy black bulb of the mike, a soft glow warms the underside of my arm from the palms all the way up to the shoulder blade. "Man, oh man," I murmur.

"Ring it up, then," my father says in a resigned, dehydrated voice. He pats his front pants pocket, slides out a stained caramel-colored wallet, from which he extracts a credit card. "BankAmericard."

We walk across the slick parking lot. The clouds blow to the ocean now, the undersides glowing pink, umber, "muscular with gods and sungold," as Joni would say. The air's cooler, drier on the tops of our heads. Tomorrow I'll be back on the train to Baltimore, but why dwell on that now? "Thank you," I say. "Very much."

The dorm's a brick building on the east side of the college campus beside huge dramatic stands of pines. To get to my room, you walk through the lounge with the piano, pass rooms thick with smells: stale sheets, apple cores browning beneath beds, Aqua Velva in toothpaste green bottles. And, of course, boys. Tonight many of these boys have assembled in my room. (First a knock on my door, and then another. "What are you doing in there, beating off?") There's Todd, lying on his stomach on the carpet, where he crosses out an algebra equation; Gregg stands by the window bouncing a red-, white-, and blue-striped basketball on his palm. There's Kenny, who's buttoning up his plaid shirt, but who's known to take off all his clothes without warning, to swing his soft pink goat dick in front of the window to get a laugh. In comes Scott, Nick, John, Fletcher. And I'm sitting on my bed. I play my guitar, hoping to find some strange, but inevitable chord progression out of which I can build a song. Everyone's here but my roommate Doug (who's called Dough behind his back), last seen weeks ago, whose presence is now represented by the poster of the grinning Farrah Fawcett-Majors above his bed. The heater wafts through the room. There's a small, half-eaten container of excessively wet pasta salad sulking on the desk. Everyone's edgy, agitated, tormented by their hormones, looking for something, anything, to jerk them out of their boredom. A bag of malted-milk balls appears, and it's passed around, the spiteful little stones crushed between back teeth.

The phone rings. Seven boys lunge for the floor. They grunt, punching one another's backs while the thing keeps ringing. I yell, "Will one of you get it?"

"Paul? You want Paul?" John's barely breathes beneath the pack of boys, the air squeezed from his lungs. "Hey, where's Paul. *Paul?*"

I kneel. The earpiece is pressed to the side of my face until the skin's thinned. "This is Paul."

The voice has the wholesome, heroic quality of someone who might manage a Bob Evans franchise along the Indiana Turnpike. It's so newscasterly, so deprived of the omnipresent Baltimore accent with its diphthongs and swallowed vowels, that it might as well be Danish. "Lawrence Nilsen. I'm calling from *Folk Mass Today* magazine in San Jose, California."

Yes, yes! The publisher of my liturgical music. Why would he call at this hour, minutes before midnight?

The pile on the floor separates. Everyone's winded. Then Todd staggers backward, leans over, grabs his ankles. Without pause, Fletcher grinds his hips into Todd's butt. Both moan, big mouths stretched in mock-comic ecstasy.

"You guys!" I smash my hand over the mouthpiece.

"Sounds like quite the party there," Lawrence says.

"Rah rah," I say blandly.

"God, those college years. I'd give anything to be back at old San Jose State."

And before the sigh's escaped my mouth he's telling me about plans to record the music of four different composers who've published in the magazine. "We've been in the red for the last year and a half, and it's the hope of Don O'Byrne that more people will sign up for subscriptions if the individual artists are better known. We think you're one of the finest young composers of liturgical folk songs today. We think your work could be as big as Ray Repp's or the Saint Louis Jesuits', and we'd like to bring you out here to make a recording." The more he talks, however, the queasier I feel. I reach for the bag of malted-milk balls and pop five, six, seven in my mouth, sickened by the glossy coating, the density of sugar on the tip of my tongue. My stomach feels full, tumescent. I tear open a second bag.

"When would we do this?" My voice couldn't sound more distant. I should be jumping around the room like some love-mad bunny, but I can't stop envisioning my future: it's 2001, and I'm standing in front of a group of nuns in Bowling Green, Ohio, leading them in a responsorial psalm in a pink-beige cardigan with hair that's too thick on the sides and a salt-and-pepper toupee on top.

"What about winter break?"

I give him a date less than six weeks away.

"Okay, I'll book studio space for the first week of January. In the meantime, I'll start on the arrangements. Bass, guitar, piano, two flutes."

And then he hangs up before I've said thank you. Could it be that simple? Could life change so quickly, unfathomably, so radically? Kenny's up on top of the heater, in front of the window, wearing nothing but a belt. He squats slightly, legs turned out at ninety-degree angles, like some ancient Egyptian goddess with a thick dick. A girl under the streetlight outside sees the spectacle: she drops her books to the ground as the boys hoot themselves silly.

"What's the matter?" Kenny says, glancing over his shoulder.

I bite into my lower lip. "I'm making a record."

"And I'm Stevie Nicks," Todd says.

Fletcher sings "Rhiannon" through his nostrils, pushing it up toward earsplitting range. The others laugh, so full of vitality and the possibility that we'll all lead lives of great joy, that I can't help but laugh along with them. Until the skin tenses and folds above the bridge of my nose.

"I'm serious," I say in a pained voice.

Everyone stops, stands taller. "When, where?"

"California."

Todd's eyes betray a curious mixture of the sympathetic and the resentful before settling on the latter. "So I guess you're already out of here."

"I didn't say that."

"You're too good for Loyola."

"No, no," I wail, hanging my head.

I'm sweating. It drips and runs down my back, pooling into the elastic waistband of my underwear, though it's certainly not about the heat in my room. Six puzzled faces fix their attention on me. I'm about to walk out the door to get some air (let the six of them move forever into my room, I don't care) when Kenny, now in faded pink sweatpants, walks back in the room with a case of Rolling Rock. One by one, green bottles are passed out to everyone. "To Lisicky!" he cries. "To the glorious state of California!"

By my fourth beer, I couldn't be more excited about giving up my dreams of becoming a noted singer/songwriter to lead the Catholic churchgoers of the nation in song: the Ray Repp of my generation. I drink another beer, and then another, astonished by the cool black splash against the back of my throat. What have I been missing? Who knew how refreshing such a common, lowly beverage could be? On the TV, Deborah Harry murmurs through "Heart of Glass" on *Saturday Night Live,* with her eyes half shut. (At the same moment, one hundred miles to the east, my mother's friend Dolores Dasher stands in front of her own TV, on her Anchorage Point porch, offended, with her hands on her soft, upholstered hips. "So damn blasé.")

"Go, Lisicky!" someone cries.

"Yah!" And when I toast myself, half the bottle sloshes

down my shirtfront. I pull it over my head and stuff the sleeve in my mouth to everyone's delight.

I wake the next morning, face pressed to the floor, a rug burn beside my mouth. The alarm rings wearily, as if it's been working overtime. There's a cold, precise knife in the core of my head. My sinuses are stuffed. I take in breaths of air, trying to still the snow squall inside me, when the blurry numerals on the clock face start coming into focus. Could it possibly be ten minutes to nine? Shouldn't I be at the lectern in the college chapel, leading the congregation in the opening bars of Lucien Deiss's "Yes, I Shall Arise"? Didn't I promise Father George that I'd fill in for the regular cantor? No! I scramble to the shower, but can't keep myself on my feet: the floor's coated with—ice? oil? What is this howling in my head? I think: beer, malted-milk balls, Deborah Harry—all coalesce into an etherous winter cloud beneath my nose. I lean against the shower stall, open my mouth, and silently, with fingers touching my brows, barf an orange-yellow plume down the bright green tile.

Bottles chink, faucets gush. The bar's loud and rowdy, packed to the walls with workers from the office parks around I-695, all of whom appear to be engaged in various drinking contests. A waitress with a twinkling, harried face weaves in and out between tight tables. My friends Libby, Maya, Julie, and Bernardine have driven to The Fat Fox, a club in nearby Towson, to hear Amy Goldfin, a local singer/songwriter who's been dubbed the "Joni Mitchell of Baltimore." She sits on a high stool near the street window, tuning the pegs of her Ovation guitar, a largely artificial instrument with a rounded, fiberglass back. She adjusts a knob on an electric tuner. It's hard not to be flummoxed by so much equipment. But her ritual is clearly as much a part of the show as the actual performance—a demonstration of her expertise and high standards. A boozy voice calls: "Take It Easy." And across the bar: "Margaritaville." Amy pulls in her lips, tosses her blond hair over her left shoulder with a remote expression, not even bothering to acknowledge the banality of their requests. She's in absolute control here—or at least she wants to give that impression. She takes no shit. And though it's a hard crowd, it's a familiar one.

"Would you like something to drink?" the waitress asks.

"Absolutely not!" I say, to the woman's alarm.

I can't stop looking at Amy. She opens with Karla Bonoff's "Someone to Lay Down Beside Me" followed by Joni's "Black Crow." (How strange, even awkward, to hear the chord changes in standard tuning.) Over the course of the performance, I pick up on something poignant: she swings her guitar, bends her knees, leans backward as if she's playing to a concert hall, not to some smoky, cramped space designed to hold a hundred people at best. After each song there's applause, but if anyone is wildly enthusiastic or has fallen privately in love with her, he's not letting Amy or anyone else at the table know about it. Clearly the audience would rather she stick to her covers of Tom Petty and Eagles songs so that they could sing along and show off for their friends.

She follows a crowd-pleaser with one of her originals, "Shoot the Stars." I like it—the chiming harmonics, the open chords fingered high up the neck. But something's not quite right—is it her phrasing, the slightest exaggeration of emotion? I think about her moving hands, her artfully pained face, that crease above the bridge of her nose, and see something of myself in her wanting, and soon enough she opens her eyes, fixing me entirely with her attention. She's watching all these thoughts move through my head like black transparent shapes that I'd rather hide. And I know what she knows. And she knows what I know, and *we* know that she's going to play in places like this until she's too old and tired; we know that she's going to spend half of her time haggling with two-bit club owners who don't give a damn about anything but how much money she brings to the bar tab. And she hates me for knowing it. And I hate her for not being more. No Elektra/Asylum recording contract, no chauffeured limousines, no audience members holding lit matches, crying out her name for one of her songs instead of some stupid cover, but alone, alone, alone, lugging her amps in the back of her station wagon, driving 200 miles to play to 6 people, scrambling to pay the rent on her studio apartment with a conversation pit in Pikesville. But, in truth, she's never going to be anything more, because she'd never risk anything more. She loves her comfort, loves her proximity to her parents, her brothers and sisters, her Siberian husky too, too much. She'd never take off for Los Angeles, for there she'd have to confront the fact that there are hundreds, probably thousands of her. (Better to be the queen of the field here than to give it all up.) So she'll put up with the catcalls and the indifference and the waitresses who'll stand right in front of her during a quiet, intense moment to take an order for buffalo wings. And how can I blame her, really? It's certainly a better life than working fifty hours a week in an office park. Still, all these thoughts are enough to rattle me to my core.

She keeps her head turned to the left—nowhere near my direction—for the rest of the performance.

The four of us step up to her, with caution, to pay homage once she's finished for the night. She lays her guitar in her velvet-padded case as if it were something living.

"Thank you," she says, wiping down the neck, the fingerprints on the body. "Thank you very much." Although her appreciation is restrained and her voice is hoarse, she's clearly touched that someone's come up to talk to her. This is the kind of moment she'll take with her to bed, long after she's run a hot shower over her shoulder to ease the ache from the weight of her guitar strap.

"What a gorgeous bracelet," Libby says, picking up Amy's wrist.

"Thank you. I got it in Manteo last summer. Some little shop off the causeway."

Then talk about jewelry, the Outer Banks, the undermined cottage in Rodanthe where the waves are corroding the pilings. I shift my weight from one shoe to the other. I can't conceal my impatience. To make matters worse, I can't stop sweating: the fabric of my shirt's practically soaked beneath my underarms.

"Amy?" I interrupt. "I'm sorry—Miss Goldfin?"

Amy looks at me with a cool, inquisitive face. It's not a mean face, but it's not without strains of superiority. She looks as if she'd just dropped a Seckel pear beside her green felt slippers and is assuming, quite naturally, that I'll wash, core, and slice it, before serving it to her on the finest china. "What kind of guitar is that?"

A Kenny Loggins tape churns in the background. Why ask a question that I plainly know the answer to? Am I that filled with admiration for her longing and will, in spite of what I know about her limitations, that I'm willing to make myself stupid for her? If I were in her place, I certainly wouldn't want such a thing. Still, I can't keep myself from performing as the dutiful supplicant. We both inhabit the roles expected of us, though I'm not sure it's exactly what either of us want. Who in his right mind would really want to be an object of reverence? Who'd be willing to transform himself into a mirrored phantom onto which strangers project their own fantasies and dreads, giving up, in effect, what makes him real: his longings and failures and strange, inchoate needs.

Perhaps she knows that I wish for her courage and persistence more than I wish for my name.

"Paul's making an album of his own songs," Libby says suddenly.

I shoot her an angry look, which I soften the second Amy registers it. Gradually, the back of my brain warms. My smile feels false, wider than it's supposed to be. The change in Amy's face is palpable: it says, *you're alive, enfleshed, there's blood in you. Tell me how you got to be who you are.* And here's where I could change everything. Here's where I could say, listen, I am in trouble here. Did you ever feel yourself pulled between two things you loved? How to be solo, yet a part of the whole? To be turned toward God and Lucifer at the same time? But I want to talk so much that there's a pain sluicing my throat. My voice fails; I'm helpless, as a big man in a trenchcoat pulls Amy toward the back of the bar.

▲▼

"You're never going to believe it."

If my mother were a coffee percolator, she'd be bubbling all over in sheer joy, gushing all over the countertop, washing beneath the dish drainer, pooling inside the open drawer full of twist ties and silverware. I swear that she's ten years younger than the last time she was in the kitchen: her face glistens with a slight shine about the forehead and nose, the green of her eyes as warm as steeped tea.

I cross out the last word of the refrain. I put down my pencil. "What?"

"Michael's gotten into All Eastern."

Her voice thrills, though it's not without uncertainty. (Does she already envision him packing up his instruments and clothes to leave for good, though he's only sixteen?) On the other side of the kitchen, past the hearth room and the foyer, Michael plays the opening passage of "Carmina Burana" over and over again. Like a weather instrument, something inside me is spinning, powered by part joy, part dread.

"That's great," I say.

She pulls back a chair from the kitchen table and looks at me, smiling. Love has transformed her face. Now she knows why she's been a mother, why she put up with shepherding us to music lessons in Moorestown and Cinnaminson, or driving periodically to Paul Laubin's workshop in northern Westchester to look at oboes. Our family will never be the same. Every time we walk through Clover, or the St. Thomas More church parking lot, it will be known that Michael triumphed over hundreds of other high-school oboists from the entire East Coast who wanted his position. People will greet us, will ask to sit near us at concerts, will think the most banal comments we proffer are witty, worthy of passing on from person to person.

Our lives are changing. And yet I can't help but feel a disquieting spasm of jealousy.

I glance down at the song I've been working on. *Kids kick a soccer ball, hot dusty street. Not much to laugh about, not much to eat.* Immediately its lyrics feel forced, willed into being, more conventional than I thought it was.

I get up and walk to Michael's doorway.

"Michael, that's brilliant."

"I mean, I thought I'd probably get in, but I'm still sort of shocked."

"You've worked so hard," I say. "I'm really, really excited for you."

He shaves cane for a new reed beneath a high-intensity desk lamp. He puts down the knife on his desk, then raises his face, beaming. "Can you believe it?" he says.

Even he's been transformed by the news. His lower lip looks fuller than it typically is, tinged with vermilion, bright with moisture. He's lost any bit of baby fat around the jaw; his whole face is leaner, as if sharpened with a reed knife. I scan the cluttered shelves of his room—a small bottle of aspirin imprinted with Julia Waldbaum's face, a container of Ann Page Pure Ground Sage, a candy tin from Gimbels, a thimble from A&S: his shrine to fading American retail—and feel a love so ferocious and strong that I'm almost sick. If we weren't so close, if I didn't see him all the time, I might hug him, but such a demonstration would only seem showy, formal, making the two of us stiffen.

"When's the concert?"

He pulls in his lower lip, wraps twine around the reed. Such methodical precision: he holds it but two inches from his face. "May."

"I can't wait," I say and leave.

I lie in my own room with the door shut; my mind wanders as his music penetrates the walls. He's playing something older now, more harmonically traditional—is it Mozart? Haydn? The lyric leaps; the splendid, dazzling, red-gold feeling: where does it come from? How has he tapped into its source? The emotions feel almost pure, unbidden to me. Every time I've been trying to sing these days, I can't get my voice to do what I want it to do. There's a complex feeling in my head, but as soon as I open my mouth and try to translate it to sound, I'm frustrated. Either the pitch wavers or the phrasing's too deliberate or the timbre of my voice blurs and muddies when I want it to paint sharp, sharp lines. I can't even sing a note without stepping outside of myself, judging. Could it be that Michael is the real talent in the family? I bite myself just below the knuckle of my ring finger, almost breaking the skin, and leave two little fences of indentations, before the flesh stretches back. On the other side of the house, a soup ladle clangs against a pot. I can't help but think that the mother I've known and loved for eighteen years is lost for good, that the lighthouse beam of her attention will be turned toward Michael from here on out. Already she's the president of Band Mothers; already she's the love and delight of Rob Soslow, Cathy Wiener, Andy Susskind—all of Michael's musician friends. How could she possibly have the energy and interest left to care for another son who has the ego and audacity to think that he can be an entire All Eastern Orchestra on his own—not only to be all the musicians, but the conductor, the concert meister, and the composer of all his works?

(But what would I expect? Should my parents know all my Laura Nyro albums inside and out? Should they follow me around to the bars and coffeehouses of the Mid-Atlantic states? Ridiculous!)

I slap my guitar strings over the soundhole, a sassy trick I've picked up from Joni. I have no problem with the refrain, in which the speaker asks a big boat to spirit him away, but the whole project collapses, at least lyrically, when I try to examine and specify what the speaker's sailing from. (What would Sister Mary Jonathan make of *that*?) Although I have a hard time admitting it to myself, I have a tough time writing about love. Why do my attempts to explore the terrain of relationships always make me feel like I'm trying on someone else's shoes? Love—how does one write about the difficulties of romantic love without saying the same thing that's been written two hundred million times? If the truth be told, I know as much about love as I know about the workings of my father's car or the wires linking an amplifier to an electric guitar, and in my stingiest moments, whenever I flip through the packet of the twenty songs I've written in the past year and read the gassy, hyped-up lyrics of love hoped for and squandered, I think: *What's all the fuss about? Get up, for God's sake! Live!* What makes anyone think he's even worthy of love? So much mewling and heartache while people go hungry in the world or are hostaged in cells by militant fundamentalist students in Iran. At least when I set the line "My God, My God, why have you abandoned me?" to music I can convince myself I've contributed something serious and profound to the world.

Perhaps I just think that love—like wars, or hunger—is something that happens to other people.

Just as I'm putting my guitar back in its case, my father stands at my door in the orange jumpsuit he wears while working on the car, a caged flashlight in his left hand. Once again, he's fixing the car that we worked on together weeks ago. His face—ashy, unshaved, with new gray whiskers about the jaw—is smeared with two bars of axle grease below the left cheek. I tense, thinking I'm going to be summoned to help.

"Is that a church song?" he asks.

He smiles; his voice glints with a sharp edge. He knows that I haven't said three words about the liturgical album proposal ever since Lawrence Nilsen's call, that I've been willing myself to think of anything but. Simply put, he suggests that I'm giving myself over to pleasure, when, if I were truly hard working and disciplined, I'd be engaged right now in the hardest possible project, as he is at the moment by working on his car. I should be in front of my new four-track recorder (which hasn't gotten much use, I'm ashamed to tell) rehearsing passages from the songs over and over until my throat feels as if it's been rubbed raw with steel wool. And the second I fall back on the bed, telling myself that I can't go on anymore, I should get right back up to the mike, breathe calmly, with sureness, and start all over again.

"Don't forget to practice." On the other side of the wall, Michael's back to playing the opening measure of "Carmina Burana" again.

"I can sing those songs with my socks stuffed in my mouth," I mumble.

My father picks up the copy of *New York Tendaberry* on the bureau and studies the cover. Laura bundled up on a street corner, eyes closed, chin raised in defiance, black hair flying in the wind.

"What, you don't think I'm going to do a good job?"

Of course I'm asking for it. I know I'm practically begging him to say something thoughtless, slightly cruel, in order to feel superior: to let him know he's offended me. I say, "Daddy?"

"Of course you'll do a good job." He puts the album down. But there's something hidden inside his smile. It's both playful and aggressive, like splashing someone at the beach who's been shirtless in the hot sun.

"You know what you're doing," he says.

"Daddy!" I yell.

I look at him, challenging, but there's only blue, weary sadness in his eyes. Why is it that we always manage to misunderstand, to misconnect these days? We don't seem to be able to get ourselves out of these roles we perform—the ruthless father and the touchy, unpredictable, self-righteous son. We know it's more complicated than that between us. And if his words are sometimes marbled, I can't stop fixing my attention on their darker sides, as if they should be truer, should mean more than his lightness and his love.

Two hours later, the four of us are seated at the kitchen table. Jimmy Carter's face appears on the TV, which prompts my father's usual derisive imitation: "Jimmy Cah-tah." I'm not sure what sets me off: either it's his notion that the military should storm the embassy in Tehran, forgoing the hostages' welfare, or it's the lingering effect of his walking into my room earlier. But something's been building inside me for hours, and I'm seized suddenly with the notion that I barely exist, that I'm fleshless, that if I don't open my mouth within a matter of ten seconds, I'm going to evaporate, fizz like a drop of water in a saucepan on high heat.

"I hate that school. I'm dropping out of that fucking school."

The skin around my mother's mouth tightens. She makes a small pit in the mashed potatoes on her plate with the back of her spoon.

"What do you plan to do?" she says.

I pause, emptied.

"Paul?" says my mother.

"I have to move to Los Angeles."

Everything stills outside: the pin oak leaves, the blue-jay's plunge toward the rooftop. Then the three of them break into laughter.

"What's so funny?"

My father reaches for the gravy boat, then knocks it, splashing the tablecloth. He slams a butter knife down beside his plate. "Tell me how you're going to live. You tell me how you're going to feed yourself."

"I'll make do."

They look back at me with slackened, hurt faces. For a moment it seems that I could take things in a different direction. Raise the corner of my mouth, open my eyes wider, and the rest of my face wouldn't have any choice but to respond to that lift. And within a split second, I'd be smiling. And they couldn't help but smile back. And we'd crack a joke about Mrs. Fox or Dolores Dasher or any of the characters who populate our family's collective imagination, and we'd know, without uttering a single word, how lucky we were to have one another, to share our wicked, but loving sensibilities. Instead, though, I push my chair back from the table. "I hate you," I say calmly, with clarity. I grab my jacket, walk toward the back door with the firmest footsteps I can muster, and make sure to rattle the closest doors in their frames.

My heart's beating so hard that it hurts. I'd reach inside my ribs to rip it out of my chest if I thought such a thing were possible. In the yard behind us, the Lennoxes—Tommy, Cathy, Kimmy—play flag football in the dark, thin yellow tails flapping behind their pants pockets in the wind. They pretend not to have heard a thing, but their averted faces tell me they've listened to every word.

The night's colder than I expected: steam funnels from my open mouth. I walk around the perimeter of the Circle Lane cul-de-sac and see huge, flamboyant moths—are they swallows? bats?—diving beneath the streetlight beside the Spadeases' driveway. I trudge back toward Willowdale Drive, then farther and farther outside Boundbrook. Mews Lane, Lane of Trees, Leith Hill, East Riding Drive. I march down the streets, surprised by the how different the houses look on foot. Here, even in the dark, I see everything: the oil stains rainbowing the driveways; the bronzing pachysandra, the dewberry; the thinned-out rhododendrons with their stripped lower branches.

How could I have told them that I hated them?

I stop at the corner of North Riding Drive and Millhouse Lane to tie a double knot in my left shoe. Where will I sleep? I look over my shoulder and catch a glimpse of the nearest house. Lights spangle the Japanese maples outside the window. Inside the kitchen the mother wipes down the countertop. She looks down at her son, who walks up to her with his homework. Once she gives him an answer that satisfies him, she goes back to her task with such attention and pleasure, working circles with her arm, that I can't help but imagine myself in her skin, living inside her house. I put down the sodden sponge as I walk toward the family room, where I sit on the couch and lean into my son's shoulder, my mouth practically touching his ear. To turn oneself to the world. To live without the burden of death informing every gesture. She doesn't worry her time in the vain, vain hope that something she might make could outlive her. She doesn't need to prove that she's real. Not just an inkling: a drop of water, a pool of light beneath a lamp shade.

▲▼

Running, panting, banging my suitcase against the hall of my quad. Somewhere north of the Havre de Grace Bridge an electric problem stops my train for an hour, and now I'm late to Madame Sommerfeldt's 12:45 Introduction to French I class. My door's propped open. Boxes and Hefty bags are spread out all over my bedspread. My songbooks have been taken out of their box, and the Farrah Fawcett-Majors poster is rolled into a pipe. There's no sign of Dough anywhere. How the hell could he do this to the room—and to leave it unlocked, for that matter—without checking with me first? I'm about to holler, to pound on the doors of the other rooms in the quad when a wide, slow-eyed boy in a stained orange sweatshirt and a carbohydrate pudge about the chin and neck walks toward me with a box.

"Would you mind, pal?" he says affably, handing the box to me.

He affixes a Grateful Dead sticker to the wall. Inside the box: a can of Play-Doh, a sugar bear magnet, a baby spoon, and a magazine titled *Jugs, Shakers and Headlights* that features a blond woman in a leather vest, who grins over her shoulder as she spreads her naked butt over the wide seat of a motorcycle. The box has a vulnerable, human smell like a drawerful of sweaters that hasn't been opened in five months.

"Where's Doug?"

"Where to put all this stuff. *Mom.*" He looks at me confusedly for a second, blinks, smiles, then plunks down on the opposite bed. His eyes roll back just slightly in his head, the whites visible beneath brown irises, lids fluttering. He feels around for imaginary walls. "Time for a snooze," he declares. And with a single flourish of his arm, he pushes something off the mattress, and white plastic spoons spill out all over the floor.

There's a crick between my shoulder blades, a spur between the vertebrae of my neck. A wind blows down the slope behind the building, puffing out the curtains, which are ripped, mysteriously, the hem mended with duct tape. Am I angry? Surely, I should have been warned that I was getting a new roommate, that I'd have to get used to someone else's habits. As usual, though, the school seems to believe that its students are about as significant as the goldfish inside the tanks of the Woolworth's over on Old York Road. The guy sits back up, using the edge of my guitar case as his footstool. The vision in my left eye blurs: I know how vicious I must look by the swift way he removes his shoes.

"You play the guitar?" he says.

What am I bottling up inside me these days? "I'm sorry."

He holds up two hands and rattles them. "Listen, if we're going to live together, you need to tell me what's what. No feet on the guitar case, asswipe!" He laughs a brusque nervous chortle, then leans farther back on the bed, sighs, fingers joined behind his head. He blows a thin stream of air across his lower lip, practically vibrating the skin. "Play something."

I pause for a moment. Already Madame Sommerfeldt must be going around the room, demanding conjugations of the most irregular sort. I know I should make my way down the hill, but for some reason, I reach for my guitar. I play elongated, awkward shapes, as if my left hand alone is doing yoga. It's not much of anything, really, just a series of three chords too complicated to name, but the guy listens with such intensity and care, chin jutting forward, brows raised till the skin above his nose crinkles in vertical lines that I somehow manage to pluck the strings with more nuance and feeling than I ever thought possible.

He pants a little. "You ought to be in a band."

When I tell him that I'm a singer/songwriter who plays in nightclubs, who's—pause, deep breath: should I tell him this?—preparing to record my first album in a matter of weeks, his eyes dim, before his face glows a healthy red. I know exactly what that head holds; it's the same look I turned toward Amy Goldfin not long ago, and I try to receive that intense light, to take in what it expects and demands of me, without turning on my heels, and stampeding down the hall.

"A singer/songwriter? Like Bruce? That's absolutely fantastic. Let me shake your hand, man."

▲▼

"You packed your toothpaste?"

"Mother—" I say, expelling air. Outside the car window, the split-levels of Haddontowne twinkle with lights and electric menorahs in the windows. It's 6:45 in the morning. Christmas has already come and gone. Flurries swirl. We drive toward the sky blue towers of the Walt Whitman Bridge (I think of upside-down tuning forks) and Philadelphia International. Up ahead, traffic thickens, brake lights glowing red in the cars and trucks.

"What about your shampoo? Did you see where I left it?" She eases her foot off the accelerator and turns in my direction. "You left it on the bed, I bet."

I close my eyes. "I'm trying not to throw up. I told you I was sick. You're not helping one bit."

She clicks on the turn signal and pulls onto the on-ramp of the North-South Freeway. "You're not that nervous."

"You sound like Daddy."

"You're not making sense."

"What?"

"Stop telling me how I feel."

She turns off the "Moonlight Sonata" on WHYY and aims toward the cash lane of the tollbooth. "What's there to be afraid of?"

I sink lower in the passenger seat and exhale an

extended, ragged breath. She phrases the question with such concern and sincerity that I can't help but be hushed. "Okay," I say. "Imagine agreeing to make an album of liturgical songs you've written when you're not even certain that you believe in them anymore, when you've moved into another life."

It's the first time I've uttered such a thing aloud, or even to myself. My words leave a ghost of a smell, like a lemony dust cloth that's just been shaken out in a tight interior space. I crank open the car window to let in the frosty air.

She says, "You don't believe in God?"

"That's not what I said."

"Oh, honey," she says in a heavy voice.

A ship's horn in the river below, a humming bass; it reverberates against the winter sky like a struck tuning fork. We're silent. Then just by looking at the fullness of her lower lip, the soft glow of her forehead, I can tell that she's kicking herself for not booking a ticket on the plane with me. It wouldn't be entirely unlike her to meet me on the other side of the country, at the gate in San Jose, with the shampoo and toothpaste she's convinced herself I've left behind. And then I'm reminded of the time she followed my brothers and me thirty miles from the shore house to the Cape May–Lewes Ferry terminal. There we were, standing high on the third deck, waiting for the workers to untie the ropes, and there she was below, running toward the stern past the other cars in line. She held up a tiny white bottle. "Paul!" she cried. "You forgot your saline solution."

"I'll be fine, Mom," I say now.

"You'll be *wonderful*. I know it, I feel it."

"Thank you."

"Daddy and I are so, so proud of you."

And that's enough to keep me going for a while. An hour and a half later: liftoff. My left cheek presses into the blue plastic lining around the airplane window; the houses and streets of Cherry Hill, Voorhees, and Evesham fall away. There's the angular Towers of Windsor Park, the emptied aqua tub of the Woodcrest swimming pool. There's Temple BethEl, the St. Thomas More Parish Center, the model houses of Elysium, Chanticleer, The Beagle Club, and Charter Oak, a hidden gravel pit that might have been dug out with a teaspoon. How tender it all looks from this height. No Mafia slayings in the middle of the night, no impossibly bored teenagers setting brushfires in the orchards. Why can't this be enough for me? Why is it that I spend every last bit of my energy trying to change my life, and when the possibility of change finally comes my way, I don't take it as a gift, but make myself sick with worry, scrabbling like a raccoon caught in a garbage can, frantic that I'm only going to lose, lose? I see the floors of my childhood bedroom filling up with clusters of dust, the shirts and coats in my closet stiffening with age on their hangers. And hasn't my family already stopped bringing up my name? There's Michael ascending the steps of the high-school stage to warm applause. My parents' eyes well. I see the Cherry Hill Inn, Irv Morrow's Hideaway, the boxwoods at McNaughton's Nursery like little rows of garnish, and think all it would take would be the simplest thing, a fire, an ice storm, a bomb dropped.

I'm not sure exactly where I am over the course of the next several days. I know I'm somewhere in Santa Clara,

California, in a paneled room in an industrial park abutting the freeway, but I can't take in the date palms, the jacaranda, the dry sun-warmed air blowing across the down on my forearms, or even the occasional tremor that trembles the car that I'm in with anything but the most glancing attention. I'm entirely caught inside some protracted conflict inside my head. Certainly I'm inside the recording studio at least seven hours a day. I'm wearing a pair of black padded headphones trying to sing with Lawrence Nilsen's bass, guitar, and woodwind tracks, but the voice that comes out of my mouth isn't my own. It's the voice of someone who wants to be—well, he doesn't know exactly where, but in a different place and time. And although he wrote these songs not long ago, and although he toiled over every cadence, chord, and lyric, he doesn't know what they have to do with who he is now. The voice inside his head is bright, forceful; it strikes the notes like sunlight on a ski slope. Unlike the voice that comes out of his mouth, which is chronically just a shade below pitch and is slightly nasal, muddied. It requires laborious breaths between phrases to keep forging ahead, to the annoyance of the engineers in the booth, who moisten their lips and tap their fingers against the console. He finishes "Magnificat." He thinks all he needs to do is to close his eyes and imagine himself in Laura's skin. He's singing "Captain St. Lucifer" from *New York Tendaberry,* banging the keys of the grand piano, trying to hold onto the inner "fuck you" she must have summoned thirteen years ago when she was booed off the stage at the Monterey Pop Festival. But even this exercise feels absurd to him, so he asks to go outside, where he stares down into a patch of poppies and silvered desert plants beside the door. A thin black boy throws rocks against a red aluminum shed by the freeway. Then he walks over to a car in the parking lot and starts scratching at the paint surface with a piece of broken glass.

Lawrence steps up from behind. He kneads my shoulders, pushing and pulling the muscles and tendons with such concentration and—is it anger?—that I have to pull in my belly button toward my spine to stop myself from feeling. Violet lights pinwheel before my eyelids. "You're tense."

I drop my chin to my chest and push my jawbone into my clavicle. "I can do better than this."

"You're doing just fine," he says merrily.

"Not good, no good. It's just not good enough."

"Now, now." I attempt to turn and look at him. There's something about his tone: he's lost the chipper edge he'd had at the airport the other day, the cheery, blank voice he'd use to command the high-school marching band he directs.

"But I *can* sing better."

He frowns, but laughs out the corner of his mouth. "So let's hear," he says and pushes me along toward the door.

What a riddle I must be to him: he seems as confused by my response as my father would be. I stand at the mike, sing through "You Are the Potter" two, three, four times, but it feels as if I'm murdering the song over and over and over again. Every inner proclivity toward failure I've ever kept hidden is now revealing and asserting itself. And it goes on like this and on like this and nothing ever changes.

In the control room the engineer leans back in his chair with a tense and mannerly face.

I turn first to God and then to Laura, but neither of them says a thing.

Seven people sit around a dinner table one night and ladle spaghetti and meatballs onto Melmac plates. We're in the kitchen of Don and Claire O'Byrne, the owners of Folk Mass Today, Inc. Their house isn't in a new development of zero-lot-line ranchers like Lawrence's (I've been staying in his guest room since my arrival), but on the west side of Santa Clara in a tract of houses with mottled cedar-shake roofs and burglar bars in the street-side windows. Our table faces the sliding glass doors. From my place at the head of the table, I see a sad palm with unclipped fronds, an orange tree with green fruit on its limbs, and broken toy cement mixers lying on their sides in the mashed grass. The house smells inexplicably moldy inside, with short piles of outdated engineering magazines lining the foyer. Three towheaded children shriek, run back and forth across the length of the living room, and aim at one another with clear water pistols. On the coffee table I see the proofs of the next magazine cover (JOY!) lying atop an open electric bill stamped PAST DUE. Something doesn't feel right to me here, though I know it's about more than the lack of money. Maybe it's just that it feels a bit too much like home: the whole house seems to be held together with musilage; all it would take would be a cold rainy night to wash it down.

I tear off the end of a loaf of bread. Lawrence, sitting across from me, lifts a bright blue bowl filled with Brussels sprouts. "Eat these," he says. "Calming vitamins and minerals."

Don takes off his square black glasses. Immediately his face looks kinder, almost vulnerable, less like the engineer he was for twelve years before people started strumming guitars in church sanctuaries. "You've been nervous?"

His voice is higher, pitched forward in his throat, inquisitive, yet incriminating. Has Lawrence told him something? "Yes," I venture. "It's a lot harder than I'd expected."

He squeezes, massages the bridge of his nose.

"It's not so easy to sing with those earphones on. I sound muffled to myself. Like I'm singing with cotton in my ears. And the room's dark and—"

Where is my nerve? Why do I feel so ridiculously raw and green, without any tough, protective coating?

Across the table a woman named Pam leans forward, resting weary elbows on the tabletop. Her eyes glitter flatly. "Maybe you'd like to pick out a banner from our church to bring in. We have some pretty ones. Some crosses and uplifting words. Something to help you think about the Lord."

And everybody just looks at her. She might as well be cursing softly, uncontrollably at the table. I drift off for a moment, imagining myself entirely alone in the dark, as I pitch my voice upward to a felt violet banner.

Don says, "You're not pleased with your performance?"

I think about the broken toys on the floor, the chaos of unopened bills, the chandelier with the missing bulbs over the foyer. Around the corner there's an unfinished room with unpatched drywall that hasn't been touched in years. He wants me to tell the truth. Yet, if I do, he won't want to hear it: he'll have to lay out more money for studio time, money that doesn't exist. To date this album has cost him $15,000, a figure Lawrence has quoted to me, with tightened throat, at least 3 times over the course of the week. How to tell him that I don't care about liturgical music anymore, that the boy who worried over those songs on the braided blue rug of his Cherry Hill bedroom is dead now? The one he's become can't find his way back inside the skin of that other creature.

"I'm happy," I say.

The corners of his mouth flex. He puts his glasses back on. "I don't want you to get back on that plane if you're not completely, entirely satisfied."

I laugh uncontrollably. "Of course not."

But his tone says: *You better get this right. You better do everything you can to get me out of this mess or—damn you.*

"In a couple of months we'll get you out on the road to start selling these things. We need to sell at least two thousand units to break even."

I call my parents collect from Lawrence's guest room. It's two-thirty in the morning back East. They're listening on two separate extensions: I picture my mother sitting on the edge of the orange paisley spread of the king-sized bed, my father hunkering over the desk in the kitchen, in white jockey shorts with a stretched-out waistband. I don't hold back. Whispering, I tell them that my performance has been ghastly, that something inside me will not permit me to sing, that I've given something that was once mine—deeply, unquestionably, irrevocably mine—to someone else, and I can't find a way to get it back.

"I've lost it," I tell them.

"I'm sure you're doing much better than you think," my mother says finally.

"You have a beautiful voice," says my father.

"You do," she says.

"I still remember you leading the congregation at Christ the King," he says. "I didn't even know you could sing, and there you were, strumming your guitar."

"Daddy—" I blush, yet somehow I feel strafed by his praise.

"Listen," he says. "We'll buy 200 copies. We'll send one to Aunt Myra and Uncle Steve, Uncle Alfred and Aunt Vicki, Mr. Forte, Mrs. Fox—"

"No!"

And the intensity of my cry silences them. They've never heard such talk from me. For so long they've both admired, and been confused by, my desire. Now that they're seeing what lies beneath it, they don't quite know what to do. It's as if they'd been expecting me to nose-dive all along, and they're both despairing and re-lieved all at once. They stop countering me. They stop trying to say the right thing. They don't tell me that I'm the greatest singer who ever lived; they don't say that I'm making something out of nothing. They're just silent, utterly open, and ready to listen. I stare at the orange plug-in night-light glowing in the socket. The white electric blanket on my bed ticks twice. Outside my closed door, someone shuffles on carpet, then runs water in the bathroom across the hall. Is that an ear pressed to the door?

"I can't talk now," I whisper.

"I know I should have gone out there with you," my mother whispers.

"You couldn't go out there, hon."

"Why not?" she says, her voice gathering volume,

force. "Sometimes you need somebody to speak up for you. It's not so easy to do things by yourself."

My father's cry is harsh, guttural. "Aaaah."

"Will you both *stop*," I say. And again, footsteps. I press the receiver to my breastbone, tugging the phone cord between my fingers, and turn the doorknob to the right. I look down toward the master bedroom door, but nothing. At hall's end, the minute hand of the clock jerks forward.

When I get back, my parents are still talking to each other from opposite rooms in the house.

On my last day in the studio, I'm hoarse, a taste of burnt grapefruit peel in my mouth. My shoulders have curved forward for so many days that they've practically solidified into a bow. There's nothing to prove anymore. Too much has already gone wrong to care. I stand up to the furred black microphone and start singing the final song. I listen to the bass line, the flute and clarinet duet recorded days before my arrival. For the first time, I don't try. I channel so much into my voice that I seem to fall away from it. How freeing it is not to be, not to work so hard, or build my house in resistance to—*what*? To let go of that nagging, incessant urge. All there is is sadness: fierce, unquenchable sadness. Tomorrow I'll go back home. I'll step through the metal detector, walk down the jetway, take my seat in the rear of the plane, and eat every last bit of the lukewarm chicken dish placed in front of me, but the way I hold my knife and fork will be different; the chair ahead will be tinted, less likely to be plaited with light.

I step up into the booth to listen to the playback. The voice I listen to is young. It isn't at all distinguished in terms of phrasing or timbre. It wouldn't even be enough to cause an A&R man at Elektra/Asylum to sit up even slightly in his seat. But it's simple and true and full of longing.

Both Lawrence and the engineer look up from the mixing board, faces suffused with warmth, blood. "Now we're talking," Lawrence says.

But they're tired, too. Neither offers to suggest we start recutting the other songs. And it doesn't even occur to me to think I have the right to ask for it.

For the rest of my winter break, I work. I take down the Christmas lights off the house and the tree; I wrap the ornaments in torn sheets of toilet paper. I throw out old songbooks from my desk drawers; I clean up an old baritone ukelele from the back of my closet in the hopes of giving it away. I make sure I'm in motion from morning through night, and when I sleep, I sleep so deeply that when I wake, I can't keep from being startled, heart banging, at the sunlight pouring in through the bottle on my bureau. Outside a plow scrapes the snow off Circle Lane, and the smell of waxy burning Duraflames drifts from my neighbors' chimneys. I'm sluggish and dehydrated, as if I'd taken sleeping pills before going to bed. But all it takes is a swift, violent rub to the face and I'm off again.

One day, on her way out the door to Clover, my mother buttons her wool, gray-green coat and stops by the piano. I dust the lower rungs of the love seat across the room. She stretches her hand across the keyboard and tentatively plays a note. Then plays it again, more crisply this time. Middle C: sturdy meridian. Its coherence and elemental optimism reverberate through the room. Its mocks whatever it is I'm feeling. "Would you like to go to the store?"

I stand and stretch my arms with an involuntary squeal. "I'm going outside to weed."

"It's the dead of winter."

"There's weeds out by the Lennoxes. I noticed them last night."

She presses her finger to the key again. "You haven't played the piano in two weeks."

I spot a single spruce needle on the carpet. I lean over, pinch it between my fingernails, and drop it into my pocket. "I'm just taking a break."

She turns her back to me and plays. "What note is this?"

"C."

"Which C?"

"Middle C."

"This was my mother's piano."

"I know."

And although her eyes are glossed with the slightest sheen of tears, she smiles, as if my ability to name random notes on the piano gives her the answer to what she's looking for. I stare at her, exasperation and expectancy tightening the skin around my eyes. But I don't understand what she's getting at, and I don't quite know how to give her what she needs. I get up and walk out of the room and start pulling at the frozen soil, even though nothing's grown there for months.

By the beginning of the following week, I'm back at Loyola. The campus seems to have gotten more cramped. The tree limbs crowd the space above the sidewalks, the classrooms are tight with junked chairs that appear to have been gouged, punctured with ballpoints. Even the students have changed. A couple have put on some holiday weight around the middle, while many more have gotten skinnier, with more prominent features and shadows beneath their eyes. I step into the cafeteria line my first night back and fix on the hooded bronze lamps tinting the bins of chicken cutlets orange. Suddenly, the back of my shirt is swamped with sweat. I know for sure I'm going to be asked how the recording went. I start to fabricate. To say, sorry, sorry, it didn't work out this time, the album's been postponed till June, we're looking for better session players. But when I sit down, someone heaves a lump of chocolate pudding at the white shirt of the person sitting across from me. In relief, I toss some back. And within seconds, chocolate's flying through the air, sticking in our hair, dripping into our faces, down the fronts of our shirts. Everyone howls, joyless and driven as fratboys. To the right Lauren keeps busy by running back and forth between the salad-bar tub and the table to replenish the supply. I think of her greedy, wild expression, and all at once I see her twenty years from now. She sits at her desk at some law firm, fingers massaging her temples until her mouth falls open. I look at the others, and they, too, have aged twenty years. They stand at their windows and look out onto their splendid lawns and wonder how and when their bodies thickened, their children started hating them behind their backs.

I walk to my room with my new blue rugby shirt—a Christmas present from my mom—coated in wet chocolate. To my shock, my roommate and two of his deadbeat friends are sprawled out across the floor; they lean against the sides of the beds. The sliding glass window is wide open, the screen out of its track. A bitter wind ripples the *Greetings from Asbury Park* poster. Golden mud tracks the carpet and my old chenille bedspread from the Anchorage Point house. Impossibly, there's even a crusty print halfway up the cinder-block wall.

"What?" I say, only it comes out like a whisper.

"We decided we're going to use the window from now on instead of the door," Joe says. He holds up a sky-scraper of a bong, the tall red cylinder half the height of the room. He squeezes his eyes shut. He draws on the pipe with such frenzied energy that the water inside practically boils over the top, bubbling. A bottle of chalky pink capsules is spilled at his feet. "Here," Joe says, holding out the bong to me.

I shake my head. I turn, pull my shirt over my head, and toss it in the wash pile. Why can't I feel? I'm stranded, standing with a shy, pimply back to Joe and his friends before I think to reach for another shirt.

On the floor a guy's picking some poorly tuned guitar. He plays the individual notes of a D-minor chord, then fiddles with the tuning knob of the third string. There's a glassy, bombed-out joy in his eyes. "You must be a saint," he says with a grin.

"Why?" I sit on my bedspread and try to rub off a muddy print with my fist.

"I couldn't live with this guy," he says, brows raised through the hair in his face. "I'd rather die than live with this guy. I'd rather live with my *father*." His laugh is moist, intractable, pushed through his nostrils.

"You know something?" Joe says. His looks in my direction, but his eyes fix on somewhere other than my face—my shirt collar? "I couldn't live with myself either." And with that he takes another hit off the bong; he inhales with such pure exuberance that he chugs up a lung full of water. He coughs, spraying everything within five feet of his mouth with a ghastly, bacterial mist.

My eyes rest on the soundhole of his friend's guitar. It's more beautiful than I could have predicted, with its intricate pattern of ivories and blacks. I think of putting my nose to that opening to breathe in the warm saw-dusty interior, the smell of craft and devotion. I see the instrument maker gluing the curved pieces of wood together, the skin between unwieldy brows tensing in concentration. He brings the soundhole to his mouth and sings, *Ooh, ooh,* listening to the sound of his own baritone as it's magnified, nourished.

I look at the peeled place atop the neck—dark purple wound—where a capo must have clamped.

My mind stills.

The poster on the wall flaps between its tacks.

And then, without pause, I drag the guy up to his feet, take my guitar out of his stunned hands, and push him up against the wall until the back of his head hits hard. "Take your hands off my guitar, fucker. Don't you ever touch my guitar again."

He looks back at me with equal parts awe, hatred, re-spect. I feel large, powerful, bigger than my body. But that power tastes terrible in my mouth. My hands and arms cannot stop shaking. The boy staggers from the room. And Joe Lubo rolls down onto the carpet, fast asleep, his left cheek pressing into his own muddy footprint.

In the west ballroom of the Atlantic City Convention Hall, on a stage framed with pale green-gold sea horses and Nereids, the musicians of All Eastern Orchestra tune up. The strings, woodwinds, horns, piano, chimes, and tympany swell in dissonance and mass confusion, prompting the spectators in the audience—mostly dressed-up parents, siblings—to sit up with straighter spines. They tighten their diaphragms. After all, they've looked forward to and, yes, dreaded this occasion for months. (What if something goes wrong? What if someone gets sick before the performance?) Michael, along with four other musicians, walks out onto the stage in concert black, squints in the glare of floodlights, and after a startled pause begins making his way through the music stands, between the stand-up basses and the cellos. He sits, leaning forward in his chair, and switches on the light above his music stand. Is he nervous about his solo? Does he want to get this over with? Maybe he's thinking about stopping at the closed-down Lit Brothers department store tomorrow where he'll take pictures through the front windows. Whatever's on his mind, he looks older tonight, more solemn about the eyes, with less weight in his face, than he did when he was sitting next to me in the car just two hours ago. My parents, reddened, sit on either side of me. They scan the program, trying to pick out the names of Michael's friends. More than anything, my father wants to tell a stranger that that's his son in the second row, that, yes, he'll perform the solo in the Beethoven after the intermission. But for some reason he decides to control himself. Then Michael: his face turning toward the audience. Is he looking at me? Impulsively, my hand flies up in a wave. I want people to know that I know him. But he doesn't answer back. Instead, he turns a page, moistens the end of the reed in his mouth, begins playing a flourish of notes, all of which are lost inside the swell of tuning instruments.

Outside on the boardwalk it must be twilight. The lamps, one after another, must be blinking on.

It's Tuesday, a gorgeous evening in May.

My father leans back in his chair. Arms folded across his chest: a look of impossible calm in his eyes. Then he puts his arm across the back of my chair and bends toward me, head nearly touching my ear. "What do you want to leave the world?"

His words are so full of meaning, so entirely outside that character I've built of him, that I can't even begin to look in his direction. I look straight ahead at the woman ahead of me: the cut of her jacket around her shoulders, the dark brown ponytail falling down her slender white neck. She's talking animatedly about so much at once: hydrangeas? Whether the ocean temperature's warm enough for swimming?

My father repeats his question.

I can't begin to find my way around or inside the answer. It's a tower with too many floors. I try to climb its exterior wall, but keep slipping off, falling down onto the previous ledge. The surface is too slick. But all at once I tell him of a box. It's full of songs, tapes, pieces of songs. No one may ever see it in my time, but that's beside the point. All that matters is that someday, far-off in the future, someone opens it and finds pleasure in what's inside. Taken together, the items in the box might not be useful. They might not help hunger, or hatred and indifference between people, or bring an end to terrorism and hostage-taking, but they will say one thing alone: someone lived.

My father rubs his bottom lip with his forefinger. My

words seem to vex and wound. His eyes narrow; the lower half of his face slackens, which vexes me back. Clearly, I haven't told him what he wants to hear. (He's still thinking about the phone calls from *Folk Mass Today* that I haven't returned; the unopened letters in which promotion plans are desperately proposed.) My collar's tight around my neck. I'm ready to call him on his unwillingness to understand. (Here we are assuming our old roles: the ruthless and the touchy.) I want to tell him that my desires are absolutely legitimate, that it's okay not to make records, to refuse to allow him to give away the album I made. I'm thinking all these things (how to separate one concern from the other?) as the concertmeister starts his long A and silences the ballroom in sections.

The conductor's polished shoes tap across the floor. He walks out in impeccable tails to the sound of ripe applause. He acknowledges us with a cordial, if aloof, nod. Then, turning, he raises his baton. The players of the orchestra lift their instruments with a collective gesture, and with a downstroke, the sound rushes forward, like a wave breaking over us at once.

I stare up at the figures on the proscenium. The music is so fluid and alive, so intricate and driven, that it's hard not to imagine the mermaids moving, the chandeliers overhead turning in response. The people around us are intense: some sit on the edges of their seats, some look almost frightened as if what they're hearing, if they truly, deeply listened, could possibly be dangerous. They don't just listen to the performance itself, which seems so weirdly seamless, but see and hear all the work that went into it. So many layers: the algebra homework undone, the rides to and from lessons, the heads cradled in palms after struggling through passages that were impossible to master.

Then—could that be Michael? Not that anyone but us would know; he's buried far too deep in the mass of moving instruments to be visible to anyone even in the front row. But there's his unmistakable voice. If it were a color, it would be the tint of old-fashioned licorice, that greenish purple you see once you bite off the end. The houses he builds of that color are animated with such beauty, feeling, and intelligence. It hurts as much as it salves; it's almost too much to take in at once. It's Michael's voice that I hear; it's Michael's soul turning into form, but that's not the truth of the moment. Michael, the composer, the musicians, the audience— all have fallen outside time; they're speaking backward and forward at once, to the past, the future. And no one is separate, no one an oboist, a concertmeister, a Beethoven, or a security guard standing beneath the exit sign. But we're all parts of it, the movement, the wholeness, the bright living thing.

My elbow touches my father's sleeve. We hold together without tension or shyness until the strings stop reverberating.

The applause in the ballroom startles the building. I try to lift my arms, but they're heavy; they prickle as if they've fallen asleep. Michael stands. The spotlight captures his startled expression. Then I clap so hard that my skin goes hot, my palms red, like hands that have been working for hours in ice water.

Sometime over the next couple of days I sit at the piano, playing chords, if tentatively. I don't want my

PAUL LISICKY

mother to hear, to cheer me on. It's the first time I've
played since January. For a moment, I think I feel Laura
inside my voice and skin, but she's gone as quickly as
she came. She sits on the other side of the room, utterly
separate now, wry, with raised brow.

SAME SITUATION

The crowd throbs, raucous and agitated, heat wafting off bare muscles. Bicycles with bells, pedestrians, roller bladers, gym boys, baby carriages—the street's a pachinko game; we roll in and out of each other, miraculously avoiding collision. Although it's an Indian summer weekend on Commercial Street, it might as well be July—at least *my* idea of July. "You think this is insane," says my friend, Hollis, "wait till you see the real summer." Someone crushes the back of my shoe. *"Hey,"* I say, annoyed, but the stranger's already out of earshot. On the wharf-side of the street there's a red rectangle in the window: SUMMER BLOWOUT. People stream from the store with dazed faces and plump shopping bags, and like the good gay boys we are, we lurch toward the door.

"What about this?" I hold an aqua-striped, olive-gray sweater to my face.

"Nn nn." Hollis says, shaking his head. "J. Crew doesn't work here."

I must look wounded, though I try to hold my smile. It's not that I feel any particular allegiance to my old style; still, it's disconcerting that there's so much I don't know about Provincetown culture and customs. Only last week I slept with a certain townie who biked up to me on the street and introduced himself by saying, "Hi, do you want to get high and have sex?" When I proudly (yet discreetly) pointed him out the next day, my friend Billy winced as if he'd caught me snacking on a loose Oscar Mayer wiener I'd found on the sidewalk.

"Listen," Hollis says, more softly now. "You're a spring. Not a summer. *I'm* a summer." He squeezes my shoulder, then picks through the overstuffed rack. He hands me something meager. "Try this on."

I put on an absurdly tight Tom of Finland tank top over my button-down and try to imagine standing on my parents' front porch in Florida. (*Uhh,* says my mother, covering her face, crumbling to the floor.) I put it back. I've been in town but two weeks, since October 1st, and already it seems that half the populace has participated in my makeover. Billy has accompanied me to the optician in Orleans, where he's tried to persuade me to buy lipstick red frames, which I almost assent to (does he want them for himself?), until I choose a more sensible tortoiseshell pair. My friend, Jimmy, has already shorn off the hair on the sides of my head and left the dark, foppish waves on top—a look that really seems to understand who I am, an aging boy who has one foot planted in his past, the other in who he wants to be. I can't help but wonder whether this kind of tutelage is part of any boy's welcome to town. Who, for instance, facilitated Hollis's, Billy's, and Jimmy's welcomes, their respective entries into the frat? And who before them?

I couldn't be more grateful for my new friends. Certainly, they want to see me flourish and thrive. They must get that I'm hungry to slough off my old skins, that I've had enough of being a good boy, so desperate to please. They must know that I need to be a little bad before it's too late.

"What did you get?" I say to Hollis outside the store.

He holds up a cluster of socks—mustard green, graphite, cadmium yellow—like some mad bouquet while I show off my new polo shirt.

"Paul," he says, eyes rolling.

"What?"

Instantly he takes the shirt from me and rips off each sleeve in two expert tears. I don't know whether to thank him or to weep.

"Now that's a Provincetown shirt."

It comes in like a white speck on the water. Then appears as something with more dimension: a wedding cake, an igloo, a string of white boxes in descending order, hooked together on a floating raft. It's the last arriving ferry of the season. I stand on the town beach and herald its arrival. I wave stupidly, then dip my hand in the harbor. On this fine, fair Columbus Day morning the water's freezing, cold enough to scald.

I step through the kelp on the shoreline. The smell of the water, the tolling of church bell and foghorn. How intricately lovely the world seems, how precise and expansive. Who knew what I'd been holding back? I see things more deeply; clouds tower; even the pale pink roses outside Billy's apartment window seem to vibrate. I've already written thirty pages of a new novel; I've already made more friends in two weeks at the Fine Arts Work Center than I'd made in the past ten years. My shoulders ease backward; I hold my head higher as I walk into yet another party. I speak more fluently, expressively, not afraid to display my silly side, the cast of selves I've kept expertly hidden for too long. One minute I'm the "Sissy Priest," the next I'm a comic-strip character, "Fancy Boy," the next I'm devising theme nights for a fictitious nightclub: *Lola Falana! Jack Wrangler and his Corn Cob! Star Boy in Flames!*

And yet?

Why is love still missing from my life? I haven't been in town all that long, but I don't understand why I haven't been asked out. And why is it that every time *I* ask someone out, he only seems to be interested in fooling around? Not that I have anything against sex, but I'm frustrated that the boys I've slept with don't seem to be much interested in anything more. While we certainly say hello to each other on the street the next day, it's all a bit casual. I think, if it was good that time, well, wouldn't it be even better the next? My hints at further explorations seem to be appreciated but it stops at that. Is something wrong with me? I tick off all possible permutations—body type, body chemistry, smell—and kick myself for even entertaining such common thoughts. Or does it have something to do with New England culture, where the direct, forthright expression of desire seems unseemly, if not low-class, even among those who are convinced they're above all that? Obviously it would be mistaken to expect an extravaganza of everlasting devotion from the aforementioned guy who biked up to you on the street with a lit joint between his fingertips, but *still*. I wake up in the morning, groggy, a bar of sunlight blinding my eyes. I feel hope—what will happen today?—before the melancholy settles: dust beaten from a mop. If only someone's face were on the pillow next to mine. If only to watch another man sleeping, his mouth twitching as he dreams.

I am thirty-one years old. Do I already sense my future creeping up on me: the narrow bed and the Crock-Pot, the smell of cooked cabbage wafting up from the one-room apartment below?

I certainly can't live in Provincetown forever.

I try not to fret. Maybe it's just that what I want is too specific and my desire is caving in on itself, the roof of my soul buckling under that weight. Or maybe it's this *place*: maybe there's no point in being coupled if there's so much fresh "talent," as Hollis says, waiting to be discovered at the town version of Schwab's every weekend. Still, I'm not ready to let go. One night, I walk into Gallerani's with my friend, Polly, and see two handsome men, obviously a couple, sitting along the opposite wall of the restaurant. Their faces are underlit by the candle between them. One reaches across the table for the other's hand, and in that easy, intimate gesture, I know everything I need to know about them. We're not talking about Idea here, but something earthier and sexier than that. I just know: you can see it in their eyes.

"Who are they?"

"That's Mark and Wally," says Polly. "Let's go over and talk to them."

"No, no, don't bother." I stay seated in my booth, stopping her. "They're so sweet together."

The food is brought to the table. I lift my wineglass to my lips. And Polly reaches over to touch my hand, as if she realizes that I can see suddenly, in the deepest sense, what I've been missing.

▲▼

I decide to be practical. Billy has already indicated an interest in joining the gym with me. He's been spending far too much time inside, he says, and his doctor thinks working out would be good for his health. So one day, after squeezing my paltry biceps before the medicine-cabinet mirror, I give him a call: "Let's do it." If I cannot find a boyfriend, then I can control other aspects of my life.

Yet joining the gym is a bigger commitment than I first realized. It entails entering into a complex relationship with the body in which nothing is ever good enough, in which one's always examining one's failings. I'm not sure I'm ready for this intensified scrutiny. Doesn't my body already take up far too much of my attention? And aren't bodies succumbing to illness all around me? At certain moments I can't help wishing I were born something other than human, mammal. I look down at the gray-beige pebbles around the shrubs outside my window and think how much more reliable to be stone—not to worry about temporality, perfection, and the mucky place where love and lust meet. At least not to be goaded by these hormones, which prickle the skin, and lead me to all sorts of charged, complex situations in which I'm not even sure I want to participate.

We sign up at Betty's. Although Billy has promised to suggest a program for me (he's worked out at other times in his life), he immediately wanders off toward the free-weight area and leaves me on the floor like a seventh-grade girl with braces and thick, thick glasses who's just been publicly dumped at the junior-high canteen.

"What should I do?" I call out.

"Try the leg machine."

Well, thank *you*, Mr. Forlenza. I plop onto some Frankensteinian contraption, then lift my legs feebly. Dumbbells thump and chime; everyone's focused; everyone seems to know exactly what he's doing. Unlike me, who's too ashamed to let anyone see how inept I am. It's one thing to look like a big old sissy among straight boys, quite another to earn that distinction among men you want to look sexy for.

"What in Christ's name are you doing?"

Is that man with the shaved head talking to *me?* I swallow hard.

He steps toward me. "You're cheating. Make sure you squeeze your legs at the top. Go for the full range of motion. There, there, that's right." And he stands beside me as I execute a perfect rep.

There's something lulling about the authority of his voice. I can't help but be drawn to its parental quality: that conflation of concern and control. I'm partly flattered, partly offended: who asked for his help? I let him watch me. Without my realizing it, his face (half hard: mouth, brow; half soft: eyes, nostrils) imprints itself in my consciousness like a deer paw in clay.

"I have to go, honey," says Billy, huffing, his hand to his chest. "I'm exhausted."

"Are you okay?"

But he's already hurrying down Commercial Street to his apartment.

▲▼

The doorman's a big black fellow in a floor-length duster and a red, rubbery hat with points like a jester's crown. He makes me think of an oversized, overage Little Rascal. If only he were so charming, though. Does he grimace at everyone else the way he seems to grimace at me? He seems to take particular offense at my desire to be admitted into the A-House for free. Five dollars, he barks. But aren't all Work Center fellows allowed in for free? I squeak. Five dollars, he says, more softly now, and jabs my chest with his finger. I fork over my cash, hurrying past him, a little pissed, but still hoping that one day soon I'll be recognized by him as the townie I truly am.

I've worked hard all week on a book that makes me deeply uncomfortable, if only because I'm writing about things I'd rather avoid feeling. I've been waiting for this night the whole week. I order a Rolling Rock from Ken, the bartender, and practically shotgun it. The voices around me are booming, baritone. The boys stand around the postage stamp of a dance floor, heads nodding to the beat, clutching their bottles to their chests or belts. The fireplace roasts the room. Everyone's waiting for something to happen. I'm all loose and woozy, as if the beer has dripped down into the emptied cave of my stomach. I stroll onto the floor. Perhaps I'm lucky that my eyesight is so poor, that I still have on the same pair of gummy, protein-coated contacts I've worn for the past three and a half years; otherwise, I'd feel self-conscious if I could see those faces looking back at me. But my body feels right tonight, that pleasant combination of tensile and supple. I'm ready for trouble. I chug my arms and I shimmy, focus on the bass line rumbling the floorboards.

I raise my head. I'm unnerved to see that the man from the gym is dancing not two feet from me, his palms facing outward at his collarbone, eyes closed. His grin is sly, the left corner of his mouth turning upward. For the first time I see how muscular his body is, how thick across the chest, and for the first time I see that he's attracted to me, which quickens my heart, in part because I hadn't known it before. He grasps my hand, drags me off the floor, and buys me another beer. It's too loud to talk. He puts his lips to my ear, says something wickedly cutting about the boy to our left, and I laugh, pretending to understand every word, though all I can think of right now is the warmth and weight of his shoulder through his sweat-drenched T-shirt, its dense, meaty quality.

"Let's get out of here," he says finally with a controlled triumph. As we walk past the boys at the bar, I try to maintain a look of cool composure. My pulse beats inside my back teeth. I tell myself: Of course, *of course.*

To this day I can't even recall the route to this house: did we walk, ride bicycles? Was it cloudy, or did the moon silver the surface of the harbor? All I know is that we're inside his living room. He latches his fingers together, stretches his arms overhead, and to his shock, I tear up his shirt out of his waistband and fix my mouth to his left nipple. "Oh, Jesus," he says, as his knees weaken.

Soon enough I'm leading him to *his* bed (how sexy, how profound this feels), just the way he led me off the dance floor. We lie down for a minute, still, a little shy, then all at once we're on each other, thrashing, voracious. He lifts his face from mine after a while. "That's one fierce mouth on you, boy," he laughs.

I lick my way down to his tight, tight stomach. I am hungry for forgetfulness, greedy to be an animal.

I'm still awake at four-thirty in the morning. The bedroom is too cold, the floodlights outside shine through the blinds, throwing slatted patterns on the ceiling.

V. sleeps beside me, absolutely calm and contained. He snores delicately. What is it about me when I have sex with someone I'm excited about? Why can't I sleep afterward? Why do I feel this lump in my throat as if I'm about to have a heart attack, but a satisfying heart attack?

"I have to kick you out," says V. affectionately.

Sunlight pools on the floor. As I focus, V.'s face is just inches above my own, the tiniest thread of spit jeweling the space between his open lips. "What time is it?"

"It's ten," he says, glancing at his watch. "You have to leave before my boyfriend gets home."

I sniff. I almost say it: *Boyfriend?*

His voice is calm and rational as he explains the situation to me, how he and and his boyfriend of three years spend one night apart each week to sleep with other people, even though they're deeply devoted to each other. The sincere expression in his eyes suggests that he doesn't think he's hurting me and that there's no reason in the world why I should be offended. And while I know in my heart that it's his absolute right to be in an open relationship, I wish I'd had access to this news a little earlier. And yet it would seem indelicate to express such feelings, akin to wearing sneakers at a Park Avenue dinner party hosted by the princess of a long-gone republic.

I step into my jeans as expertly as I can.

"Well, bye," I say, extending my hand at the door.

A tinge of sorrow flickers in his eyes (the color of tea leaves in this light) as he pulls me close to him. His hug is tight, unguarded. His shirt collar smells of fabric softener, a hint of shaving cream. "I had a wonderful time," he says.

A branch cracks outside. "Me, too."

I walk home. Sunlight shines on the shards of a broken Coke bottle by the street.

Danella thinks it's time to lie low. We're in her Work Center apartment with its knotty-pine paneling, its sweltering fireplace. She stirs the contents of an enormous pot, preparing one of her low-fat soul food recipes she's trying out on me. (A dud of a cook, I couldn't be more grateful.) She's on vacation from men after having ended a long, exhausting relationship with someone with whom she shared a Kings Croft condo in my hometown of Cherry Hill, of all places. This hard-won detachment gives her a special assurance, a self-effacing, Zenlike wisdom. We adore each other like brother and sister. (She calls us Laurel and Hard-on.) I walk over to the stereo and put on our favorite music of the day: first De La Soul, then Queen Latifah. Before long we're moving our arms, dancing casually around her apartment. I've never been at such ease with my body, and it pleasures me no end that she doesn't make fun of my white-boy moves. Later, slouching on her bed, we'll watch John Waters's *Desperate Living* until we laugh so hard that the tears run hot down our cheeks.

For now, we sit down to eat. The greens are fabulous: zesty, spiked with lemon and garlic: church bells on the tongue. Once again, I'm talking about my lovelornness, a topic that must tire the patience of even the best of my friends.

"You're kicking and fighting," she says.

I lift my head. Do I detect the slightest hint of scorn in her voice?

She salts her corn, takes a spoonful, then cocks her head. She salts it again. "You're going to get what you want, honey. But you can't force it. It will come to you." She has a way of investing these tired, New-Age expressions with such freshness. But why am I so unwilling to have faith?

"There's not very much time."

"You're *young*," she insists.

But then a tender recognition settles inside her gaze. We've just been talking about how many people are sick in town, how so many of them are not going to make it through the winter. Even her beloved younger brother has been in and out of hospitals for years. As far as I know, I'm healthy, but, like most of my friends, I'm scared to death to go to the doctor.

"Eat." And she spoons another helping of greens onto my plate.

▲▼

The tide advances on the town beach outside the gym's sliding glass windows, foam swirling around the boats' rusted red hulls. It's twilight. A northeaster gangs up on the coast; ions rush and tumble through the atmosphere. Yet everything's safe inside this little corner of the gym: no water seeping under the sill. There's Polly, leaning on the Roman chair. There's Hollis, by the window, doing his shoulder shrugs. There's Tim Callis, who's just passed a homemade cassette of dance music—"Butt Party"—to S., the woman behind the counter. There's Jasper, up from New York; there's Jack Pierson; there's Scott Frankel; there's Ryan Landry—all the people I'm fond of, the inimitable combination of souls who give the town its peculiar vitality and panache. Unfortunately, Billy's stopped coming: I can't tell whether he isn't feeling well or whether he's lost interest.

I'm much more committed to working out than I'd ever expected. On my better days I'm convinced that I've actually remade my entire body (look: a blue ropy vein has popped out on my biceps!), and when I tell my friend, Elizabeth, whom I haven't seen since our time together at Iowa, that she might not recognize me when she comes to town, she'll kid me mercilessly for years to come. Of course, it probably helps that I've shaved off my hair and grown a goatee, which gives me a certain Luciferian quality.

We're all engaged in our reps and our sets when S., the woman behind the counter, switches off "Butt Party." She claps her hands like a drill sergeant. "All *right*," she bellows, "Who in this gym *smells?*"

We're silent. The room positively vibrates with collective shame. She has tapped into our deepest dread. *It's me*, each one of us thinks.

Then a few of us start snickering, nervously, quietly, expelling air through our nostrils. Immediately, S. herself seems to realize how extravagant and over-the-top her outburst was, how it expresses some lurid deep phobia. What rage has she kept bottled up inside? It probably makes it worse for her that no one's willing to back her up; all at once all the shame in the room boomerangs. She crumples down in her seat. We might have stepped onto the set of *A Woman Under the Influence*.

The combination of the approaching storm and the complex energy in the room has my hair practically standing on end. *Is it you? Is it you?* Now everyone wanders about the gym, sniffing, laughing. Arms are raised. We smell; we're smelled back. And all at once we're

creating one of those quintessential Provincetown moments, weirdly intimate, something we'll remember for
the rest of our lives, when people who've never spoken
before laugh together. All the while S. sits up front,
moistening her lips as if she's on the verge of tears.

On my way out I feel a tapping on my arm. V. smiles,
slinging his gym bag over his shoulder.

"Were you here the whole time?" My voice sounds
harsher, more authoritative than I'd intended.

"Can you believe her? Maybe she'd like to spray us
all down like little piggies in a trough."

We stand outside in the howling wind, leaves rasp-
ing the pavement around our feet. Like me, he, too, is
caught up in the spirit of camaraderie and happy feelings. He lifts his head. A door swings open inside me. In
the porch light his eyes smile and gleam with just the
right hint of wickedness. "Your place?" he says.

I grab for his hand. Where is death tonight? We walk
down Pearl Street. The world couldn't be more achingly
beautiful; the sky glows beyond the stark, thrashing trees.

And so it starts, the events that conspire to make love, or
whatever this is, the center of your life. At first, you don't
even realize how much of your attention it consumes.
You still have a life, don't you? You still get up to brush
your teeth and pour your milk on your honey puffed
wheat. You still send off your student loan payment on
the first of the month. And yet you jump when you hear
the phone or a knock at the door—is it him? You keep
yourself sexually focused and groomed at all times because you never know when the opportunity will arise.
Worse, you don't leave town when your brother offers

you a free plane ticket to Miami for fear that when you come back he'll have revised his feelings. You don't even insist on your right to see him because he tells you—quite cheerfully, in fact—the story of Renaldo and Bobby. The single Bobby, who's having an affair with the coupled Renaldo, has started to make demands, and the way V. sees it, "That's going to kill things." The whole thing becomes more precious to you because it's provisional, forever on the verge of vanishing. You lacquer it the way an oyster lacquers a grain of sand: layer upon layer until it shines.

You're walking down Commercial Street. You think you see the back of his shaved head in a group of people standing outside Café Express and your steps quicken. He's happy to see you, and you him, but when you talk you can feel a tension, the possibility of sex beating beneath everything: Should we do it? Are all the conditions right? In public, you carry on something resembling a friendship, but you wonder whether the others know what's going on between you. You *hope* they can see it in both your eyes, for at the very least it will prove to you that there's something real between you, that it's more than just sex, which is what V. thinks it is. Or so he says.

You look at his unchanging gaze sometimes. Is he hiding something? How could he not be as torn-up as you are?

But in spite of the fact that the terms aren't equal here (he's unavailable a certain portion of the time; you're *always* available), you must admit that it's incredibly intoxicating. Life has never seemed as dense and as rich: a fancy Italian cake. You love the way he makes fun of you. You love his warmth and his wit, his sweeping assessments of the pretentious and the absurd.

He takes particular pleasure in exposing the true es-
sences of people who present themselves one way and
are actually something else. One man, who's known as
sensitive and sweet by many of the available straight
women in town, is branded a "cunthound." Truth be
told, he's hard on everyone. The fact that he approves of
your character makes you feel like a million bucks.

Now if only you could sit at your desk for more than
five minutes at a stretch. Your new novel has come to
naught. You stare out the window, then get up to pee.
You stare again. You wonder whether you have Adult
Attention Deficit Disorder.

You're standing outside the First Old Store one night
when his boyfriend bikes toward you. A valve in your
heart flutters. Too late to run. You know you should
probably be feeling guilty and contrite about what you've
been doing (once is one thing; again and again is
another), but you know he's probably doing the same
things himself with somebody else. And besides, you
must confess that you feel some warmth toward the fellow. You talk about Alicia Henry's show of new paint-
ings at the Work Center, which both of you happen to
like very much. You both complain about the music at
the A-House. You look in his Nordic blue eyes. You can
see the edge of asperity in them. He knows; of course he
does. You are breaking up the relationship. Still, this
doesn't stop you from wanting to tear the flashing red
light from his handlebars and throw it against a building.

Danella offers me a cup of Earl Grey as I sink into her
sofa. Over in the barn there's a party still going on for

a visiting writer. Things have been getting a little wild around the compound. Is it just the cold, the fact that there's nothing much else to do out here on the edge of the world besides our work, and we need to blow off some steam, in a manner of speaking? Or is it simply that we trust each other? Within the last couple of weeks we've heard rumors of all sorts of couplings: lesbians with straight boys, black girls with white boys, straight boys with gay boys—every possible combination you can imagine. Only last week, as part of a collaborative art project, Itty poured an assortment of canned foods from her cupboard over my naked body and photographed the results—something that we both found amusing, compelling, and a little kinky.

Sometimes, though, one needs to take refuge. Through the window I can hear the strains of Public Enemy drifting out across the parking lot.

"We haven't gotten together since last month," I say to Danella. "Do you think something's the matter?"

She tosses carrots into her juicer, a thoughtful, sleepy expression on her face.

"I mean, if things were really great between them, this wouldn't be happening. I can tell what he thinks when he sees me. It's just too much for him to take in right now."

The sleek machine makes a grinding noise before she switches it off. She will not proffer the easy answer, though she knows that's what I want from her. "Then why are you so worried?" she says finally.

"What?"

She pushes the dreadlocks off her forehead and presses her hand against the small of her back. She sips from the carrot juice, which leaves a pale, Creamsicle-colored mustache on her upper lip before she wipes it off. "If he's the one, he'll come to you."

"You mean I shouldn't try to bring this up?"

"Sit tight for now." She walks over to the sink and rinses out her stained glass. "Just trust me."

"But what if this is it?"

"It's not over, sweetheart."

I lift the cup. The tea burns the tip of my tongue.

A burst. I've been writing since dinnertime, and now it's half past three in the morning. I've accumulated two chapters, fifteen more pages of my novel. I think they're good, but who can tell such things when you're in the storm and fire of it? Whatever's transpired, though, I've had a conceptual breakthrough: my protagonist till now hasn't been active enough. He simply hasn't taken charge of his daily affairs; everything's been done *to* the poor guy: a baffled, inert observer. I want to shake him; I want to whack him upside the jaw. As soon as I make him choose, the stalled narrative takes off. He comes alive. The story sings for the moment, one unexpected event leading to the next.

Is my book trying to tell me something about myself?

I decide to sit tight. Outside my bedroom window the entire compound's dark, with the exception of Jim and Jane's window, in which a little lamp burns. I lie down on my spongy, narrow mattress. I think about what Danella told me, but her words don't stick. What's the worst that can happen? Am I only going to make an ass of myself? Or am I going to find out that he really doesn't care about me, that I simply don't have that much meaning for him? Well, if that's the case, then screw it.

I down cup after cup of coffee. I must have courage. I must keep hold of my convictions. I throw on my leather jacket, my scuffed Doc Martens, and a pair of torn 501s. I am walking down the stairs, walking out the door. The town couldn't be more beautiful this mild December night. A loose clapboard bangs softly against a building. A white star fires, fizzling out over Long Point. The breadth and depth of the landscape. I shudder inside. And I couldn't be more pleased with myself, for I'm thinking: This is what it means to be an adult. This is what it means to throw off the yoke of childhood uncertainty and be able to ask for what you want.

The lights are on in V.'s bedroom window. I creep up the driveway, careful not to make too much noise on the gravel. Music plays inside: Is it Joni? "The Same Situation": *Still I send up my prayer / wondering where it had to go / with heaven full of astronauts / and the Lord on death row.* I take a step further, sidle up against the car, and stop at the foot of the stairs. Voices. Not two inches from my shoes a skunk ambles by, white tail flaring. My mouth opens. My arms move about frantically as he wobbles away down the hedgerow, as scared of me as I am of him. Luckily, he keeps his scent to himself. I prop myself against the sideview mirror, practically falling to my knees. Then another step. Voices again. And this time I see them—V. sits in the hot tub, his arms wrapped around his boyfriend from behind. Steam hovers over the deck; the water bubbles. I think I should be angry, but it only feels like I've been hit by a bicycle and I can't feel anything. Their backs are pale and broad in the moonlight. V. nuzzles the bluish hollows behind his lover's shoulder blade; the leaves shiver, and that's enough. I see it all: the heft of their time together, their successes and missed opportunities, and suddenly I know why they're up this late. They've been talking about me, them, how they're going to move onward from here. Their eyes are closed. They're too caught up in the moment to notice the intruder standing on the deck.

I turn back down the steps. I wait till I'm far enough away from the house. I glance back over my shoulder, and this time I really do fall down on my knees. I stay there until it hurts, the gravel digging into my skin.

I shouldn't be surprised when V. tells me that he and his boyfriend have broken up. He tells me in the calmest, most workaday fashion, two years after I happened upon them in the pool. I've been involved with someone else, Eric, fresh from India by way of Montreal, and my attentions are too much turned toward him to feel anything like surprise. I suppose I'm still a little in love with V., but I've tossed that love aside, turned it inside out and lost it like a sock beneath a bureau. All over town, seemingly in-it-for-the-long-haul relationships are falling apart. And much, much worse, people are dying. How many friends have we all lost over the last couple of years? It's 1993, the height of the Epidemic. Billy, Lon, Richard, David, Chico: even if they haven't yet died, they're getting sick. The medicine is lousy, the doctors have thrown up their hands, and we all know it's only a matter of time. And now Wally—I've been looking in on him while Mark's away teaching at Sarah Lawrence— isn't doing so well. One night I walk by their house to see a clear-glass votive burning in the living-room window.

A couple of days later, Eric and I attend Wally's memorial service inside the white clapboard Unitarian church. I'm reasonably composed throughout. I reach for Eric's warm, broad hand, and think of that scene back in Gallerani's, which seems like so many lives ago, when I first saw Mark reach for Wally across the candle-lit table. Shyly, I walk up to Mark after the final hymn. He says, "Thank you for being in Wally's life." And he says it so plainly, with such simple austere truth, that I burrow my eyes into the soft part of his shoulder. The world falls silent. The church empties out. Too much at once: Wally's death (I should have stopped by more often in those last, difficult weeks); Mark's efforts to hold himself together; Eric's protracted indecision—whether to go back to Canada, or move on, or . . . *what?* Death after death after death in town. And V.—what about him? The fractured globe turns, the cold clear lights of its core burning through the rift in its surface, but there isn't any globe in the sanctuary, just time going round and round inside our heads, and Mark holds me tighter before letting go, and lets me know that I shouldn't be sorry for losing my composure.

Some days I can't believe that Provincetown is still standing.

But there it is along the beach: a little battered, some days a little unsteady on its feet, but walking forward, a trace of wryness in its expression.

And who could have imagined that the story would turn out this way? Polly certainly saw it; so did Jenny,

Dan, and Pam. Lynda, who caught me on the street a few days after Wally's death (she herself would die in a car accident outside Plymouth in two months), hugged me, saying, "Don't forget about Mark."

How would things have been different had we not started out in anguish, had someone else not died first?

Love in the New World.

Mark and I stand in our living room, stepping back from the windows, and wait to see who takes what from our giveaway pile at the foot of the driveway. Sometimes it feels okay to let a few things go—not all, but a few. I'm ready to go back to work when I see a young man sifting through a milk crate full of my old shirts. He's new to town. He has that hungry look; it barely masks his vulnerability, the squint, the touch of trouble in his eyes. He picks up a shirt, chews on his lip. It might very well be the shirt from which Hollis tore off the sleeves all those years ago. The trees shake for a moment. The clouds part, sun bronzing the tips of the leaves. I want to tell him, watch out, dangerous currents in the forecast. Instead, Mark and I stand side by side at the window and wait to see what he'll do.

MYSTIC ISLANDS

A padded brown envelope arrives two days before my birthday. It's from my youngest brother, Michael, so it's bound to be entertaining and a little weird, with all the loaded significance of an in-joke. I think of his other recent gifts: a cassette tape of songs from Russ Meyer's *Beyond the Valley of the Dolls*; a photo album of Greenbriar, an aging Levitt development in Fairfax, Virginia; a coffee mug adorned with the face of Faith Seferis, failed Channel 27 newscaster, from a snapshot he took of the TV screen.

Still, nothing quite prepares me for what I'm holding in my hands: a customized "memory calendar" of Mystic Islands. I laugh and I laugh, absolutely delighted and bewildered by this painstaking, nearly obsessive gesture. I flip through the spiral-bound pages to find NOVEMBER: a green box with a flat roof, faded pink trim, and two 12 x 24 jalousie windows masked with strips of frosted contact paper. Its front yard is but gravel and weeds. Beside the carport: salt-burned hydrangeas, a dented trash can on its side, and a multibranched gas meter resembling something from a science-fiction movie.

▲▼

On the edge of the world, on an isolated thumb of filled-in wetlands, the original Mystic Islands bordered southern New Jersey's Great Bay, a huge expanse of water once noted for its pristine oyster beds. Its sales office first opened for operation in the late 1950s, its first house occupied not long thereafter. Over the course of 10 years, the developer built over 3,000 waterfront homes on land created through the dredge and fill method, and sold the modest properties to second-home buyers from Ozone Park to Piscataway. Mystic Islands might have continued expanding to this day if the Environmental Protection Agency hadn't wisely put the kibosh on the destruction of saltwater marshlands back in the early 1970s.

But describing the place's inimitable attraction isn't so easy; it's almost certain to point up the inadequacy and slipperiness of language. Or even worse, the ugly traits of snobbery, elitism. But how else to describe a place whose own residents seem to have mixed feelings about it; where, when you go into the local store to ask for some local postcards, you're practically hollered at: *Why would you want that?*

Perhaps it's best to take the tour. It's 1962, and you've been lured by the lively advertisements of the *Philadelphia Inquirer*'s real estate section. You drive through the gates down Radio Road past the Rotunda Lounge (a round affair in which community meetings are held), the Mystic Islands Casino (the local bar/restaurant), and the Mystic Islands Playhouse (a huge tin structure—a hangar?—built to keep potential juvenile delinquency in check). Huge blocks of concrete hunker throughout the property; you learn later that they're the footings of a demolished World War II–era radio tower. You think of German submarines cruising ominously offshore and

are fully, entirely interested. Yet nothing readies you for
the sight of all those houses. You think of porches, enclosed porches with minuscule windows and pastel
siding. The word "functional" comes to mind. But
they're waterfront; every last one on a man-made, navi-
gable lagoon, which lends the streets a festive, Venetian
air. You drive over a wooden bridge and you're out in
the marshes, signs everywhere insisting on the future:
Future Golf Course, Future Marina, Future Park. You
make it to the dead-end cul-de-sac of Radio Road. An
already faded sign says PRIVATE BEACH, but someone's pushed down the chain-link fence, and two
figures—two teenage boys—sit on the yellow sand beside the breezeless bay, slapping at the mosquitoes on
their arms.

The whole place seems to be held together by pins
and needles.

You turn back. You find it within yourself to check
out the "model home mall." The developer, for some odd
reason, has positioned the sewage-treatment plant directly across the lagoon from the sales office, perhaps
only to remind you that all properties are connected to
city sewers. You walk down the sidewalk, trying to ignore the faint hint of the fecal on the air in favor of more
pleasant things: the seagulls on the wires, the slap of a
wavelet against a wooden bulkhead. The sewage plant
hums louder now, groaning. But you've had enough,
and you walk back to your car and drive all the way
home to Anchorage Point.

Is it only that our parents took the tour that year, enumerating its deficiencies in the most energizing, exhilarating

manner? Did they fan our inexplicable attraction to the place?

I look at my calendar now, flipping past the house with the multicolored metal tulips in the window boxes. Mortville, I think. If John Waters had grown up in New York or New Jersey, he'd have set one of his early movies here. I can almost hear the late Divine—florid, loud, beautiful—of 117-25 Playhouse Drive calling out the window to her next-door neighbor, played by Edith Massey, or the amazing Jean Hill.

But real people live here with real lives.

As years went by, as soon as I was old enough to drive, my brothers and I drove to Mystic Islands twice a year to pay our homage. I wasn't even sure what we were looking for: hope, ruin, some combination thereof. Still, something about our exploration must have satisfied, or at least offered the *possibility* of it. We were so compelled by our mascot community that we even took our friends there, some of whom understood its elusive appeal, some of whom refused to. Michael's friend, Robert Soslow, got it right away, even though he seemed to be more compelled by our devotion than by the place itself. "So Lisicky," he said cryptically. (We took it as a compliment.) On the other hand, my friend, Mark Champlain, a native Wisconsiner, who would shortly move back to the Midwest, seemed both disturbed by Mystic Islands and by our tender regard for it. Even by our acknowledgment that it existed in the world. "New Jersey," he mumbled, already thinking about those cold, deep Wisconsin lakes.

His assessment was probably more on the mark than we knew at the time. Nowhere else in the world could you find this conflation of funk and glory, muscularity and decay. In some ways Mystic Islands seemed to distill the true essence of New Jersey in all its nervy contradictions. Certainly my own way of seeing developed from having grown up there; you couldn't grow up in a place in which refinery abutted farmland, where fancy custom houses were built atop toxic-waste sites, without embracing the *full* of it, without recognizing the fluid relationship between damage and beauty. I suppose there are consequences to this perspective if you don't keep it in check: detachment, cynicism, a hyperawareness of the gap between appearance and reality. (Now I get it: that New Jersey sense of humor!) But how could one not admit to the monstrous radiance of the Meadowlands, that stretch of wrecked marsh between Linden and Secaucus, that place to which outsiders point when they say: *Jersey*. All that buzzing energy. All those tanks and high tension towers, all those fires and carcinogenic streams, and the World Trade Center towers beyond, ghostly through the scrim of smog. That smell. Poisonous and fabulous. Of course, it's an ecological disaster. Of course, it embodies shortsightedness and brutality. But as much as I despair about the hole in the ozone layer, global warming, and the destruction of the rain forests, I can't ignore the otherworldly beauty of the place: the obverse side of heaven. At the very least I'd rather look at it, take it deep within, than pretend it doesn't exist.

Another question: Would Wisconsin be what it is without New Jersey? Mark Champlain cannot fill the tank of his SUV without making sure, in some part, that the re-fineries of the Meadowlands exist (not to mention wars in the Middle East).

▲▼

One more time: you drive down Radio Road to see the rushing blue sky, the wheeling gulls, the vast tract of marsh past the bridge. A great blue heron dips its bill into the tidal stream, and all at once it takes off, an explosion of flight. It drops the minnow to the reeds. The breeze off the marsh is warm, redolent of cattails, bay mud, and the sweet insides of pilings, telephone poles.

Maybe Mystic Islands seemed to us a huge gesture of faith. Maybe we couldn't help but be moved by all these efforts to make the very best of one's limited lot.

▲▼

Or maybe we were just embarrassed by the place. Did Mystic Islands give us some voyeuristic, prurient thrill, stirring up our inherent feelings of shame? Could it be, as Michael Cunningham suggests in one of his short stories, that we're "drawn to humiliation against our will?"

Think of the stand-up comic in a Holiday Inn; the aging businessman performing "My Way" in some Manhattan karaoke bar. Or the chilling crack-ups in John Cassavetes's films. Or better yet, the young newscaster from the tiny Wildwood station, who flubs her lines, angry at the cameraman for screwing up yet again. Throughout our high-school years my brothers and I watched the broadcast with an almost religious ferocity, almost praying for Faith's pursed lips to snap, which, believe it or not, they did from time to time. *Stupid,* she seemed to say with every gesture. Stupid, stupid. Human folly, incompetence, mediocrity, self-absorption—she couldn't bear these qualities in anyone, especially in herself. Paired with the vacant Mary McClaine, former Miss New Jersey, all teeth and smiles and good cheer about the world, Faith fell into a deeper gloom. Their nightly drama lasted for more than two years. Oh, the nasty glances, the sighs. Still, she wouldn't quit: persistence, persistence. Cup of our darkest thoughts: Faith filled us with as much dread as we could possibly need.

And relieved some psychological pressure. We couldn't have known what we were getting into, immersing ourselves in the drama of getting ahead (whatever that meant), as we struggled toward roles that felt so far from us. Bobby drawing blueprints for architectural-school applications, Michael auditioning for Juilliard. And what should I do: music, writing, art, some combination of the three? Didn't failure lurk around every corner? So tempting to throw it all away. Impossible not to be in thrall to flop, fiasco, and disaster, when all around us, in our township of the self-made, behind the masks of achievement and style, the costs of excessive striving were already becoming apparent. The high-school alto who finally recognized she was tone deaf once the entire audience blushed and chattered through her solo in *Fiddler on the Roof.* The divorced mother of three, burdened by the payments on her $350,000 house, arrested for shoplifting frozen dinners ("I had to feed the kids") from the 7-Eleven beneath the looming Cherry Hill water tower. Our next-door neighbor, months after installing a pool, tennis court, and detached four-car garage, standing outside his house with his hands balled in his pockets as the tax sale commenced in his living room. Even those who seemed to be on the up and up were watched with the most obsessive, exacting eye, while everyone else, with an urgency we couldn't quite name, hoped at least to be *seen.*

No wonder we were soothed by any demonstration of damage outside ourselves. I only see it now: we were only coming to love what might someday happen to us.

I'm drinking from my Faith Seferis mug, just as I do several times a week. The ultimate irony is that the place that seemed to be held together by pins and needles still stands after almost forty years, undiminished by flood, hurricane, age, or neglect, both regenerating itself and falling apart at once. Although my brother has attempted to arrange the calendar's photos from examples of the heroic to the disastrous, chronicling Mystic Islands's inevitable collapse, it seems to resist a received linear narrative. Sure, it's become a little more threadbare over time, but the houses haven't changed as much as I thought they would. In all honesty, the place doesn't work its charms on me as much as it used to. Maybe it's only that I'm getting older, and it's harder and harder to feel so detached from struggle and compromise. How much different that is from when the whole world seemed to be about possibility: *What if?*

Sometimes, lying in bed, I like to imagine myself on the streets of Mystic Islands. It's dark, and if I'm quiet enough, over the crickets and the murmurings of the la-goons, I can hear the lighted windows talking to me: *You who think you're better, you who think the towers you're building are going to save you. If you only knew how close you are to us.*

Afternoon with Canals

It's the hour when the heels are inevitably blistered, when we've strolled past as many canals, funky house-boats, and tall, glamorous windows as we can for one day. Even the obsessive pleasure we've taken in trying to perfect our pronunciations of *Prinsengracht* or *Leidesgracht*— the burr of those "g's" scratching the backs of our throats—is no longer of interest. All those rainy pavements, those brooding clouds blown in from the North Sea: we're sodden, saturated, and we can't help but wish to be warmed, to feel the heat of a candle's flame drying us out from inside.

"So now what should we do?" I say.

My boyfriend leans against a stone wall in his leather jacket. He shifts his weight from leg to leg. He holds me entirely in his gaze, brows raised, a hint of mischief in his grin. We know it's too early to head back to the guest house. We shrug at exactly the same moment, tensing our shoulders, then laugh, nervous but relieved we've been thinking alike.

Of course, it shouldn't come as any shock that we're strolling past these burnished cherry red boxes (I think of elegant Japanese furniture) inside of which handsome men, in varying degrees of light, lie back with their

hands latched behind their heads or on their stomachs. Now that we've calmed down—the fingers fill with
blood; the pulse slows—we're tempted to walk downstairs till I'm reminded of my tattooist's instructions: no
steam room, no hot tub. I press my hand to the freshly
pierced flesh, bewildered that the crown-capped heart
will be on my arm for the rest of my life.

Then my boyfriend's arm is around my waist.

Just across the hall, inside one of the boxes, sits a
man with an amazingly hard chest. A honeyed light
shadows the planes of his rough, bearded face. What
does he want? Is it just me, or am I simply in the way?
Are we, together, two large Americans with our shaven
heads, just the ticket for a dreary, lowlit afternoon? We
try our best to read him, the flares of interest, the averted
eyes, as he shifts inside the frame of the box, soulful and
startling: a Vermeer in the flesh.

Only hours ago we stood before a still life in the Rijks-
museum. Tulip, dragonfly, conch shell, lemon peel: all of
it entered me, soaking through my skin and bones, like
dye. If only for a moment, I stood before the easel, mixing paints. Poppy seed oil, lead, red upon blue—twilight
falls, while just outside the window, on the other side
of the wall, horseshoes clomp on cobblestone, bakers
pound their dough. Time hurries away from me as I try
my best to still it, to anchor it within its frame.

We walk around the system of boxes. It takes us
but two minutes to find out that our dear Vermeer is
gone, his space emptied but for the impression—already
disappearing—of his body on the mat. We look at each
other and shrug, smile. No matter. Maybe this is what
we'd wanted anyway. Without saying a word, I draw my
arm over his shoulder and lead him inside the box. It

doesn't take long. The warmth beneath my fingers, the density and heft of his muscles—he feels like gold in my hands as I touch my lips to his neck. His palms press against my skull. Then what: a kick against the wall? We laugh. So many footsteps down these halls, so much longing and release, little cries, and breaths pulled in, while far from the range of our hearing, the car horns beep, the motorboats chug in the canals, cell phones ring, forks chime against the dinner plates of Amsterdam. *"Prinsengracht,"* he rasps. *"Leidesgracht."*

We walk down the street again, arm in arm this time. In two days we'll be back on the plane, rushing off to meetings, appointments. My feet hurt inside my shoes. But we've framed time at least: we'll travel back inside it, again and again, and beyond.

PYGMALION SALON

Tonight you simply can't afford to be a-
n eyesore. But no one will ever see a

dog in mascara this time of year.
Ash Wednesday'll come but Carnival is here.
What sambas can you dance? What will you wear?
                ▲▼ Elizabeth Bishop, "Pink Dog"

My love of clothes interests me profoundly: only
      it is not love, & what it is I must discover.
                ▲▼ *The Diary of Virginia Woolf*

Please bring back Gimbels, Korvettes, Kress,
Ohrbachs, Alexanders, McCrorys.
    ▲▼ Graffiti from a New York City Public Rest Room,
                            November 2001

I.

My father's robe is made from a lustrous black wool
with magenta piping along the hem, pockets, and
sleeves. Its belt assures a jaunty fit around the waist.
Although a little shopworn, it's still in decent shape. I
never in my life expected to get much use out of it, but

believe it or not, I'm wearing it as I write this, almost enjoying the scratch of its seams against my bare shoulders on this frosty May morning in Utah.

But I wasn't so sanguine about receiving it. Six months ago, visiting our December rental in Key West, my mother gives me my Christmas presents seconds before their departure. Two bright pink boxes from Burdines hold two black shirts, always something I can use. But this third box ... what's inside? It smells faintly of napthalene, Right Guard, of being packed away somewhere. Something aches above my heart. I can't help but picture my father wearing it in the basement of the Cherry Hill house, which they've finally sold after six long years. He's standing beneath the bare bulb, paging through an engineering magazine, one of the thousands he's been saving—and promising to get rid of—since 1959.

"You don't like it," says my mother.

I look at her. There's not a trace of irony in her expression. "Oh, no, no— I'm just—"

"We have to go, dear. The boat parade's at six." She kisses me faintly on the lips, walks past the peppers and mango trees, and drives home to Pompano Beach with a merry toot of the horn.

I spend the rest of the day riding my rented bike down the woeful, palm-shrouded streets of Key West. It's hard not to be troubled by the gift. Is my father okay? Only three weeks ago I've visited them for Thanksgiving to discover he's developed a swelling, the size of a tea strainer, on his tricep just above his elbow. Although it's since receded, baffling his doctor, it's reminded all of us of the nascent terrors of the body, of how fragile we are. Or is this about something no less dire, but protracted?

Are they losing it? Thanks to good genes, my parents look quite young for their age, but they're in their seventies now, struggling with cataracts, arthritis, and high blood pressure. Just last night my father forgot that I'd been teaching every summer for the past three years.

I stand at the beach, watching the winds whipping up the milky green. A squadron of pelicans mimics the fighter planes over the Florida Straits. Maybe I should truly feel honored, grateful that they think I'm worthy enough to inherit my father's mantle. Yet I can't stop wondering if the situation were reversed: How would he like it if I boxed my worn Levis and gave them to *him* for Christmas? Would he feel so honored? Or would he only think I was cheap? Actually, it's quite amusing to think that we'd be able to trade clothing at all, given that I'm six foot two to his five foot seven, a five-length sleeve to his three. The robe *is* a size Large. He used to wear it with the sleeves rolled up. Not once, but twice.

Could it be that he hasn't any use for wool now that they've moved full-time to Florida?

Perhaps I obsess.

When I come back to the house, I walk into the master bedroom to find the black robe lying on the bed as if my father had just stepped out of it. A shroud of sorts. I'm so startled that I lurch out of the room and shut the door behind me. Our dogs, Arden and Beau, look puzzled. They bark and shimmy, demanding that I take them to the White Street Pier.

It's not till we're walking past the house with the roosters and the pot-bellied pig out back that I realize what the gift was about: B. Altman. Sewn into the collar is a strip printed with a witty elegant script circa 1968: B. Altman. Of course.

2.

My brothers and I never called it Altman's. It seemed as crude as calling draperies "drapes" or Provincetown "P-town." It was always *B.* Altman, actually B. Altman & Co., and the store carried a special distinction in our family, not because we loved the clothes so much (who in South Jersey wore tartans and tattersalls?), but because its single Philadelphia location seemed to embody a faded elegance, a worndown optimism, qualities that made sense to us. Although impeccably neat, the store hadn't been updated since 1962. It stood alone, unmalled, a white brick building surrounded by circular planters, gracing a lush green knoll in Devon. Already on the way out. Even the logo seemed charmingly passé by the time we made our monthly pilgrimages to it, and it was no surprise to us that the whole chain—including its Fifth Avenue flagship—closed in the early 1990s.

Its Main Line address probably had more allure than we were willing to admit. Like just about everyone else in Cherry Hill, our burgeoning suburb carved out of apple orchards and sandpits, we were eager for what was hard to get. Not that we didn't have opportunities; there was the Cherry Hill Mall, of course, with Strawbridge & Clothier, Bamberger's, and enough tropical foliage to resemble Miami Beach's Lincoln Road. It was one of the first enclosed shopping centers in the country, and our community—formerly the lackluster Delaware Township—was even renamed in its honor after busloads of tourists came to pay their respects from as far away as Baltimore and Boston. But it's like that old line: *Who wants to belong to any group that would admit you as a member?*

(Which makes me think of my friend Lisa Marx's mother and the way her eyes misted whenever she spoke of her longing to live on the Main Line.)

The charm of B. Altman, no doubt, shaped my youngest brother, Michael, who's been drawn to fading and unusual department stores for as long as I can remember. Three months short of six, he opened his own personal branch of the chain in our summerhouse living room in which he sold my mother Scotch tape and Russell Stover chocolates. He's one of the few people I know who will actually buy his clothes solely on the basis of the store's label, no matter how inappropriate the piece. ("Get me a tie from Porteous," he says, when he hears I'm spending the weekend in Vermont.) He can recite lists of defunct chains with all the solemnity of the Kaddish: Ivey's. Hutzler's. Steinbach. Sakowitz. S. Klein. Pomeroys. Lit Brothers. Gimbels. John Wanamaker. The names of the dead are endless. He deplores the globalized market, any systemized effort to eliminate the regional, the quirky, the specialized. Lately, when he has time off (in between playing oboe for the Richmond Symphony and traveling with his wife, Sandy, to the regional pageants of the Miss America "scholarship program," another hobby), he travels across the country and photographs individual stores that he thinks are on the brink of closing. (Even their daughter, Jordan, is named in honor of a lost scion of American retail: Jordan Marsh.) Ninety percent of the time his speculations are correct. Only a couple of years ago, he made a point of making the final purchase at Thalhimers in downtown Richmond on its final day of operation. He stood in line to buy a violet blouse, of all things, so he could hold the cherished title forevermore. ("There wasn't any men's stuff left.") The local newspaper even interviewed him upon his departure. "I loved this store," he said, shook the blouse in the air, then walked out to his car.

3.

I'm less drawn to department stores these days than to a sale. Although Michael thinks this deplorable (the reason behind the demise of so many smaller chains), he's forgiving enough—at least for the moment—not to call me on it. Today we drive to a huge outlet mall in western Broward County. It's one of my favorite things to do when I visit my parents, whose high-rise is ten miles to the east. And though I'm appalled by the location of the place—it's located quite literally across the street from the Everglades—I'm breaking into a cold sweat as we spot it on the horizon. Its parking lot shimmers beneath bronzed cabbage palms and glary subtropical clouds.

We park beneath a post that says UU, which we always do just in case someone gets lost. The place is enormous, arranged in arcing semicircles, almost a mile from one end to the other. (How many times have we seen lost tourists, separated from their loved ones, on the verge of sobbing, after they've fallen under the spell of all those good buys?) But that doesn't stop us. I walk faster. From ten years back, I hear the sad, giddy laugh of B., an old acquaintance from grad school. She kids me about my third new shirt in as many days, wondering aloud about the state of my character. I laugh along with her, though it's hard not to be miffed. When I admire a visiting writer's outfit, she says later, "I expected more from you." I can still see B. slumped at a conference table with a cup of tea, her sweatsuit the outward expression of her inner gloom.

I know exactly what I want. My shirt must be gray, collared, both casual and formal at once, bridging the elusive gap between nightclub and poetry reading. My project takes all of twenty minutes. When I'm finished, I walk to the checkout line with two pairs of shoes, a gleaming windbreaker, and a nubby gray shirt with blue stitching around the placket.

Michael, on the other hand, has turned his attentions toward Sandy, who's asked him to buy something for her. The blackberry-dyed snakeskin vest (now where are his politics?) he brings to the register is both hideous and fabulous at once, marked down to $75 from $1,750.

I stand outside the store window. I step right, left, then right again, shuffling in place as Michael disappears beneath the moist inky foliage to find the rest room. My shirt is wet beneath the underarms; my nervous system revs with a blend of accomplishment and guilt. I reach into my bag and rub the soft gray fabric. Within minutes—is that B. pulling up a chair in my brain?—I hear engines chuffing, supervisors yelling. A lethally sharp knife slices through fabric. And a seventeen-year-old girl from Beijing guides the yoke beneath the focused light of the sewing machine. She's bored, yet careful (see the lines already around her eyes?) to keep the needle from piercing her finger. The factory is too hot. Coins clink in her pocket at the end of the twelve-hour day. And at the same time, on the other side of the world, cotton bales roll in on trucks or trains, once warm from the workers' hands, now glowing with grease, seed, spray, and dark red drops of human blood.

I blink myself awake. My palate is dry. In front of me, beneath the moist inky palms, a single mother walks by in a nylon track suit. She's carrying a baby over her left hip. He turns and twists; he won't stop crying, screaming into the well of her collar socket. Another hard life. No decent apartment, no sturdy lock on the door. The refrigerator broke down last week, spoiling all the food on the shelves, and the management will get to it only after chasing out the drug dealers in the courtyard. Car alarms whoop throughout the night. And, despite everyone's efforts to clean up the place, the apartment next door is filled ankle-deep with broken bottles, used syringes, and wadded sheets of newspaper.

A question for B.: How to deny the baby's mother the pleasure of stopping a young man cold with her new track suit? *Hey, girl.*

The imagination breaks down here. No answer, no reply.

4.

From Oscar Wilde: "The truth of masks."

5.

How much of my current interest in clothing is exacerbated by spending the semester in Salt Lake City?

In a recent poll, my temporary city rates lower than Birmingham, Alabama, on a ranking of the country's "well-dressed" places. Walking past the big wedding cake of the Tabernacle, I'm not sure I believe that, though the fashions you see on the street do strike me as dated. (What could "dated" mean, however, in a world in which the cycles move faster and faster, when bleached denim is declared "in" again the second dark, raw denim hits the front table at the Gap?) Around Temple Square, kids still wear oversized pants and child-sized tops emblazoned with the emptied, smiling faces of Kate Jackson and Farrah Fawcett-Majors. Or more poignantly, ripped T-shirts that yell FUCK OFF in dripping black letters.

It goes without saying that fashion means more here than it does in, say, New York or Los Angeles, where personal style is taken for granted, where trying too hard simply translates as neediness. But something is clearly at stake for those Salt Lake kids who refuse to dress in button-downs and khakis, who chose to distinguish themselves from the pack and the underlying notion that they're effortlessly, endlessly duplicatable. Their clothes are nothing less than political. They're saying, *Listen, I have a self. I have the right to stand out. I'm not merely a member of the group. I don't want to be married at sixteen, I don't want to go off to Kampala for two years.* Et cetera. I'm reminded of a recent TV commercial for the Salt Lake City transit system that promotes public transportation during inclement weather. A cartoon snowflake cries, "I'm unique, I'm unique!" seconds before it's smashed brutally, joyfully by an oncoming bus.

6.

Is my lust for clothing a sort of fashion penance? Am I just paying the debt on all those mistakes in my past, the childhood garments from Grant's or E. J. Korvette, the adult attempts at, say, grunge? Last week, while organizing some old photographs, I came upon a picture of myself from 1993. I'm grinning, wearing a vintage olive green coat with fur collar, something I found in the thrift store of an Episcopal Church in Chatham, Massachusetts. I loved that coat at the time. I wore it everywhere from poetry readings to the opera, but now I'm just alarmed by the sheer wrongness of it. Such a tube-like fit: What on earth was I thinking?

7.

Do such revelations cause us to look down at what we're wearing right now? In five years will we look back at pictures of ourselves, flustered, humble? Or will the evident changes in our faces help us resist that?

8.

(insert to manuscript, January 16, 2002)
What I have on right now, from the bottom to the top:

Two-tone brown Camper bowling shoes from Santa Monica Shoes, December 2000; white Dickies work socks from Urban Outfitters, 14th Street and 6th Avenue, New York, September 2001; white jockey shorts from Banana Republic, Philadelphia, May 2001; G-Star raw denim cargo pants from MAP, Provincetown, October 2000; black leather Diesel belt, Elisabeth, Prague, July 2000; long-sleeved gray-violet thermal shirt with white stitching, Urban Outfitters, Houston, fall 2000.

And there you have it, a layer cake of time and place.

9.

Ladies and Gentlemen, Welcome to The Paul Lisicky Hall of Shame: 1971—a sheer brown shirt with four-inch fringe at the sleeves. 1973—a pair of oversized aviator glasses with a strange trapezoid above the nose that trapped skin oils. 1979—a body perm (enough said). 1983—a black Ralph Lauren polo shirt with yellow collar and lavender horizontal stripes. 1985—an oversized pair of black velour corduroys. 1988—a colossal black overcoat (vintage again) worn solely because it was bought on St. Mark's Place. 1992—cranberry-colored Doc Marten boots. 1993—grunge! 1994—double-processed white/blond hair that the hairstylist came close to dying a Windex blue. 1995—earrings, earrings. 1996—pointy vampiric sideburns.

10.

On our way back from the outlet mall, Michael and I take the long route home down Sunrise Boulevard. We're in traffic. Outside a beauty shop, The Pygmalion Salon, stands an older lady in a boxy bright orange dress imprinted with windowpanes. It's breezy, and any work that's been done to her hair suddenly doesn't matter anymore. It stands up in wild white tufts through which bits of her freckled scalp are visible. I'm in awe; I can't take my eyes off of her. How fearless she looks beneath that rushing sky, standing beside the bus stop in her bright orange construction. The Peggy Guggenheim of Fort Lauderdale. It wasn't so long ago that she was beautiful. Her entire look is shaking its fist at time's ruthlessness, its steady, exacting damage. It says one thing alone: Not my style. You're not going to take that from me.

II.

I'm fascinated by someone at the gym.

With her impossibly shiny hair, in her ankle-length black coat, the Cher of Salt Lake (my private name for her) sweeps past the stationary bikes in a skin-tight, low-cut top in the dead of winter. She resists eye contact, silencing the whole room, albeit briefly. Some gawk, some simply pretend that she doesn't exist. (Didn't that old man with the holy undergarments beneath his running suit feel a twinge?) Yet there's no way you can't take notice. The Temple is literally across the street after all, and there's something heroic, finally, about her fierce little waist, her topknot inspired by Sharon Tate, her decision to display her sculpted, surgically enhanced breasts. There's a side of me that wants to yell out and cheer. It's not that she's particularly charming, cheerful, or available. I'm not even sure she'd ever acknowledge my hello. But I can't help projecting myself into her, imagining what it might be like to walk through the world that way. Oh, to silence with beauty. My eyes roll back in my head as if I've been shot up with heroin.

It would be simplistic to say that her appearance is about asserting her superiority over us. Of course, that's a part of it, but it would seem ungenerous to attribute her work to hostility. Her appearance indicates that there's a larger world outside the mountain-walled valley of Salt Lake. She gives us permission to take delight in ourselves, to stand in resistance to the towers of the church across the street and all of its concomitant prohibitions.

She embodies an eagerness to know the terms of the world, to try them on, then discard them when need be. She tells us that you don't have to live the life that was handed you, that you may indeed claim your self.

Could it be that just beneath the constructed surface of every glamorous person there's a ghost of somebody else, awkward and sad, who refuses to stay dead?

12.

I go through my closet and decide what to keep, what to give away. Luckily, we're moving from Salt Lake in exactly two weeks, and I probably should be doing anything but writing. But moving is always the occasion of reevaluation and of taking stock. It stirs up time, and one can't help but go through all its attendant activities without looking backward and forward at once. It doesn't get any easier. Even if you've moved a dozen times in as many years, as I have. Cherry Hill, Anchorage Point, Provincetown, Iowa City, Key West, Salt Lake City, Houston, not to mention shorter stays in other places: London, Los Angeles, Amsterdam, Prague, San Miguel de Allende. All these names and places fade as we turn our eyes toward New York.

I stand before an open box making myself sick over my decisions. There's no law saying I have to get rid of anything; certainly I could just pack up every T-shirt and pair of jeans and send them off with the mover. But moving seems to necessitate something like paring down, so that's the way it will be.

To keep: the plaid yellow jacket with the slightly threadbare collar.

To give away: the black rayon shirt with the pockets over the chest.

But it's harder than I think it is. There I am, six years ago, standing at the register of a now defunct store, pleased with my new jacket (there's nothing else like it at the time), hopeful about my new life in Provincetown. In only a few short weeks I'll wear it every Wednesday night to the Crown and Anchor, where I'll take it off as soon as I pass the bouncer. I'll fold it precisely, then tuck it beneath the stacked chairs. I'll dance for two and a half hours straight, without a break, utterly alone and *with* people at once, almost convincing myself the whole experience is sealed, safe from the workings of time. I'll put it back on when I'm finished, my sweat soaking into its sleeves. I'll wear it walking through the dunes one brisk October morning. I'll wear it when I've heard a female friend, the window washer who says hello to me on the street every morning, has died unexpectedly of pneumonia. I'll wear it for hours and hours until I've latched onto the next jacket, and I'll lose interest in it, until I've stopped wearing it at all.

But maybe I'm just being the worst kind of sentimental. Maybe I'm investing my memory with a significance it doesn't merit.

I stare down into the yawning dark with my flashlight. Shirts and jackets and shoes and trousers: I have hours of work ahead of me. I'll be up all night if I keep up like this. *Good-bye, you.* And I drop the jacket into the giveaway pile.

13.

It's evening now, a breeze through the open window. It's chilly enough to merit something warmer, so I reach for my father's robe, which I haven't yet packed, and slide my bare arms into its sleeves. It's looking shabbier by the minute. A few nights ago I lay down on the living-room floor in it, the lustrous wool picking up more animal hair than I thought possible. I sit before my desk now, naming the sources of each individual strand, courtesy of our two dogs and two cats.

(Not long ago Mark told me that his friend, Mekeel, had a dream in which she learned that he must buy me a new robe. He thought she was probably right; he's hinted on more than one occasion that I might look better in something else.)

I stare at the picture of my father sitting on the dock behind my childhood summer house. With my chunky black horn-rims, I now look just like he did in 1962. He looks amazingly content, fully himself, no sense of doubt about the future. I'm resembling him more and more by the minute. On my last visit he introduces me to their downstairs neighbor, Jim Malone, a retired dentist, who cries instantly, "Man, you look just like your dad." Something that would have flustered me when I was younger.

(I push my glasses up the bridge of my nose. Will these, too, end up in the great Hall of Shame?)

Once again, I've forgotten to call. Now if I could only get him to keep his word. Although my father's been promising to set up an e-mail account so we could stay in touch more easily, six months have gone by without any progress on the matter. This seems to be his method of dealing with getting older: delaying choices as if the passage of time isn't quite real.

But who am I to judge? For the moment, at least, everyone I care about is well. I hold in my breath. Like

Virginia Woolf, I want to whisper to each passing moment, "stay, stay, stay."

I tie the robe tighter around my waist. If I'm lucky enough to get old, I wonder how I'll be? Like my father, putting things off, moving through the years as if he's convinced he'll escape death? Or like the elderly woman in her shocking orange dress, saying no, *no* with her style, lunatic, defiant, refusing to accept the inevitable?

Famous Builder 3

I was glad when they said to me,
   "Let us go to the house of the Lord."
                                          ▲▼ Psalm 122: 1

The man and his friend Denise drive down Route 73, groaning at all the trophy homes behind the big box stores. He's not entirely surprised that the 32-foot globe at the New World entrance is gone. So much of what they remember has been torn down, refurbished, paved and planted over: the Holly Ravine Farm and its petting zoo, the Clover supermarket, the broad green entrance lawns of Wexford Leas with its brick tollhouse. Still, he sighs. A wince, a film falls over his eye, and it's 1972: the boy and his mother stand in a field to watch a pinpoint above the South Jersey farmland. Blades beat, crowds mill. Drivers pull onto the shoulder of the road to see what all the fuss is about. And then the big, bald revelation, just as the Friday *Courier Post* predicted: REPLICA OF UNISPHERE TO BE TRANSPORTED BY HELI-COPTER TO ROSSMOOR DEVELOPMENT. The boy and his mother gaze skyward, a little skeptical, yet certain that change is on the way. They clap, giving themselves over to the collective shock and thrill (wasn't a

statue of Jesus transported like this in a Fellini film?)
when the great globe falls from thirty feet above. The
ground rumbles. The helicopter blades go *trk-trk-
trk-trk-trk*. The boy and his mother feel more than
they have a right to—weren't they just making vague
fun of the developer's appeal to the good life, even as the
boy clutched the brochure to his chest? The crowd scatters. The sky darkens with the passage of the cold front.
And yet mother and son keep watch until their backs
are tired, as the banged-up world's lifted onto its
pedestal.

Denise looks out at the serviceable two-story Coloni-
als that have taken New World's place. "Whatever happened to it?"

"The world?"

"The development. These aren't the models I remembered."

The man tells his friend—have they really known
each other for eighteen years?—about the sewer mora-
torium that stopped the project. (Among all that fills
his head, he can't believe he's cataloged this lowly
fact.) Only a few dozen homes—Tudors, Haciendas, and
Contemporaries—out of a proposed thousand were built
before a local firm later took over the project and renamed it Willow Ridge.

"This is just"—she gestures at the boxy, bland houses
beside the road—"isolating, *grim*. Do you remember
what New World meant?"

He nods vigorously. And then they both roll their
eyes, smiling at the gap between who they were then
and who they've become.

"I mean, those homes were like"—Denise takes a
breath, "I don't know, wrapped Venetian candies."

"Hollywood soundstages," the man offers.

"They *fizzed*. And it wasn't like they flexed their muscles. Not like the trophy homes these days."

"A little populist glamour."

A few miles later they pull into Sturbridge Estates, the model homes they've decided to check out. Something about what they're doing feels deliciously subversive, a little dangerous. After all, neither would ever choose to live in a new suburban house. But that doesn't stop them from wanting to revisit every now and then what captivated their childhood imaginations. How many hundreds of houses did they explore with their parents every Sunday afternoon after church? Impossible to name and number them all, but the ritual is part of who they are. It dyes their blood, indelible as the ink of all those hymns, responsorial psalms, Eucharistic prayers. If it wasn't its own religion, then it was a coda to the Mass, an extra occasion to exalt. How they walked from room to furnished room, hushed and holy, as if they were already passing into the next world, the better one to come.

But time has worked its changes on them in ways that are deeper than they can articulate. Today they're trying on who they might have become had sex, art, books, and years of school not complicated things.

"This is it?" says the man. "Whatever happened to five furnished model homes?"

They stare out at a 5,000-square-foot château with a stucco veneer and plastic punch-in window dividers.

"I guess this is the one we get to see," says Denise.

They get out of the car and stare at the impeccably sodded lawn, shadowed at this hour by the stretched pattern of a weeping willow. The yews glitter in the sprinkler water. There's only one other car parked in front of Denise's.

"I don't know about this," the man says.

"We'll just breeze through. We don't have to stay very long."

"It looks mean," says the man. "I think it's glaring at us."

"Oh, stop."

They nudge open the front door. They feel smaller than they're used to: the foyer is the size of a small ball-room, and the second floor soars thirty, thirty-five feet, bordered by a staircase with a railing of bleached wood. The ceiling above sparkles with granulated spray. Every-thing smells adhesive. A circular window on the landing overlooks the treetops in the backyard.

The man steadies himself. "Whoa."

They step lightly in their shoes. Music tinkles through the sound system. The living room, the dining room, the family room: all are so enormous that the furniture looks lost in them. A violet orchid glowers on the coffee table. A boxy sofa hunkers beside the gray wall, trying as hard as it can to command. But it seems to feel as they do. It clears its throat, pats down its sleeves, and wishes it were inside a warmer, more congenial space.

"This is a house for the family who doesn't want to spend any time together," the man says.

"This is a house that wants to bully you the minute you step into its mouth," says Denise.

"But it's cheaply built," the man says. "Look." And he runs his palm over the woodwork, as something catches. He shows his hand to Denise, who scowls at the blond splinter piercing his thumb.

Carefully, they ascend the staircase. No other visitors

this afternoon. No salesperson coming forth to welcome them, to shake their hands and pass out a price list. Denise is entirely immersed in the finer facets of the interior (is that because her ex-husband lives in an earlier section of the same development a few streets away?), while the man's attention has scattered like the flock of sparrows he watches through the circular window. All he wants is a brochure. All he wants are names, maps, renderings: the lyrical essence made concrete. Perhaps that's all he ever cared about, really, all those years he wanted to be a builder. Names, maps, renderings: loving the particulars of a world inside and out, upside and down, until it made the brain glow.

"Oh, my God," Denise says. "Look at this bedroom."

They stand, dazed, inside a chilly white room with clerestory windows. Like the sofa downstairs, the king-sized bed's dwarfed by the room. The orchids this time are a deep violent yellow with crimson threads. But the enormity of the space strikes him as more severe here: the man feels as if they're caught inside a chilled glass cathedral, without pews or a congregation, which doesn't permit anything resembling spontaneity or laughter or a casual human touch.

"Can you imagine someone fucking in here?" the man says.

"Sweetheart," Denise says, "this house isn't meant for someone who fucks."

And when they look up, a colossal salesman with a green golfing cardigan is standing in the doorway.

He doesn't say hello. Or turn up the corners of his mouth. He holds them entirely in his gaze, making it plain he's heard everything they've said. He knows exactly who they are, not the husband and wife they were sure they'd resembled, but something stranger, impossible to categorize: excommunicants who've wandered into the realm of particularly righteous church.

"Beautiful home," the man says.

"Thank you so very much for your time," Denise says.

They squeak past him. And they walk down the stairs, first slowly, then a little faster, nearly tripping over their laces before they run, run, run to the car.

CODA:
Perennial Lane
Botany Lane
Slender Place
Radium Lane
Manikin Lane
Hepburn Lane
Galaxy Lane
Unique Court
Merry Turn
Wisp Lane
Wafer Lane
Ballad Lane
Exhibit Lane
Panorama Lane
Bendix Lane
Wisdom Lane
Wicket Gate
Trousdale Drive
Quicksilver Lane
Privacy Lane
Tardy Lane

REFUGE OF THE ROADS

We're not talking about the shard of a saint's bone. No pamphlet of spiritual lessons from the bottom of a well. Just a pen. Not even something handed down to me by some long-dead ancestor I never laid eyes on, but something I picked up in Provincetown on the last days of August when the crowds on the street were thinner and quieter than they'd been, when the light was such a deep, scalding pink over the rooftops that I couldn't stop from walking into that shop—just as the first stars appeared overhead—to anchor that moment in my memory. It certainly helped that the pen was my favorite color (marine blue) and had the same anodized surface as the aluminum drinking cups of my childhood from which I drank iced tea after spending entire days at the beach. Still, I never thought it had meant so much to me until I'd given it up for lost a few weeks ago, until I'd already decided, with overwhelming reluctance, to forgive the stranger who grasped it between his fingers.

But what's this? I wave it about like a sparkler. "My pen! My pen!"

Mark crosses our front yard in Houston, a cat carrier in each hand. "Well, look at you."

"I was reaching inside my jacket pocket. The inside

pocket? I can't believe this. It must have been there the whole time."

I hold in my sigh. I'm so full, hot, so taut about the face, that I might just roll and blow across the lawn. There I am, rubbing up against the ferns, the live oak, the mottled clay pots of the sago palms. I'm rising, aren't I? Right through the limbs of the trees. Then . . . *pop.* Certainly I'm only confirming my tendency toward dramatics. Our elderly cats, Portia and Thisbe, bleat at me from behind the bars of their respective cages.

"Didn't I tell you you were going to find it?"

"Yeah, but I'm always losing things."

"And you're always finding them, too." He places Portia and Thisbe side by side on the backseat, stops, then looks directly into my face. If there weren't some glimmers of warmth inside that gaze, if he didn't so clearly get a kick out of this facet of my personality, even though he pretends he's had it, I think I'd be inclined to fuss.

But listen: while I admit to losing my wallet at least once every two weeks (a smack to the forehead, "My wallet! My wallet! What have I done with my wallet?") only to find it next to the bathroom sink or under another pile of laundry, I've lost all kinds of things within the last six months. My driver's license. A tank watch. Several gym locks. My address book with the leather cover—years of collected names left beneath the seat of a rental car in the airport at Portland, Oregon. My weight-lifting gloves—*twice* within the last week. This wouldn't be such a problem if I didn't try to be so exacting, if I weren't always listening for the jingle of my keys in my pocket. Is that my father's voice I hear, from twenty-seven years back, on a family trip, as my mother and I sort through the trash bin of a Denny's in San Diego for my clear pink retainer? *Didn't I tell you not to take it out of your mouth?*

I squeeze my pen tighter in my palm.

Here we are, packing up the car in the hopes that we can drive the 2,200 miles—along with our two cats and two large retrievers—back to Provincetown in four days and three nights, so that Mark can get back in time to catch a plane to D.C. the following morning. As we've divided our time between at least two places for the last six years, we should be used to these harried feelings, but no. All those books, clothes, papers, objects—perhaps the prospect of carting our home along with us just one more time seems about as daunting as cleaning a cathedral with a toothbrush. Or maybe my mind is so saturated with making mental lists of everything I want beside me that I need a good squeezing out: a sponge that's scrubbed one too many cups and dishes. How to say yes to one thing, and no to another when confronted with the task of imagining yourself so thoroughly into the daily routines of the future? If I'm not thinking hard enough, I won't have my camera with me if I need to take a picture of Arden, our copper-black retriever, when he decides to sit on the back deck during a mid-March blizzard, perfectly poised and cheerful, brown eyes shining, flakes sticking to his curly coat like a dog inside a snow dome. Or I won't have *The Hissing of Summer Lawns* when I need to think about it in relationship to *Hejira*. And what about the green box patterned with the yellow beetles given to me by my brother, Michael? I'll need it on my desk, surely I will, to remind me that he carried it all the way back from Ocean City for me, when he had ten thousand other things to think of, and a new wife and Jordan, their baby.

Mark walks down the porch steps with one arm behind his back as if he's hiding something from me.

"What do you have there?"

"Nothing." He tucks whatever it is beneath his seat and gazes at the neighbor's ivy. The dogs' tails thump the back window from inside. "Ready?"

"So you're doing it, too."

"What?"

I hold out my palm for the house key.

"*Baby.*"

"Just one more thing." Then I walk inside and grab the bottle of seaweed-peony shampoo from the corner of the tub.

Mark and I take the bed by the window. Big Beau harbors between us, pink-nosed and golden, white snout resting on splayed paws. Portia wheezes by my feet; Thisbe stares at her face with horror in the full-length mirror, while Arden, it goes without saying, stretches out his legs as far as he can, claiming the opposite bed entirely for himself: *mine.* We're at a Holiday Inn in Laurel, Mississippi. The food bowls have been filled and emptied, the litter box appropriately moistened, and we're all lying in our room with its plum carpet, plum bedspreads, and plum lamp shades. We work to keep our minds still, trying not to think of all the churches, billboards, pines, and yellow crosses (always in threes) rushing by. The heater flutters the curtains. *The Sopranos* flickers and fades on the TV screen. Given that we're five hundred miles from the familiar scents of our rugs and our cushions, we're all holding up just fine. Arden heaves a huge, stunned, luxuriant sigh.

Headlights glow through the window. Now what: the manager, a squadron of housekeepers? A crowd marching up the hill with nooses, torches? "And you said it was one miniature pinscher," the desk clerk cries, jerking the curtains aside. *"Homo!"* But it's only the man next door. I get up and decide to check out the flat wrapped soaps, and wonder if I should just stash them in my bag.

At the mirror, I stare at my eyes, corners creased from looking ahead. Seventeen hundred miles away, the streets are still sandy from the spreaders, the SEE YOU NEXT SPRING signs curling in the shop windows. Mid-February, after all. Could the house remember us? Old, dear house: steep roof, waxy, resinous smell, thick with the lives of all the generations who've lived and died inside its rooms these last two hundred years. It couldn't be further from the house of my childhood, strong with its scents of fresh paint and adhesive, no nicks or scratches on *that* woodwork, a house in which we did our best to fill up that newness with talk, arguments, music, living with the now-touching conviction that the view outside the window (see that swing set with the forest green seat? the cluster of cherry trees by the dog house?) couldn't be anyone's but ours forever. So much longing inside those walls: Bobby sanding the finish off a battered Ib Koford-Larsen chair he'd found along the street, Michael playing a six-measure passage from "Carmina Burana" over and over on his oboe. There's my father working out an especially recalcitrant equation at the table, my mother pulling in her lip, threading a sewing needle just inches in front of her face. (And

269

outside, though never very far away, Mrs. Fox leading a hushed tour past her front-loading washer; Dolores Dasher watching the blinking red light atop her flag-pole; Bill Levitt talking up his next new city; Joni Mitchell; India Wills; Amy Goldfin; Aunt Goldie; Lisa Marx; Kate Papagallo; the Cher of Salt Lake; Laura Nyro; Billy; Beethoven. . . .) Who would have thought that we'd all leave for different parts of the country and become the kind of family who'd make dutiful phone calls to one another on the occasional Saturday? No wonder my mother had that lump in her throat when, one morning, during the week of her moving, she saw her mother's old upright—the very piano on which I'd practiced for so many years—carted away to the church on that flatbed truck.

I turn back toward the room. If it were mine to do such a thing, I'd secure this moment with the heaviest anchor: Arden taking up all the space he needs; Beau resting a thick paw on Mark's forearm; Mark touching my leg as I walk by, just to let me know he's thinking of me.

And Portia and Thisbe: Could the two bitterly com-petitive cats already know they'll both be gone soon, within days of each other?

But a long, long drive ahead. Tomorrow, we'll leave the room exactly as we found it, no pet smells, no spilled food, not even a trace of our being here but for an im-possibly heavy trash can. And my pen, which I'll leave beside the sink, or under Arden's bed, though we'll be miles past Nashville before I'll even realize my pocket feels deep.

ON BROADWAY

Sidewalk and pigeon
You look like a city
But you feel like religion to me.
▲▼ Laura Nyro, "New York Tendaberry,"

Jasper soldiers up lower Broadway, vulnerable and fierce as the buildings above our heads. He doesn't care if anyone rolls his eyes. He's not consumed with thoughts of running into one of his patients, or someone from his building, or even his mother, for that matter, who might be in from Manhasset to catch a show. He's walking down the street with his shirt off. Not because he's exerting his power over anyone, not because he's expecting anything returned from another stark, handsome face, but because he wants to feel the world on him: every song, taste, and smell penetrating his tall flexed torso this unseasonably warm November night.

I'm walking beside my friend. Faces surge toward us, casting the occasional glare. Everyone else is fully dressed, in coats, suits, jackets. Why is my brow hot? If shame has a taste, then it's the cheapest wine on the list. It trembles the palate, dries out the mouth, slides down

271

the gullet where it takes up in the stomach and sours, making you want some aspirin.

"Let's head over to Fifth," I offer.

We're stopped at the corner of Astor Place. "I thought you wanted to walk on Broadway."

"Yes, but—"

Who could have known he'd leave the gym like this? His eyes fix on my face. And he sees purple-black shapes moving inside my head. And it pains him that he's embarrassing me. And it pains me that I'm embarrassed for him, and we balance on the curb for a second, stranded, before the WALK sign flashes on.

"We're in Manhattan," he says, with a hurt smile. And though I'm not quite sure what he means, and I can't quite ignore those purple-black shapes, I can't help but see that he's part of something larger: just as the sleek black woman with the plaid bag is part of something larger, as is the thin Japanese kid with the absurd blue tassel swaying back and forth from his cap. And we walk on and walk on, past the drunks slumped outside the ATM, the bus to Fresh Meadows puffing out its sprays of exhaust, the salted golden pretzels tied to the sides of a vendor's silver cart absorbing every scent, texture, and cry of anguish.

And yet? And yet?

Ahead, a coffee shop. Pendant lights hang from the ceiling; a white moth hovers above the raspberry pie in the window. Jasper stands with a smile around the edges of his lips, like some enormous, alarming child who's been presented with a tray of cupcakes. "Would you like something?"

"Sure."

"Stay here," he says. "Hold this for me." And he

hands me his gym bag full of sneakers and sweatpants and God knows what, so heavy that my shoulder hurts, and I have to put it down on the sidewalk, lest I run out of breath.

I watch him through the frame of the window. No fear that he's not behaving like the rest. No fear that he's going to be asked to leave or put his shirt on. He walks right to the counter, past all the faces he's silenced, the cluster of muscle boys, the NYU student who wants to gaze up at him but can't because he's the most beautiful thing he's ever seen. The girl takes Jasper's order, talking with incredible animation about the tattoos that rope around his shoulder, and all at once I'm reminded of my father, who's walking in and out through the steakhouse in some distant corner of my memory, and filling up the doggy bag with the scraps from people's tables for Taffy, our miniature collie. He doesn't care that I'm beside the door with my mother and brothers, arms folded, blushing. He doesn't care that Michael's calling for him to come to the car, or that the couple by the salad bar is so perturbed that they've actually stopped eating, holding their knives and forks in stillness above their plates. All he's thinking about is Taffy, how her eyes will gloss over once her bright blue bowl fills up with the meat.

"Drink up," Jasper says, passing me the cup.

"Thanks." And it's bitter and delicious. So weirdly delicious that I imagine he's slipped something inside it, something to keep me nervy, opened to the city and everything beyond in all of its wildness and danger and beauty.

And yet? And yet?

When I look up from my sip, he's gone. Hats bob up and down like inflatable balls on the waves. The street's darker, chillier. Second by second, it's losing its luster. Wind silences the horns. It catches the loose trash on the sidewalk, blowing air into the bags, lifting them up, up above the city before they fall, like emptied paper lanterns. And then I spot him again, soldiering on, defying anything that tries to tell him to cover up. Time's a bullet fired, his walk says. Planes are flying toward us as we speak. You are the buildings protecting us. You are the boy slamming the sidewalk with his skateboard wheels, the woman with the plaid bag slung over her shoulder, the cold salted pretzels served up night after night by the vendors. The bones groan beneath the layers of Washington Square Park. Be mighty, his walk says. Be struck, pierced by the light on your skin. I spill hot coffee down the front of my shirt. "Wait!" I say. And I run down the sidewalk after him, trying to catch up.

Acknowledgments

Books, like houses and cities, are never built by one person alone, and I'd like to thank the following people for their contributions to this project. Karen Brennan, Bernard Cooper, Alice Fulton, Denise Gess, and Elizabeth McCracken all read the earliest, fledgling versions of these pieces, and I'm grateful for their friendship and feedback, in addition to the inspiration of their work. I'd also like to acknowledge Jo Ann Beard, Polly Burnell, Stephen Briscoe, Kathleen Cambor, Allan Gurganus, Barbara Hope, Robert Leleux, Jonathan Rabinowitz, Katrina Roberts, Joy Williams, Lisa Zeidner, and my late friends Agha Shahid Ali, Betty Jones, and Robert Jones for their support. Enormous thanks to Barry Goldstein for the photograph. Thanks, too, to Carol Houck Smith for her encouragement and astute suggestions. And Deborah Lott—her keen-eyed feedback was crucial at a late stage of this manuscript.

I couldn't have wished for a better editor than Fiona McCrae, whose steady attention, gentle push, and fierce intelligence helped to make this a better book. Thank you, as well, to Anne Czarniecki, Katie Dublinski, Janna Rademacher, J. Robbins, and everyone else at Graywolf for their interest and generosity.

To the Lisickys: my brothers Bobby and Michael must be thanked for their contributions both great and small. Love and bright wishes to my parents, Tony and

Anne, who gave us enough room to be ourselves. I dedicate this book to them.

Finally, most important, I want to thank my partner, Mark Doty, for his support and belief, and for going along with my occasional need to drive through an old Levitt development.

PAUL LISICKY is the author of the novel *Lawnboy* (Turtle Point, 1999). His stories and essays have appeared in *Ploughshares, Boulevard, Sonora Review,* and in many other magazines and anthologies. His awards include fellowships from the National Endowment for the Arts, the James Michener/Copernicus Society, the Henfield Foundation, and the Fine Arts Work Center in Provincetown. He teaches fiction and creative nonfiction at Sarah Lawrence College and in the low-residency M.F.A. Program at Antioch University, Los Angeles. He lives in New York and Provincetown and is currently at work on a new novel.

The text of *Famous Builder* is set in Clifford, a typeface designed by Akira Kobayashi. Book design by Wendy Holdman, endsheet design by Kyle G. Hunger, set in type by Stanton Publication Services, Inc., and manufactured by Maple Vail Book Manufacturing on acid-free paper.

Key to Endsheets

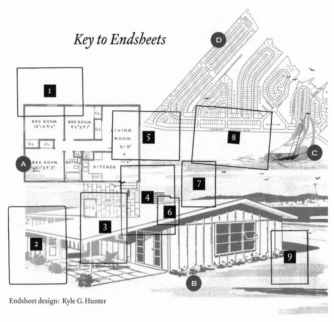

Endsheet design: Kyle G. Hunter

Anchorage Point Promotional Materials

A. Model Home, "The Sea Breeze"—Floor Plan

B. "The Sea Breeze"—Exterior

C. Anchorage Point Brochure, 1960 [yacht detail]

D. Lot Map

1. 15 Circle Lane, Cherry Hill, 1990

2. Anton and Anne Lisicky, 1956

3. Anton Lisicky, Paris, 1945

4. Anne Homan, 1951

5. James Lisicky and Lisa Burker (cousins), Grammy, author, 1964

6. Anton, RCA ID-badge photo, 1960s

7. Paul Homan (Anne's brother), 1938

8. Author and Anne on boat, 1964

9. Author, Provincetown, 1992

Graywolf Press is a not-for-profit, independent press. The books we publish include poetry, literary fiction, essays, and cultural criticism. We are less interested in best-sellers than in talented writers who display a freshness of voice coupled with a distinct vision. We believe these are the very qualities essential to shape a vital and diverse culture.

Thankfully, many of our readers feel the same way. They have shown this through their desire to buy books by Graywolf writers; they have told us this themselves through their e-mail notes and at author events; and they have reinforced their commitment by contributing financial support, in small amounts and in large amounts, and joining the "Friends of Graywolf."

If you enjoyed this book and wish to learn more about Graywolf Press, we invite you to ask your bookseller or librarian about further Graywolf titles; or to contact us for a free catalog; or to visit our award-winning web site that features information about our forthcoming books.

We would also like to invite you to consider joining the hundreds of individuals who are already "Friends of Graywolf" by contributing to our membership program. Individual donations of any size are significant to us: they tell us that you believe that the kind of publishing we do *matters*. Our web site gives you many more details about the benefits you will enjoy as a "Friend of Graywolf"; but if you do not have online access, we urge you to contact us for a copy of our membership brochure.

www.graywolfpress.org

Graywolf Press
2402 University Avenue, Suite 203
Saint Paul, MN 55114
Phone: (651) 641-0077
Fax: (651) 641-0036
E-mail: wolves@graywolfpress.org

KAUFMAN AND BROAD INC.

July 10, 1972

Mr. Paul Lisicky
15 Circle Lane
Cherry Hill, New Jersey 08003

Dear Mr. Lisicky:

We appreciate very much your interest in the housing
industry and particularly Kaufman and Broad. We are
proud to be your favorite.

I have enclosed some brochures from around the country
as well as some extra literature you might enjoy such
as our quarterly publication "Spectrum," and a company
history and fact sheet. I have also added your name to
our mailing list so you can expect regular information.
Homebuilding is a very good career choice for you,
especially since the housing need in America is so
great. It will take eager, young people like you to
solve the problems and meet the challenges of this
dynamic industry. And unless I miss my guess, you
will make a very fine homebuilder.

Best of luck to you.

Sincerely,

Jan Hunsinger
Jan Hunsinger
Assistant Director of
Corporate Communications

JH/bpt

10801 NATIONAL BOULEVARD   LOS ANGELES, CALIFORNIA 90064   AREA CODE (213) 475-6711 or 272-9914